Gentleman Jim

To our great and gracious God and for my parents

Gentleman Jim

The Wartime Story of a Founder of the
SAS and Special Forces

Lorna Almonds-Windmill

Pen & Sword
MILITARY

First published in the UK by Constable, an imprint of
Constable & Robinson Ltd, 2001

Published in paperback by Robinson, an imprint of
Constable & Robinson Ltd, 2002

This edition published in 2011 by
Pen & Sword Military
an imprint of
Pen & Sword Books Ltd
47 Church Street
Barnsley
South Yorkshire
S70 2AS

Copyright © Lorna Almonds-Windmill 2001, 2002, 2011

ISBN 978-1-84884-424-7

The right of Lorna Almonds-Windmill to be identified as the Author of this Work has been asserted by her in accordance with the Copyright, Designs and Patents Act 1988.

A CIP catalogue record for this book is available from the British Library.

All rights reserved. No part of this book may be reproduced or transmitted in any form or by any means, electronic or mechanical including photocopying, recording or by any information storage and retrieval system, without permission from the Publisher in writing.

Typeset in 11pt Ehrhardt by
Mac Style, Beverley, E. Yorkshire

Printed and bound in the UK by CPI

Pen & Sword Books Ltd incorporates the imprints of Pen & Sword Aviation, Pen & Sword Maritime, Pen & Sword Military, Wharncliffe Local History, Pen & Sword Select, Pen & Sword Military Classics, Leo Cooper, Remember When, Seaforth Publishing and Frontline Publishing

For a complete list of Pen & Sword titles please contact
PEN & SWORD BOOKS LIMITED
47 Church Street, Barnsley, South Yorkshire, S70 2AS, England
E-mail: enquiries@pen-and-sword.co.uk
Website: www.pen-and-sword.co.uk

Sergeant 'Gentleman Jim' Almonds, one of the 'Tobruk Four', was in many ways to the desert born. In this environment he was totally at home. He excelled in the velvet darkness and revelled in the vast emptiness of North Africa. His nickname was apt; six feet and four inches tall, his gentle, quiet and considerate manner hid enormous self-discipline and control which left him cool, efficient and deadly when the situation demanded it ... [He] was held very high in Stirling's esteem.

Alan Hoe in *David Stirling: The Authorised Biography of the Creator of the SAS*, Little, Brown & Co (UK) Ltd, 1992

> We are the Pilgrims, master: we shall go
> Always a little further: it may be
> Beyond the last blue mountain barred with snow
> Across that angry or that glimmering sea...

excerpt from *The Golden Journey to Samarkand* (1913) by James Elroy Flecker, inscribed on the clock tower of the barracks as a memorial to their dead, 22 SAS, Stirling Lines, Credenhill, Hereford

Praise for *Gentleman Jim*

'An authoritative history of the founding of the SAS –
as well as a terrific read.' *The Spectator*

'Jim Almonds was one of the great SAS figures of his day and
it is splendid that his daughter has now told his story.'
Sir Max Hastings

'Exceptionally well researched … highly recommended.'
Guards Magazine

'A remarkable story, told stylishly.'
Soldier Magazine

'This fine and meticulously researched book captures quite
brilliantly the special spirit of the early SAS.'
The 2nd Earl Jellicoe

'Lorna Almonds-Windmill has written an exceptionally well researched
and interesting book about her father…highly recommended.'
Guards Magazine

'Incredible true story …'
Bristol Evening Post

'In view of the SAS's crucial involvement inside Afghanistan
against the perpetrators of international terrorism, the story of
this extraordinary man and the effect he had, and still has, on our
lives could not be more prescient…Read it and be thrilled.'
Lord Hanson

Contents

Foreword by The Rt. Hon. The Earl Jellicoe KBS, DSO, MC,
FRS, PC xi
Acknowledgements xiii
Preface xv

Part I	The Guards, the Commandos, the 'Tobruk Four', and the Founding of the SAS (August 1928–October 1941)	1
1	'L' Detachment – SAS	3
2	Lincolnshire Poacher and Guards Commando	16
3	Into the Breach	26
4	The 'Tobruk Four'	44
Part II	The SAS Desert Raids, Capture at Benghazi and Two Escapes from Italian Prisoner-of-War Camps (November 1941–December 1943)	57
5	Reserves of Courage	59
6	First Strike and Regroup	67
7	Engaging the Enemy	82
8	SAS to the Rescue	101
9	Partners in Crime	112
10	Attack on Benghazi	126
11	Living with the Enemy	141
12	'Empire' Effort	149
13	The Italian Picnic	159

Part III	1 SAS in Scotland, Behind Enemy Lines in France and Leading the Advance into Germany (January 1944–May 1945)	179
14	The French Picnic	181
15	No GAIN without Pain	198
16	Mission Accomplished	216
	Notes and Sources	230
	Glossary	248
	Bibliography	250
	Index	252

Illustrations

1. Almonds in the Coldstream Guards, Tower of London, 1932
2. Almonds, 'L' Detachment, 1 SAS, Kabrit, 1941
3. Jock Lewes, hand bandaged from desert sores, Kabrit, 1941
4. Three of the 'Tobruk Four': (*l-r*) Jim Blakeney, Almonds, Bob Lilley, Cairo, 1941
5. Pat Riley, who described Almonds as 'one of my best pals', Kabrit, 1941
6. SAS training: jumps and rolls from trucks at 30 mph, Kabrit, 1941
7. 'Paddy' Blair Mayne, when still with 11 Commando, 'The Scottish', at Lamlash, Isle of Arran, 1940
8. Almonds off on one of the first SAS raids, Kabrit, late 1941 – the slight lean forward is due to the weight on his back
9. Almonds building Stirling's boat
10. The boat taking shape, Kabrit Point, 1941
11. Almonds (*top right*), with two Italian POWs, building the parachute training rig, Kabrit, 1941
12. The finished parachute training rig Almonds built for Stirling, Kabrit, 1941
13. Survivors of the Nofilia raid: (*back l-r*) Alan Nutt, LRDG, Brown, LRDG ('Sensor Box'), 'Snowy' McCulloch, LRDG; (*front l-r*) Almonds, Bob Lilley, 'L' Detachment, SAS. Note the early white SAS berets
14. Weapon cleaning before a raid: (*l-r*) O'Dowd, Rose and Storie who took part in the attack on Nofilia aerodrome
15. Dennis Basset, LRDG, immediately after leading the marathon walk from Jalo. Merlyn Craw said, 'He looks all in, doesn't he?'
16. An LRDG patrol at Howard's Cairn, a rare landmark in the Great Sand Sea
17. SAS jeep north of Kufra Oasis
18. David Stirling, south of Marauder, 1942
19. Mike Sadler, England, 1944

20. LRDG truck with anti-tank gun in the Wadi Tamet area
21. The Road Watch: Frank White, NZ LRDG, observes enemy convoys on the Trig el Abd road
22. Merlyn Craw, NZ LRDG, 1942
23. Johann Folscher, British South African Police, a member of the 'Empire Effort' first escape from Italian POW camp, Italy, 1943
24. The ketch *Kumasi* Almonds designed and memorised in solitary confinement in the Italian POW camp in 1943. He later built her by hand in Ghana and sailed her back to England in 1961
25. Almonds, six months after 'the Italian picnic', with John, Bristol, spring 1944
26. 'Paddy' Blair Mayne, CO, 1 SAS Regiment, Scotland, spring 1944
27. Georges Poulard, the Frenchman who met Almonds at the DZ France, June 1944
28. The château at Chilleurs-aux-Bois where Troopers Ion and Packman were murdered
29. Almonds with 'Monsieur le garagiste', Antoine Kroutchelnitsky, a member of the French Resistance
30. Almonds at the Vickers-K with his section behind enemy lines in the Forest of Orléans, July 1944
31. Cartoon by Ian Fenwick who was ambushed and killed in the Forest of Orléans on 8 August 1944
32. Almonds, aged 84, visiting the New Zealand SAS in January 1998

Foreword

The Rt. Hon. The Earl Jellicoe, KBE, DSO, MC, FRS, PC
President of the Special Air Service Regimental Association

I felt greatly honoured to be asked to write the Foreword to this fine book. I read it with interest and pleasure and it has brought back strong memories to me. It is a remarkable human story about a remarkable man. It is a true story of courage, danger, and amazing survival against all the odds. It is also the story of the way the SAS began. This book captures with a refreshing honesty the real spirit of young men at war in a special outfit, wanting to do their best but not knowing quite how to go about it.

The David Stirling whom I served under during the war was without doubt the finest leader of men I have ever known. However, he always insisted that he was not the sole founder of the SAS. There was Paddy Mayne who made his unique contribution in the early days in the Western Desert. There was Georges Bergé who brought with him the splendid French Squadron to join the SAS at a crucial time. And there was also, not least, Jock Lewes who, as our author rightly states 'had done something for the SAS that no other man, not even Stirling could have done', bringing with himself the training practice and philosophy which became the special SAS operational style. Lewes when he joined the Detachment brought with him the 'Tobruk Four', aptly described by Alan Hoe, Stirling's biographer, as 'pure gold dust'. One of them was Jim Almonds, for a long time the oldest surviving member of the SAS 'L' Detachment originals. He was one of the first twelve men who joined David Stirling when he founded the SAS at Kabrit in early September 1941. Physically tough, with the self discipline and mental strength never to give up whatever the circumstances, he yet showed the personal humility that led to his nickname.

In spite of being torn between love and duty, Jim Almonds always ran *to* the battle. He chose to operate behind enemy lines during the siege of Tobruk. He went forward for David Stirling and drove straight at the enemy with all guns blazing during the raid on Benghazi. After escaping twice from an Italian prisoner-of-war camp, he risked his own life while still in enemy territory to reconnoitre an enemy minefield, no doubt saving many Allied lives later. On arrival in England, he insisted on returning to the SAS so that he could parachute into enemy territory in France. For these exploits he rightly received the Military Medal and Bar and the French Croix-de-Guerre with Silver Star.

His family appear to have carried on the tradition. His son John – the baby in the story – was brought home to die after his mother had defied the doctors. He went on to pass SAS selection, command an SAS Squadron at Hereford and become the SAS Chief of Staff. Lorna Almonds-Windmill, also for a time a Regular Army Officer, is well placed to write this book, being a daughter of the Regiment and having a thorough understanding of both the Army and the psyche of the soldier. This well-researched and fascinating account has drawn together the threads of many SAS personal experiences and contemporaneous reports filed at the Public Record Office, resulting in one of the most vivid chronicles of the early SAS to date.

'Either write something worth reading or do something worth writing about,' said Benjamin Franklin. This book does both. I hope that you enjoy reading it as much as I did.

Acknowledgements

I owe an enormous debt of gratitude to many people who helped me to write this book. First, to those involved in the story, who took the trouble to let me talk to them, then to read what I had written in draft and provided photographs: The Rt. Hon. the Earl Jellicoe, KBE, DSO, MC, FRS, PC, to whom I am indebted for the Foreword but who sadly died in 2007; my father, Jim Almonds; my brother, John Almonds – the baby in the story; the late Pat Riley; Mike Sadler; the late Ernie Bond; Jimmie Storie; Leslie Bateman; the late Merlyn Craw; New Zealand LRDG; and the late Alan Nutt, New Zealand LRDG. I am grateful that, in some cases, I had the immense and humbling privilege of revealing to the survivors, including my father, the full picture of what had happened at the time.

I also received tremendous help and cooperation from the family of Ian Fenwick, who died in the Forest of Orleans, and permission to publish some of Ian's cartoons.

I acknowledge with thanks the assistance of the Public Record Office (PRO) – now the National Archive. Records held by them appear courtesy of Her Majesty's Stationery Office – and the patience of the staff there who on many occasions helped me to track down the files that I was looking for. These were mainly PRO WO/201; WO/205; WO/218; and WO/373.

I received cooperation too from the Special Air Service Regimental Association who allowed me to carry out research into their own files, notably the collection of papers and photographs known as 'the Paddy Mayne Diary'.

Most of all, I acknowledge that this book would not exist without the patience, wisdom and exceptional memory of my late father. The passages in the text about him are either taken from his wartime diary or are the words he used when I was interviewing him. I also owe him a great debt for the man that he was. Any effort I have expended is as nothing compared with what he went through. I have only had to write about these things: he had to live them. I hope that what I wrote does justice to him and to the many courageous men who appear in this book. I would like to acknowledge too the courage, loyalty and determination of my late mother.

Duncan McAra, my literary agent, was a tower of strength and encouragement in helping me to shape and complete this book. His constructively critical eye, efficiency and tireless effort on my behalf have been outstanding.

I would like to thank especially Elizabeth Fletcher, whose suggestion it was that I should pick up the pen, my brother John for his expert SAS opinion, my sister Gloria for finding the key documents in the labyrinth of the family archives and the many readers of the first edition who have communicated to me their appreciation.

Lorna Almonds-Windmill
London, April 2010

Preface

I was nineteen years old before I realised the effect that coming from an SAS family had on other people. It was August 1964. After two weeks' leave following my Commissioning Parade, I was being posted to my first Army Unit as a brand new Second Lieutenant in the Women's Royal Army Corps. I felt very self-conscious wearing my officer's uniform for the first time and terrified lest I should suddenly meet the first person whose salute I would have to return. A sleek staff car picked me up from Chester station and deposited me at the Officers Mess, Saighton Camp, just outside the town.

I wandered rather circumspectly into the Ante Room for tea. Two tall, personable young Lieutenants in No. 2 Dress were standing by the delicious spread of afternoon tea which had been laid out by the Mess staff on gleaming white cloths.

'This,' I thought to myself, *'is more like it! This is what I went through all that Officer Cadet training for.'* I stepped forward to meet my new colleagues. With the most charming manners, they introduced themselves and one poured me a cup of tea. But on hearing that my name was Almonds, both reacted with horror and one even took an involuntary step backwards.

'Almonds!, not any relation to John Almonds?' said one.

'Or Jim Almonds!?' said the other. Alarmed at their reaction to my name, I tried to smile reassuringly.

'Well, actually, John's my brother and Jim's my father …' I began.

'Do you sleep rolled up in a wet blanket under a hedge bottom?' interjected the first, fixing me with a suspicious look.

'Or spend Christmas Day on top of Ben Nevis?' said the other.

'No, no,' I said hastily. 'I'm really *terribly* normal. I like nice soft beds and lovely hot baths and I'm in danger of losing my sense of humour if I don't have a good hot cup of tea first thing in the morning.' Seeing them still looking at me somewhat askance, I added, 'and, I promise you, I've never jumped out of an aeroplane.'

Twenty years later, in June 1984, at the opening of Stirling Lines in Hereford, I experienced a similar reaction to my name from the founder of the SAS, David Stirling, later Sir David Stirling. Somehow, I had ended up sitting in the middle of the very front row on that sunny summer morning. I was therefore directly in front of him as he made his brief speech. He stood tall and upright, still a very impressive figure. He spoke unassumingly but with undeniable magisterium. He was keen to reiterate that he had always been unhappy at being cited as *the* (sole) founder of the SAS.

'To ease my conscience,' he said, 'I would like it to be recognised that I have five co-founders: Jock Lewes and Paddy Blair Mayne of the original "L" Detachment; Georges Bergé, whose unit of Free French joined the SAS in January 1942; Brian Franks, who re-established 21 SAS Regiment after the SAS had been disbanded at the end of the Second World War; and John Woodhouse who created the modern 22 SAS Regiment during the Malay campaign by restoring to the Regiment its original philosophy.'

'*Jock Lewes*,' I thought, '*and Paddy Mayne, now those are names I've heard my father mention many times.*'

After Stirling had unveiled the new accommodation, I found myself talking to him.

'Almonds!?' he said. 'Not …?'

'Yes,' I said. 'I'm his daughter, and John's sister.' Stirling smiled, and looked across at my brother John, who had commanded one of the SAS Squadrons at Hereford, before going on to Staff College.

'Amazing,' he said. 'You know, your father was one of the fittest and most self-disciplined men I can ever remember. Really, it was unfair to use him as a standard for the others. And,' he glanced quickly sideways and lowered his voice in case my mother should be within earshot, 'he was such a damned good-looking chap. Oh yes. I've seen those women in Cairo eyeing him. But he seemed oblivious of it.' That was the last time I saw David Stirling, although my parents later attended a small lunch in honour of his Knighthood and my father saw him periodically until he died.

After the Regiment reformed in 1952, my father continued to serve with the SAS when they were still clearing terrorists out of northern Malaya until 1954. It is said that three factors count against being a successful parachutist: being over 6 feet tall, over 11 stones in weight and over forty. Since my father already had the first two against him, by 1954 when he was forty, it was time to stop.

As children, my brother John, my sister Gloria and I had grown up with little awareness of the SAS or what had happened in the war. My father never talked about what *he* had done. He was a quiet man anyway. We only knew that 'being fit' and not grumbling or giving up in the face of difficulties was important. Occasionally, making it very clear that it was information shared only 'within the family', he would talk with admiration about what others had done: of the determination and inspired leadership of Stirling, of the bravery of Lewes and Mayne, and of men like Chalky White who had lost a kidney and three fingers but 'never had a day off sick in his life'. In Kuala Lumpur, I remember young subalterns coming to our house for Sunday lunches and then suddenly 'Uncle Guy' or 'Uncle David' were not around any more. These young men were still being killed in action (and go on being killed) in the cause of freedom and peace long after the Second World War.

As we grew older, and became more aware, we were constantly reminded never to talk about, or even to mention, the SAS or any connection with it. As far as my father was concerned, its very existence was not to be disclosed by us. I remember very clearly the first occasion, in the early 1960s, when my sister and I heard a soldier boasting about his connections with the SAS (he pronounced it 'SASS' to rhyme with 'ass', something we had never heard before). We looked at each other in surprise since if he were really in it, or even had the right aptitude, he would not be engaging in such loose talk. We of course kept completely silent and delivered an immediate SITREP back to 'HQ', where my father and brother were outraged. It was simply not done to talk about the Regiment.

Time went by and it became increasingly clear that the public cover of the SAS was becoming very difficult to maintain. I say 'public' because it was not possible, without an elaborate and costly array of screening mechanisms, to avoid personal activities within certain parts of the Armed Forces from becoming common knowledge amongst those who had an occasion to know. The two young officers that I had happened to meet on my first day at Saighton Camp had known my brother in training and knew that he was preparing for SAS selection. My father, an original member of 'L' Detachment (the first men selected by Stirling in 1941) was also well known because he had already featured in many books about the Regiment. Throughout my own Army career, I was never posted to any unit without somebody having heard of the name 'Almonds'.

By the time of the Iranian Embassy siege in 1980, there was a moderate level of public awareness about the SAS but this was blown into a state of full-scale curiosity by the events at Princes Gate. Now, there was no point in trying to deny the fact and deadly efficiency of the SAS. In addition to the early books that had been written about the regiment, many excellent and authoritative text-books began to appear. Over the last few years, popular accounts have also been written, but these generally refer to service in the modern day SAS. This book does not attempt to replicate or denigrate any of these versions of events. It certainly does not seek to glorify war or the use of judicial violence. Rather it seeks to provide an accessible account of my father's amazing experiences, and those of other men like him, during the founding and very early years of the SAS.

The world in which my father was brought up and joined the SAS has now almost slipped away from us. Although standards of living were certainly harsher then, the men who joined 'L' Detachment at the very beginning of the SAS were not super-heroes. They felt pain, fear, hunger and despair. Apart from certain basic standards of physical fitness, such as good eyesight, they were different only because they chose to adopt a values system which denied self and set superlative standards of shared trust and loyalty. This is my father's story, and to an extent my mother's too, set in the context of the Western Desert in 1941 and 1942, of two dangerous escapes from prisoner-of-war (POW) camps in Italy in 1943 and, perhaps most perilous of all, of parachuting into France and operating behind enemy lines in 1944.

This is also the tale of a revolution in soldiering and how enemies are fought. In 1932, my father joined an early modern Army which had reformed after the débâcle of the First World War. During the raids of the Western Desert and on special operations in France, lessons were learned which turned the Army into today's post modern professional force. Somewhere during this short period, superiority through weight of numbers gave way to the triumph of quality over quantity – but at a cost. Something precious was lost in the process. We learned how to win the war but perhaps lost touch with the world we were defending. If this book awakens an interest in the moral values that underpinned the spirit of that age, which was after all a spirit of resistance against an evil regime, I shall have achieved my objective.

First SAS camp Kabrit drawn from memory by Almonds

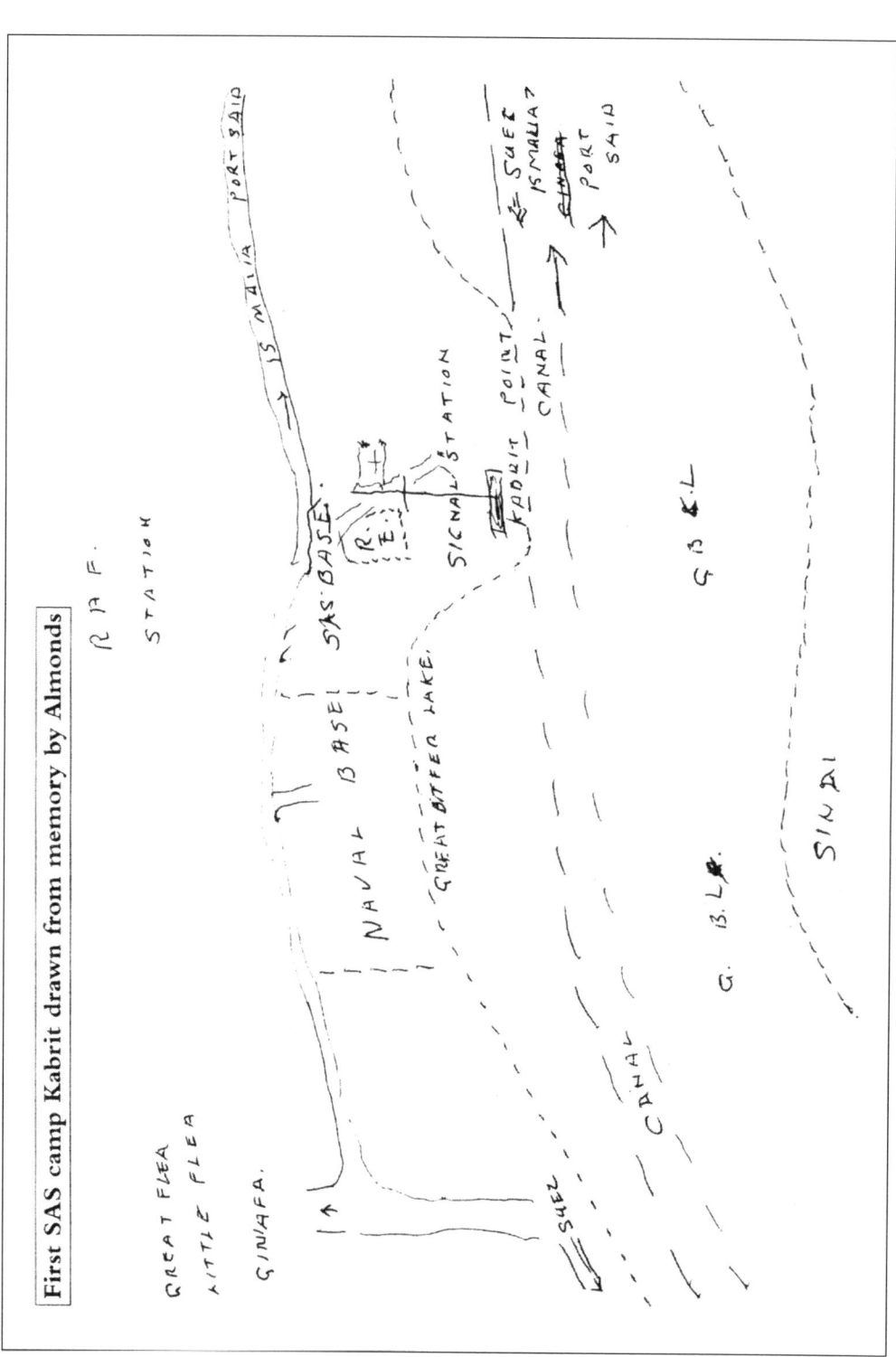

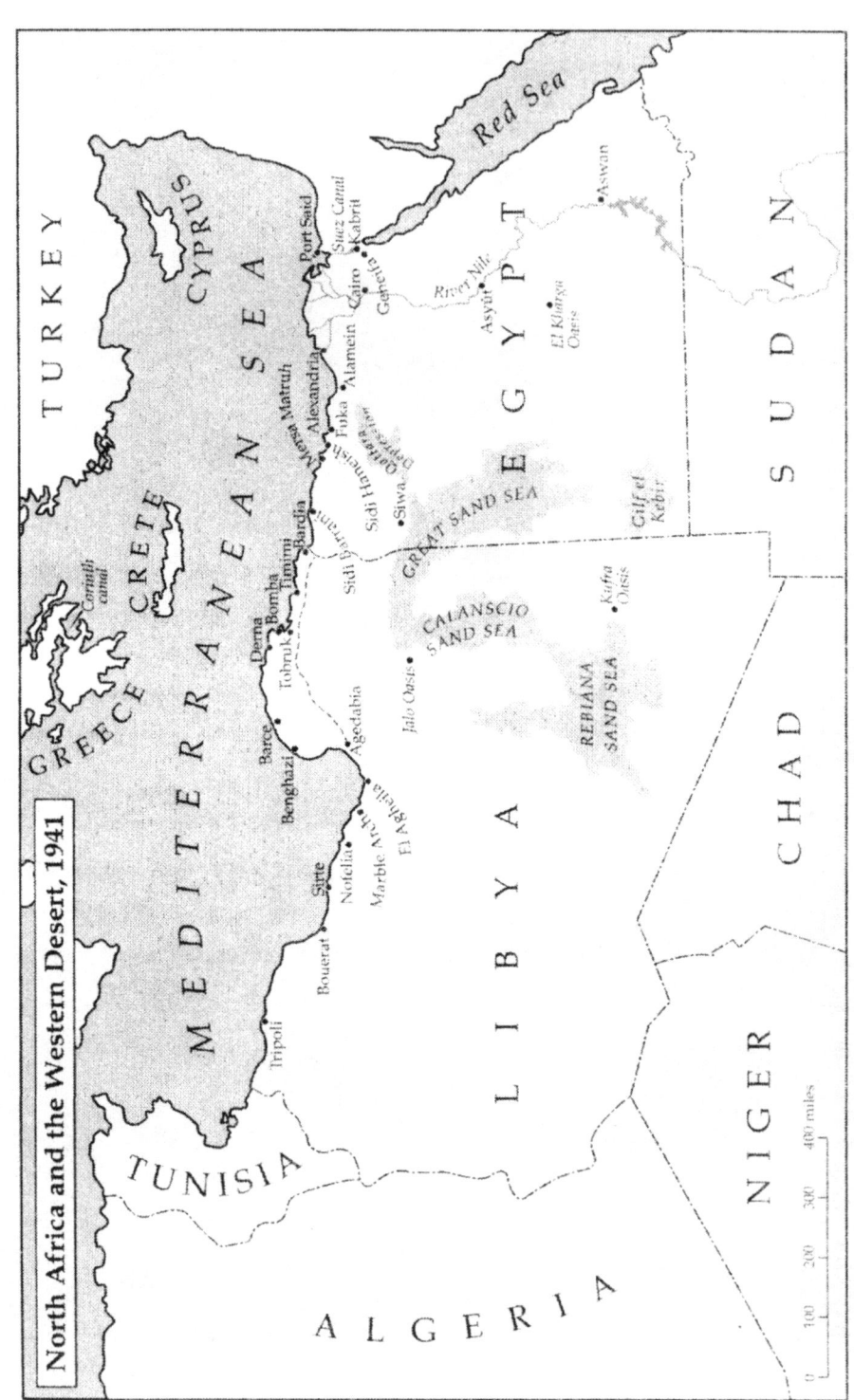

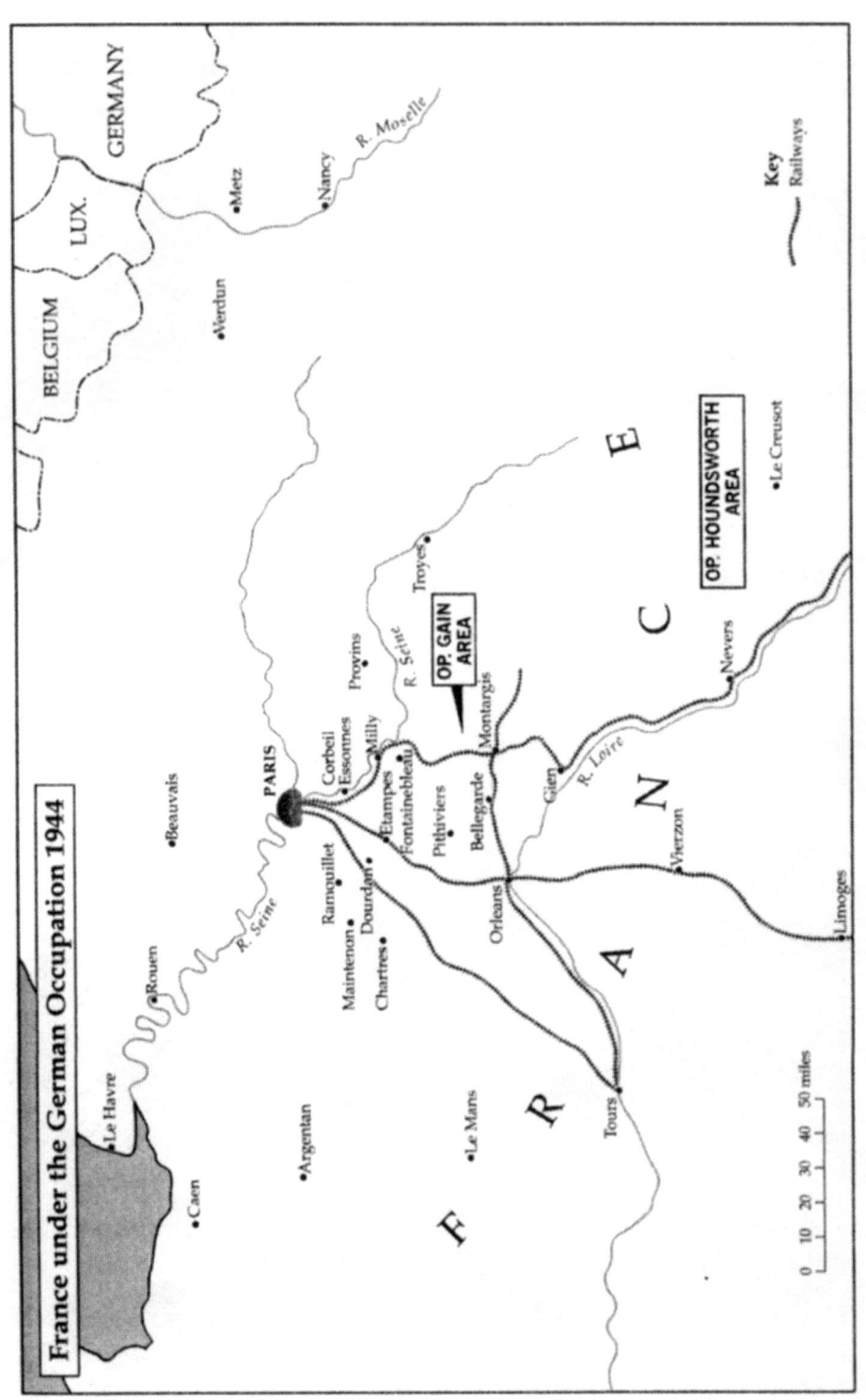

Part I

The Guards, The Commandos, the 'Tobruk Four', and the Founding of the SAS
August 1928 – October 1941

Chapter One

'L' Detachment – SAS

Geneifa, Egypt. Thursday, 4 September 1941, the first day of the third year of the war. In baking heat, a handful of Guards Commandos drew up a new set of equipment from the 'Q' stores and left by lorry for an unknown destination called Kabrit.[1] One of them was Jim Almonds, a very tall sergeant in the Coldstream Guards with dark brown hair and eyes. The others were Jim Blakeney, a big raw-boned trawler-man from Grimsby; Pat Riley, a six footer with a round, jovial face; and Bob Lilley, slim built, with a thin, dark moustache and high cheekbones. They headed towards Kabrit, east of Geneifa and north of Suez on the edge of the Great Bitter Lake.

Well out into the desert, the barren dusty little camp of a few tents was at first sight completely deserted. One or two warships anchored out in the Lake provided the only visible signs of life. It was the hottest time of the day; the sun beat down on a silence broken only by the distant muffled sound of firing practice across the water. At the entrance to a tent, heroically purporting to be an HQ, a handwritten notice on a stick in the ground said 'L' DETACHMENT S.A.S. REGIMENT.

Riley leaned out of the truck as they drew within sight of their new Unit. He had been born in America but had returned to England at an early age. In spite of his nationality, he had managed to get into the Coldstream Guards. Suddenly, he spotted a lone figure sitting on an up-ended kit bag.

'It can't be – yes it is – it's Seekings!'[2] His old friend heaved himself up and came to meet them. He had a neat fair triangular moustache and unruly light brown hair which was plastered straight back on the few occasions when he had it under control. He and Riley were old sparring partners from earlier days in the Army. His compact stocky build was ideally suited for parachuting, while his irascible nature made him a dangerous opponent in the boxing ring. Seekings helped them to unload their kit from the truck while they plied him with questions. He told them that there was a naval station just down the road, one of those dry land ships that the Navy took so seriously, where they had to talk about going ashore. There was also an Air Force base, and a New Zealand stores depot not too far away.

It was soon apparent that Kabrit itself was 'a bit of a do-it-yourself job'. Not only did they have to dig in for the tentage but, according to the CQMS (Company Quarter Master Sergeant), they were going to have get the tents from somewhere, along with other essentials. A whole crowd of other men were due to arrive soon from the old Troop of their CO (Commanding Officer) David Stirling. These included Ernie Bond, who had been with them inside Tobruk.

That evening, the SAS came together for the first time. David Stirling addressed them all in the still warm open air.[3] The atmosphere was not unlike that of the first day of a new school term. Next to Stirling, stood a young Welsh Guards officer, Lieutenant Jock Lewes. He had not been blessed with the physique, strength and stamina of the average Commando but he looked keen and intelligent. He was about six feet tall with a slim build and a high forehead from which thick sandy brown hair was swept cleanly back. He had a sharp, sensitive face with the regulation neat moustache and an unconscious slight air of superiority. He was very fit. But there were some things which fitness could not prevent. His hands and arms were disfigured by weeping desert sores.

The founder members of the SAS were gathered informally, dressed in variations on the standard theme of the Commando uniform of khaki shorts and shirts. Lewes motioned to them all to sit down. Jim Almonds and Riley, with Jim Blakeney and Bob Lilley were grouped in front of Lewes. They were the Tobruk Four, who had carried out night operations with him behind enemy lines in Tobruk. Ernie Bond was close to Stirling. Dave Kershaw lounged next to Seekings. Kershaw was tall, with dark intelligent eyes and angular features. 'Honest Dave' had fought in Spain against Franco on the Republican side as a member of the International Brigade. He and other, rather idealistic, young men had suffered and lost together but they had not given up their ideals. Dave would never do down a friend but he had no compunction about ripping off the system when it came to commodities which were in short supply.

Corporal Bob Bennett, a cheerful cockney from the Grenadier Guards, pale complexioned, thin faced and slightly intense, squatted on his haunches next to Corporal Jimmy Brough, a canny Scot with beetling brows from Stirling's own Scots Guards and Commando days. Corporals Johnny Rose and Johnny Cooper, also from the Scots Guards and among the youngest of the volunteers, sat next to each other. Beside them,

Sergeants Bob Tait and Geoff DuVivier, of the Gordon Highlanders waited patiently with Privates Jock Byrne and Jimmie Storie.[4] 'Whacker' Evans, Scots Guards, and Tubby Trenfield, Warwickshire Light Infantry, two large burly men with bluff, matter-of-fact faces surveyed the scene impassively.

Stirling was immaculate but relaxed. He had an air of effortless superiority. He thanked them all for being there, taking time to pause and let his gaze rest on each man. He had a simple direct way of speaking that got right through.

'I know that each one of you has made a personal decision to be here and I am delighted to have you on board.' A few discreet coughs covered the unexpected emotion of the moment. Then he went on to say that it worked both ways. They were a brand new Unit and could not afford to carry any passengers. Nor could they afford to 'piss about' disciplining anyone who was not one hundred per cent devoted to having a good crack at the Hun. The SAS discipline would be self-discipline. If they did not want to stay, or if they were not up to it, they would be RTU'd (Returned to Unit) immediately. The assembled men did not demur.

He went on. It was a new Unit. They must not expect to be spoon fed by MEHQ (Middle East Headquarters) or have everything done for them. 'L' Detachment would be what they made it. As a first step he suggested that they devote some time to deciding what was needed by way of stores and equipment. Then it was up to them to go and find them. There was a large Allied stores depot not far away which probably would not even miss what 'L' Detachment needed as basic essentials. Grins flashed around the assembled group. But Stirling was quick to drive home the message about personal standards. They knew that routine operational standards always fell slightly below those achieved in training. So they would aim for the highest, most testing levels of endurance and performance when they were undergoing training. Though it would be tough, they would give thanks for it when they were in action.

Part of their training, he told them, would be aimed at getting them to think for themselves. While the team concept remained important, each one of them had to develop a sense of their own independence and personal effectiveness. Finally, he emphasised that turnout and bearing were important to their morale. Although when they were out in the desert there might not always be enough water to wash and shave, nothing was changed the rest of the time. In camp, they all owed it to each other, and to the good name of their new Unit, to maintain the highest possible standards of dress and behaviour. They could get a visit from MEHQ at any time and so should not be caught napping. After wishing them good evening and good luck, Stirling, accompanied for a few yards by Lewes, headed off towards the Officers' Mess tent.

In September 1941, war in the Western Desert was coming to the end of its phoney lull. Since the British operation codenamed *Battleaxe* had failed to relieve Tobruk on 15 June and General Sir Claude Auchinleck – 'the Auk' – had replaced Wavell as Commander in Chief Middle East,[5] the numbers of men under arms in the Nile theatre had grown to around 500,000. They had quickly been organised into the Eighth in the Western Desert, the Ninth Army in Syria and Palestine and the Tenth Army in Baghdad.

Wavell's days of dearth in material resources also seemed to be over. American weapons and equipment were augmenting the supplies arriving from Britain and the Commonwealth. The Suez Canal was safe and open to Allied shipping. Apart from the continued bombardment of Tobruk, which was besieged but still held on, peace appeared to have settled over the Western Desert. But the appearance was deceptive. As the weeks passed, it became clear that both sides were conducting sedate and civilised preparations for an inevitable battle. The tide of war had slopped messily from west to east and back again since early 1940, as the Axis made gains and was then pushed back, only to advance again, always along the vital coastal strip of road, ports and airfields. Each ebb and flow left a dirty brown tide mark of mangled and broken vehicles, equipment and weapons and desert scrub scorched and blackened with oil. A spring tide was now gathering itself up in the west. Rommel was preparing to unleash his forces in one massive attempt to breach the Allies' flimsy defences and sweep into Cairo, Egypt and beyond. The outcome of the war in the Middle East was at stake.

That first night, after Stirling's talk, bank upon bank of vermilion cloud marbled the late evening sky as the newly formed SAS men began to consider their first night operation, an assault on the New Zealand Army. They clustered around the CQMS, Gerry Ward, to go over the list of stores and equipment to be purloined. Ward was matter of fact as he outlined the objectives. A stocky, slightly older man, he had been selected for his experience as a first-rate quarter-master sergeant. Most of the Kiwis were away on operations so they shouldn't have too much trouble getting what they wanted. They needed basic items like tents, the bigger the better, camp beds and chairs, small tables, receptacles such as bowls, jugs and any medium-sized luxury items they could find like mirrors, wash stands and so on. They were not to waste time carrying back anything that they could already get like basic rations, issued kit or medical supplies.

The area stores depot turned out to be huge. The moon had not risen and the stars of the immense desert night gave little light, cloaking their clandestine mission. The marauders from Kabrit prowled about in what seemed like a veritable city of British and other Commonwealth tents before getting their bearings and making for the New Zealanders' lines. Each man had a few secret qualms; the Kiwis were well liked and respected as the finest infantry in the Middle East.[6] They were also paid more than the British and lived accordingly. Suddenly, the SAS men saw the scale of their antipodean colleagues' provision.

'Blimey!' Lilley was staggered. The New Zealanders appeared to have everything except the kitchen sink. They even had a stock of every item. Kershaw was impressed.

Almonds was relieved. He and Riley were bent on equipping the first SAS Sergeants Mess to a high standard but they did not want to deprive the New Zealanders. They carried out a 6 foot folding trestle table for the bar. With it into the back of the 3 ton truck went a turned, dark oak standard lamp. Kershaw struggled up with two others carrying an old piano which they hoisted up into the three-tonner. By common assent, Bennett and Rose certainly 'had the tonsils' for singing along with it.[7]

Riley and Almonds got hold of a three-man tent and a double; they were to share with Ernie Bond, while Lilley and Blakeney shared another. Without too much difficulty, they acquired a few more decent sized tents. One or two were even taken while still fully erected by grabbing each corner and lifting them noiselessly from around their sleeping occupants.[8] On the way back, the brigands passed the camp cinema tent and relieved it of the first few rows of easy chairs reserved for the officers.[9]

A little while later, Stirling asked Almonds if he could build them some parachute training equipment. He said that he had heard from Mr Lewes, who had introduced the idea of parachuting to Stirling, that Sergeant Almonds was 'a dab hand at making things'.

'We very badly need parachute training equipment here,' he said. What do you think you can do for us?' He had a way of making the most impossible request seem perfectly reasonable and anyone who did not immediately accede to his demands feel a total spoil sport. Almonds thought on his feet. He had joined the SAS for the challenge, not to end up becoming a Clerk of Works. And making things when the right tools and materials were not available was a very tall order. On the other hand, the means to train properly was vitally important; the success of the unit and possibly the saving of lives depended on it. And he had heard that the CO was a very difficult man to refuse. He hesitated. But then saw that Stirling was looking at him with a confident smile on his face. Before he knew where he was, they were discussing the details. It was true. It *was* impossible to say no to him.[10]

The men saw little of their leader, who appeared to spend his time alternately browbeating the staff at MEHQ or importuning his many personal 'contacts' in Cairo with the same objective of acquiring the basic necessities required by his new unit. But resources were not his only problem. His small force of six officers and sixty men, and his own recent promotion to Captain, had been granted at a price. He had agreed to plan operations jointly with the Director of Military Operations, MEHQ. It was not a happy marriage. For a start, the two men had different perceptions of 'L' Detachment's role. Stirling's original idea was based on the notion that 'small is beautiful', especially when it comes accompanied by the element of surprise and the freedom of complete flexibility, to do whatever is required in any given situation to achieve the objective. His aim was to make the unit strategic. It would focus on specific targets where minimum input could cause maximum damage to the enemy. This would mean attacking and disrupting whatever was most crucial to the enemy's ability to make progress in winning the war.[11]

All this was a foreign language to the average Woolwich and Camberley-trained staff officer and particularly incomprehensible to the Director of Military Operations. To make matters worse, they were not on the same wavelength. In fact they did not even use the same medium of communication. Stirling liked a face to face meeting, possibly with a few key points sketched out on the back of a tobacco packet as an *aide mémoir*. Failing that option, he preferred to pick up the 'phone. Such methods of interaction enabled him to make the most of his considerable powers of oral persuasion and personal charm. He detested the pirouetting on paper beloved of staff officers in general and of the Director of Military Operations[12] in particular. It was to say the least an uneasy relationship.

On Friday 5 September 1941, 'L' Detachment started training for operations to be carried out in enemy territory, for which they would be dropped by parachute.[13] Each morning, while it was still dark, they went out on a route march or a long distance run, resplendent in Empire builder navy blue PT shorts. Then the daily tasks and training would begin and continue until dark. A rumour about a young officer called Blair Mayne was prominent in the minds of the men. It was said that 'Paddy' Mayne was joining the unit. Unless the bush telegraph served them wrong, Mayne had come out with 11 Scottish Commando. He was said to be good in action; perhaps a bit too good. According to Riley, the boys were all pretty impressed about him having 'smacked' his last CO during an argument, actually knocking him down. Stirling had had to get him out from close arrest to sign him up.[14]

Most mornings, the trainees were out early. When they did not run, they played rugby on a pitch with hurricane oil lamps hung out as markers. The 'A' and 'B' teams represented nothing in particular. The main aim of the exercise was to knock each other about a bit. One morning, a new officer joined in the training.[15] This, they were told by the PTI (Physical Training Instructor), was Lieutenant Mayne. He was big, with massive thighs and shoulders and huge, spade-like hands. Almonds judged him to be about his own height, around six foot three, but heavier at around fifteen and a half stones. Nothing unusual in that for 'L' Detachment. But for all his bulk, this man handled himself well. He was very alert and fast on his feet.

The desert night air was still crisp and they kept moving, even when the ball was momentarily not in play. Pools of light flooded the area around each flickering lamp, and the noisy scuffling of the game moved from the light into the shadow and back again, up and down the pitch. Once the game got going, everyone forgot the training element. Only the winning mattered. Shouts rang out.

'Here! Pass man, pass!'

'Com'on now Jimmaie! Overrrr heerrrrre! Over heerrrrre!'

'Ouch!' Almonds had run into one of Mayne's huge ham-like hands. The new arrival grinned and darted away with the ball. The word was that he had been a Rugby International before the war.

'Get away!' said Bob Bennett, who never believed anything first go around.[16]

After a game, they would rest for a few moments winding down from the physical exertion. It gave a peculiar inner glow of confidence, the rough and tumble, the getting slightly hurt and not showing it, the learning to handle themselves better next time, the not taking it personally. They got to know each other. Gradually, it strengthened that strange thing called character.

In parachute training too, Mayne was focused and nimble, rolling quickly forward and up onto his feet when he hit the ground. Withdrawn by nature, with a saturnine countenance, he said little and when he spoke it was quietly with a soft Irish lilt. He made his points slowly, with a kind of deliberate logic. He did not seem entirely comfortable speaking in front of the group, which included one or two other officers. It seemed to Almonds that there was almost a touch of shyness there, yet Mayne was obviously well educated and confident. Often, the Irishman appeared to be brooding, as if he were weighing up the situation, while underneath lay barely controlled anger. He spoke little and at each break in the training would immediately light up a cigarette and engross himself in a book.[17]

One morning, the serious training began. It was 07.30 and they had just returned from a four hour forced march across the desert, followed by a quick burst of PT.[18] Already the sun was glaring out of a cloudless sky. Lewes had expertise in the chemistry department. He seemed to spend most of his spare time in a makeshift shack of a laboratory, cooking up experiments on explosives, earning himself the nickname of 'the Wizard'.[19]

The men assembled around him, wondering what was coming next. This was the part of their training, Lewes told them, where they were going back to school. But this was a school for learning how to blow things up. Chortles of enthusiasm came from the trainees. But Lewes's expression remained deadly serious. He told them that the curriculum consisted of demolition: the recognition and handling of different explosive substances and fuses and their suitability for various tasks. They would also look at how they deployed the devices so that they did maximum damage. Again, grins flashed around the group. But Lewes immediately dampened the mood of the moment. This was a course where people could not learn from their mistakes. That was because they were usually dead.[20]

It was true that nothing concentrates the mind like the thought of one's own impending execution. 'L' Detachment settled down for the morning's lectures. For blowing up bridges, there was a neat formula. One pound of standard plastic explosive would blow 1 inch of steel, 12 inches of timber or 20 inches of masonry. So they could calculate how much plastic to use, where to place it and how to link it together. First World War gun cotton slabs could be used with a primer, detonator and length of fuse, long enough to allow the saboteur to get clear.

They studied the effective sabotage of enemy aircraft, ammunition dumps and railways. Destruction had to be 'strategic'. There was a standard policy of attack, especially in the placing of bombs, so that it was not possible for the enemy to 'cannibalize' by taking working parts from each aircraft or vehicle so as to repair and produce one operational machine. The aim in blowing railways was to spread the rails apart so that trains would be derailed. The main objectives were those parts of the track which would be most difficult to replace, such as points or curved stretches. Failing these targets, a mine was to be placed on a straight stretch. The objective was always to disable machines or installations, not to kill or injure men. Nevertheless, it was a sober group of trainees who learned the deadly skills of their new trade.[21]

Before long, they were unutterably weary in mind and body. In spite of being superbly fit, they were suffering from physical training which threatened to test the human body to destruction.[22] Stiff in every limb and joint, an unspoken fear began to set in. At times, the training standards seemed impossible to reach and the risk of death and injury almost a certainty as they hurled themselves out of trucks moving at nearly thirty miles an hour. They were also sick at heart at the apparent prospect of the war stretching away ahead of them while life passed them by. On Sunday 7 September Almonds wrote in his diary:

> Feel a real coward. Would to God I were a brave enough man to turn down this job and seek employment in a training centre. Have a horrible feeling that soon my darling wife may be caused much sorrow.

One morning he and Pat Riley lay resting after a night scheme. They had blown up a disused factory with charges of gun cotton and marched the 14 miles back on a compass bearing.[23] Ernie Bond came to tell them that 'the Wizard' was going to put on a good show. In addition to the training in demolition, Lewes had been deploying his scientific skills on some novel bomb designs. At night, the light in his 'laboratory' could often be seen burning late as he worked on customising some special device for SAS purposes. Apparently, he was set to prove all the boffins wrong. There was to be a demo' for the CO and a couple of 'nancies' from MEHQ to show that it was possible to get a bomb to blow up an aircraft *and* set it on fire at the same time.[24]

They joined a growing crowd of men and strolled over to the demonstration that Lewes had set up on the edge of the camp. An old aircraft with a gallon drum of petrol placed inside against the fuselage near the wing represented the enemy target. A small bomb, not more than a pound in weight sat on the wing. Without standing on ceremony and with barely a nod in the direction of Stirling and a group of Royal Corps of Engineers from MEHQ, Lewes detonated the device. The explosion itself was small. The crowd watched, all eyes concentrating on the sputtering flames which seemed for a moment about to die. Then with a roar, echoed by a great shout of satisfaction from the onlookers, the fuel tank caught fire and flames leaped up into the air, licking round the aircraft frame. After controlling the blaze, Lewes walked quietly away, leaving Stirling to smooth the ruffled feathers of the Royal Engineers Brigadier and the technical officers from MEHQ.[25]

In spite of his natural modesty, Lewes took the first opportunity the next day to teach the new bomb to his trainees.[26] They had to begin, he said, with 1 pound of plastic and knead for a while. Then they had to wrap thermite inside the plastic 'dough' – adding the thermite would keep the burning going after the explosion – then a detonator and a fuse would be added. Lewes was walking about in front of the group as he manipulated the small ball of plastic between his hands. Then he explained that as they put the detonator in, they had to crimp it to the fuse by biting it. He demonstrated, putting the two components together between his strong white teeth and biting hard. They had to build in the delay by using a thin metallic tube with a copper wire inside which would decay on contact with acid from a small phial – Lewes held it up and showed it around that group as he talked. When the phial broke, depending on the amount of acid inside it was possible to vary the time before the bomb went off, from about ten minutes to over an hour. The device was not very heavy so quite a few could be carried on raids. Appreciative grins spread around the class. But Lewes seemed always bound to quench any high spirits.

'Oh, by the way,' he said. 'Making the bomb and moulding the plastic gives you a headache and a bit of a queer feeling. But it soon passes off.'[27] From then on the men made their own 'Lewes' bombs for use in the field.

Lewes was a technical entrepreneur par excellence. But every successful piece of technical innovation cost him dear in the many hours he spent working on devices that were not, in the end, practicable. He was dedicated to developing any specialist innovation that would give the SAS an advantage over the enemy. But since there was no way to buy this in he used his own resources of knowledge, to utilise whatever was to hand. This was not invention, but exploitation. He was always gathering data which he then qualified by quizzing others about it.[28] Since Almonds was good at making things, he was often the target of these attentions. On one occasion, Lewes experimented with a new vehicle ambush technique by planting 44-gallon oil drums on either side of a road where it ran into a defile. By means of a trip wire across the path of the vehicle, a small charge beneath each drum would detonate and launch them into the air. A second charge would then disperse burning oil and tar over the enemy transport passing through.[29]

Gradually, Lewes began to translate his innovations into the technical training for which the SAS later became famous. Even the standard operating structure, of having a CO, a 2IC (Second in Command) and an officer in charge of Training Wing, was developed then and still survives. Stirling, Mayne and Lewes live on in their modern-day counterparts.[30] But training was never a soft option. It was deadly serious.

Lewes's great contributions to the SAS were the use of the parachute, four-man teams and the bomb named after him. Stirling's were the strategic role and the culture. 'L' Detachment's *raison d'être* was to destroy a whole range of key enemy installations: as many enemy fighter aircraft as possible whilst on the ground at their aerodromes, together with ammunition dumps and petrol stores. The SAS repertoire also included attacks on ships, port harbour facilities and infrastructures, such as roads, railways, bridges, pipelines and telephones, which would interfere with the enemy's vital flow of supplies. With every mile that Rommel advanced, his precious supply line became more extended, presenting a tantalising target for the saboteurs. Operations were to be carried out at night, well behind enemy forward troops, by small groups of about six men who would first lie up well hidden and observe the enemy, before moving in to strike after dark. It was estimated that such a team would have time to blow up about sixty aircraft – as many as were destroyed in one afternoon by the assembled British fighter 'planes in the Battle of Britain – but with significantly reduced costs and loss of life.

One of Stirling's greatest contributions was arguably the ethos. Success depended on the pursuit of excellence in personnel selection, training and team building. Having selected men on the basis of criteria which included brain as well as brawn, integrity and loyalty, Stirling engendered an approach which looked for the best in every man. He never blamed or criticised, but was quick to take responsibility himself for any failures. By focusing on achievements and praising them, confidence was boosted and he inspired trust as a leader. Stirling never mentioned his own contribution but always lauded the successes of others.[31] Mistakes were quickly learned from – and then just as quickly thrust aside. They were never allowed to sap confidence or destroy mutual trust. Personal aggrandisement and bragging were particularly eschewed. The final refreshing difference from the rest of the regular Army was mutual respect. Although *responsibilities* might vary according to rank, every man was an equal; personal qualities and what a man could *do* did not depend on class.[32] In this atmosphere, the 'L' Detachment men underwent the most dangerous and most arduous training programme of their lives.

On 21 September, Almonds sat alone with his diary, thinking of his wife Lockie and the son he had left at three months old.

> John's first birthday. On this morning one year ago today we were together and you my pet needed a little love and care. Do you remember?

In Bristol, John was very ill and getting worse. Lockie had kept the bad news from her husband in the hope that it was only temporary. She could not bear to think of him worrying when he was powerless to do anything to help. She was keeping a brave face in front of her parents. Alone, she occasionally allowed herself a silent, desperate weep.

The training continued. For the first time, Almonds was really afraid. As part of pre-jump preparations, 'L' Detachment had started taking occasional flights in a Bristol Bombay bomber. Parachute training was also well underway. He had resigned himself to the role of 'bogus engineer' and had built the jumping stands requested by Stirling. Each was a large wooden hexagon with sides which increased in height as the trainee worked his way round it from 4 to 12 feet.[33] Parachute landing practice had progressed from 8 feet, as they swung out on ropes from the frame, let go and went into a forward roll. Hitting the ground from 12 feet was extremely hard. It felt as if their knees were going to be rammed right up into their shoulders.

He also built a mini-railway line and they started jumping off a trolley rolling down an inclined ramp, to practice sideways and backward rolls. The next step was to provide for a dummy drop by parachute. He took over the work of designing and erecting two 40-foot towers for a 'wedding ring' assembly which would represent the hole in the underside of the aircraft through which they would jump when making their parachute drops. The work had already been started, mostly with materials pilfered from a nearby Royal Engineers unit, and he was presented with a large, very heavy ring of angled iron that had been joined into a circle. The massive contraption was, in his view, highly dangerous and a sure recipe for injuries so he had had to begin the work again from scratch. With his precious couple of hours' spare time after dark, he started building a canoe out of old packing cases.

Parachute training continued. The SAS was preparing for its first major drop in enemy territory. On 6 October he wrote in his diary:

> Some of the lads made their first parachute descent from the plane. Afternoon spent jumping backwards from a lorry at twenty-five miles per hour. Three broken arms and a number of other casualties. Broken bones through training now six. Sent Lockie a wire. Worried, have not heard from her for some time.

The next day, importantly as it later turned out, he wrote that the parachute static line fittings on the plane had been scrapped because they were inadequate to stand up to the job. Having finished the base of the first tower, he supervised the start of work on the erection of the steel uprights. Work was progressing nicely on the canoe. Then, on 9 October, came urgent news from home. His son was in hospital.

> Received bad news today. Wire from Lockie through CO. Sonny [the baby] dangerously ill. My God, what can I do now? Interview with Commanding Officer with a view to being returned home. He promised to do his best but fear the worst.[34]

Stirling was sympathetic but not encouraging. It seemed that the baby was not expected to live. Leave was out of the question but he suggested that Almonds take time out to write home. 'L' Detachment did a 'night scheme' and he marched thirty miles before morning like an automaton.[35] What if he too were killed or disabled?

> Canoe finished. Great success but afforded me no pleasure. Too worried about Lockie and little John. Pray that they are all right. No news from home. Wonder how things are. Construction of towers continued. They must be safe and strong or I shall be responsible for someone being injured or killed.[36]

Suddenly, he seemed to have more challenges than a man can cope with.

He had not imagined this combination of impending disasters in his life when he had first attempted to join the Army.

Chapter Two

Lincolnshire Poacher and Guards Commando

Jim Almonds was born in the tiny, ancient village of Stixwould in the middle of Lincolnshire. A human settlement of some sort has been there since Roman times.[1] His grandfather, Edward Almonds, was a farmer who lost everything due to foot and mouth disease. By 1900, he was reduced to a smallholding with a few fields. Jim, christened John, but known as Jack until he joined the Army, was born in the house that he lived in until he died in 2005. He had a rugged upbringing. In winter, children were wrapped up and put outside to play. They soon learned to run around to keep warm and to eat when food was on offer.

Jim's father George inherited the small-holding. He was a churchwarden and the family Bible was read every evening before retiring. On Sundays, it remained open on the table all day. Jack was brought up on 'Masterman Ready' stories and Rider Haggard, which instilled a need for adventure. His father built working model steam engines for a hobby and from an early age, Jack made things with his hands in wood and metal. He was always whittling a stick, or carving a new bow from a carefully selected young yew tree. Boats fascinated him and at ten years old he built his first craft, a punt made out of a bacon box with toffee tins as outriggers for extra stability. He learned knots and rope-making and enjoyed boxing the compass. From the start he got selected for things. The first medal ever pinned to his chest was the first prize in a local Bonny Baby competition.

On his fourteenth birthday in 1928, he made his first attempt to join the Army. But it did no good. The sergeant squinted at the name scrawled on the dun coloured application form and said that much as his Majesty would like to have the volunteer before the colours, he needed to stand up straight. The boy was already 6 feet tall and nobody had ever mentioned that he did not stand up straight. His chances of being accepted were slim. The Army could afford to be choosy between the Wars.

He worked at the Vicarage at Hutoft, near the coast, where he performed a range of duties: acolyte, incense-swinger and bell-ringer. There, he refitted all the bells with new pulls. When the weather was too bitter for him to cycle across half of Lincolnshire, he enjoyed pencilled letters from home. Most of the correspondence was about making things.[2] At seventeen, he built an aeroplane in the village school yard. Helped by a friend, he made it mostly out of wood and cloth, savouring every stage of the planning, preparation, assembly and finishing. The embryo aircraft had a Douglas twin motor-cycle engine without an exhaust which made a terrible racket. He took particular pleasure in fashioning the hand-carved two blade wooden propeller. The 'plane never flew. But he knew what would have made it fly, had the money been available. His photograph appeared in the *Lincolnshire Chronicle* on his eighteenth birthday, sitting in the pilot's seat.

On the same day, he set off again for the recruiting office.

'You want to go into the Lincolnshires?' said the sergeant. 'Oh no. It's the Brigade of Guards for you lad.' The ease of his acceptance was a complete anti-climax. He had anticipated a real fight to get in.[3]

Basic training was hard. At the Guards Depot at Pirbright, everything had to be done 'at the double'. And there were other challenges. A big heavy red-faced man leered at him as he lay on his pallet mattress with his knees up on his first night in the reception centre.

'Don't sleep like that lad!' he said. 'If you fart in the night you'll blow your balls off!' Almonds kept quiet and the antagonist went off to find better sport. A few young men were totally unable to cope. The recruits were deeply shocked when one young man killed himself by drinking the 'Bluebell' metal polish that they used to clean their brasses.

But there were good times too. Almonds revelled in the freedom of the countryside around Pirbright and spent most of his spare time swimming, fishing and roaming among the fir trees. He had no nickname. But if anyone called out 'John', half the barrack room stood up. He was the one to volunteer to be called something different.

'All right,' he said simply, 'I'll be Jim.'

In 1932, the tallest of the nation's offering went into No. 1 Company of the 2nd Battalion, Coldstream Guards. No. 4 Company took the second tallest while the shortest went to No. 3, known rather disparagingly as the 'Coal-box Company'. Almonds adapted easily to life in No. 1 Company. The Tower of London at the beginning of 1933 was a fascinating place. Everything about it was big and ancient. Each step on the stone stairway he went down every morning was massive. The cookhouse was giant-sized and the food came in appropriate quantities.

Discipline was tough but fair. Things had been much harder in the past. The Company Sergeant-Major, 'Woof Woof' Dobson, used to talk about conditions during the Great War. If they thought their discipline was tough, he would say, they should have been in the Army then. Young soldiers were executed at dawn for cowardice in the face of the enemy. They could have been suffering from trauma but something had to be done to preserve the rock-solid discipline of the Guards. And it was.

Two weeks after arriving at the Tower,[4] Almonds was guarding Norman Baillie-Stewart, an aristocratic young subaltern in the Seaforth Highlanders. He was incarcerated in the Tower for passing military secrets to a German army officer, after succumbing to sexual charms of his wife.[5] Each day, the subaltern was escorted to his court martial hearings in Chelsea Barracks. Dashingly elegant in his Highland uniform and kilt, Baillie-Stewart was a crowd-puller for visitors to the Tower and women waited hours to watch him exercising in the Tower grounds.

Under close arrest, he was accompanied by a young Guards officer of equivalent rank and a sentry in case the prisoner should do anything stupid. Occasionally the sentry marched up and down but most of the time he stood at ease with his rifle at his side. The two young officers decided to stroll along the Tower casement. As they walked up and down past the young Almonds, he was faced with a dilemma. The rules on saluting require that a soldier in uniform and wearing headgear must salute every time he passes an officer, or an officer passes him. So every time the two officers passed him, he brought himself smartly up to attention, heaved his rifle up and sloped it over his shoulder before slapping his arm across its butt, to give them a 'butt salute'. Now the stretch of casement was quite short so they passed him about every five minutes. After a while, he began to think that it was rather silly to keep on saluting them and the effort of picking up the heavy rifle and throwing it up over his shoulder became almost impossible. But he kept going until he was relieved by another sentry. Not long afterwards, 'Woof Woof' Dobson sent for him and told him that he had been highly commended by both the young officers for his smartness – and no doubt for his perseverance in 'the paying of compliments.'[6]

He was selected to take part in the seven centuries-old Ceremony of the Keys and soon on public duties at Buckingham Palace and St James's he began to recognise the Prince of Wales coming in and out in his Jaguar,

'AXL 1', often driving himself. The Prince would always give a cheery 'Goodnight' as Almonds presented arms. Old Queen Mary was rather more exacting. She would occasionally stop and criticise the Guardsmen's turnout and bearing. It was very disconcerting to have one's drill corrected by the Queen.

Duties also included guarding the Bank of England. A picket of the Coldstream Guards in their red tunics and red-plumed bearskins would march through the streets of London to the Bank. They were deployed throughout the building and the Bullion Yard below. Patrolling at night, there was one corridor where Almonds would pass back and forth in the early hours of the morning under a hole in the ceiling. It marked the spot where one Guardsman had put his rifle in his mouth and shot himself.

No. 1 Company happened to be on public duties again when King George V died. Almonds was selected for special duty. He and a friend brought off the King's colour at Buckingham Palace. Slowly, the two Guardsmen lowered the scarlet colour. Then they hoisted the Regimental colour to half mast.[7] On the day of the funeral, he was one of the twenty Guardsmen marching slowly behind the cortège, their bright red tunics and the Royal Standard draping the coffin the only splash of colour in the grey London streets. He was also selected for the Guard of Honour when the Duke of Kent married the Princess Marina. The Riding School behind Buckingham Palace was a kaleidoscope of colour as the wedding party and guests mingled with disabled ex-servicemen from the Great War and scarlet-coated Chelsea Pensioners.

When his four year tour of engagement drew to its close, Almonds had the option of re-enlisting but decided against it. At twenty-two, he was quiet, with a dry sense of humour. Gregarious, he was more reserved about making close friends. Superbly fit, with enormous physical strength, he enjoyed throwing the javelin and running for the regiment and the local Horsham Blue Star and Belgrave Harriers. He still thought about the sea and hankered after adventure.

In 1936 Oswald Mosley held regular parades through the streets of Bristol. Popular disaffection had been fanned by the Great Depression and at police school there was much talk about someone in Germany called Hitler.

One balmy evening in June 1936, he saw my mother May Lock for the first time. Three girls had reached the lower part of York Street in the Bristol city parish of St Werburghs. P.C. Almonds strolled casually across the bottom of the street and, changing direction, began to patrol up the road on the other side. He came level with the three girls who were lingering to chat by a street lamp. He checked them out, as a young man notes girls. The one he remembered, pretty, with dark hair, went into the house near the street lamp. Mentally, he stored away the street lamp as a marker to where she lived.[8]

October 1937. May Lock headed along Mina Road towards the bottom of York Street as water from the Bristol floods washed over the pavements. Her way was blocked by a tall policeman in front of her. His short cape gave him a Dickensian appearance but she could see that he was quite young. He told her to retrace her steps and approach York Street from the top and watched her retreat along the deserted rain-washed road. She went back and round to the top of York Street, which was not under water, and waited while her mother sent her wellington boots up to her across all the back garden walls.[9]

Autumn 1938 was mild but blustery, reflecting the pontifications of the politicians as they speculated about the possibility of war. Almonds and May Lock met again. She was working in T. W. Smith's cake shop on Tower Hill. The good-looking policeman began to come into the shop when he was not on point duty directing the traffic. Eventually, he asked her out.

'Jessie Matthews is on at the top of Castle Street in *Sailing Along*,' he said. His manner was direct. 'Would you like to see it with me?'

'That would be lovely,' she said. She would have accepted if the cinema had been showing the classified advertisements of the *Bristol Evening Post*.

By the following year, war was looming. 'And now may God defend the right' ran the newspaper headline.[10] Great Britain had declared war on Germany.

On 1 December 1939, Almonds was called up in the rank of sergeant and posted back to the Guards Depot at Pirbright, leaving behind his bride of two months, 'Lockie'. They had spent their short honeymoon in Doone Valley, staying in the house said to be John Ridd's home in the Lorna Doone story. Together they had climbed the famous Water Slide. It had been a beautiful September and they had staved off thoughts about what the war would mean for them.

He quickly qualified as a small arms instructor and field engineer. Pat Riley, whom he had known from No. 4 Company, 1st Battalion, Coldstream Guards, was also at Pirbright. It was 'a very rum place', full of men in uniform but half of them were ex-policeman while the rest were ex-convicts. The Army is not so fussy about recruitment when there is a war on.

Almonds was a very unorthodox soldier. He kept a small axe, saw, home made bow and arrows, and toboggan in his NCO's 'bunk' and frequently vanished into the woods on archery and fishing expeditions. He understood the need for discipline but wondered why personal initiative was so frowned on. The Guards placed huge emphasis on the team approach and trust. When they went into action, each man knew that the man beside him would stay there. That was due to the discipline. It was built in and became part of the man. That discipline was to be carried into the SAS but used in a rather different way.

Almonds and Riley were soon bent on getting out of Pirbright. They did not relish spending the war training recruits. On the other hand, the idea of going into action with the Guards did not have much appeal either.

'Let's face it Jim,' Riley said. 'When it comes to fighting, the Guards are much too brave for us. And we're not stupid enough for them. All we're doing here is polishing our brasses. Now who in their right mind goes into action with polished brasses? It's a sure way to get knocked off!'[11] They offered to be rear gunners for the Royal Air Force and to ride shot-gun on trawlers, but without success. The Swedish Army called for ski-trooper lumberjacks to defend Finland because of the threat of invasion by Russia. But they were turned down.

Their Company Commander was not very popular with the men, because of the rather autocratic statements that appeared in Part I Orders.[12] One day, the unimaginable happened. The Part I Orders were torn down. Without knowing who had perpetrated the crime there was not much the Company Commander could do. But he commissioned the camp carpenter to construct a strong hardwood box with a lockable glass case which was then fixed to the wall. That way, nobody could tamper with daily orders. But the men weren't having any of it and the next time a particularly stupid order appeared, the whole box was wrenched off the wall and disappeared. This caused mayhem as the men lay in bed in the morning shouting to each other.

'Hey! You seen anything on orders today then?'

'No, can't say as I have mate. Nothing at all.'[13]

Of course, they could not be charged for disobeying an order if they had had no chance to see it. Not long afterwards, their Company Commander left the unit.

Almonds and Riley waited for the first reasonable opportunity to make a graceful exit. Together with two other recent arrivals, Jim Blakeney and Bob Lilley, they were destined to become the 'Tobruk Four', an antecedent group of the SAS. With a young Welsh Guards officer Jock Lewes, who was later David Stirling's right-hand man, they were to develop and put into practice the skills of operating behind enemy lines and then join the SAS at its foundation. But the opportunity for 'escape' from Pirbright did not arise until a high level personal connection helped to make it possible.

On 3 June 1940, Churchill wrote a memorandum to his Chiefs of Staff calling for raiding units to keep German forces on the coasts of occupied Europe tied down.[14] Not long afterwards, in early summer of that year, Pat Riley recognised Second Lieutenant, the Lord (George) Jellicoe, son of the Admiral Earl Jellicoe of First World War fame, walking down the side of the barrack square.[15] Riley went through the required ritual of saluting and seeking permission to speak. George Jellicoe smiled, recognising the face but not the name or place. He told Riley that he and Mr Collins were there to assist with the formation of a new Guards Commando Regiment. 'Good, what,' he added. Jellicoe was dark, with a handsome refined face, of medium height but with a powerful frame. Riley asked him when the formation of the Commandos was due to happen and learned that it would be soon. Jellicoe told him that the Guards Commando needed good men who were prepared to do anything that the Germans could do. This included going to sea, marching for miles, driving convoys, landing on beaches, in short more or less anything required. He asked Riley if he was interested and added that they were, of course, looking for the more experienced chaps rather than the new boys.

'I dare say one or two of us would fit that bill, sir,' Riley said, trying to sound nonchalant. 'It's not as though we're doing anything here that really requires the sort of wider experience that we've got. We could easily be replaced.'

'Very good.' Jellicoe's curt reply was the signal for the end of the exchange. Riley stiffened to attention and threw up a quivering salute.[16]

The Board of officers set up to select men for the new Guards Commando interviewed a number of NCOs and Guardsmen at Pirbright. One would-be Commando emerged from the interview in a state of shock. Bob Lilley had discovered that the new venture might involve jumping out of aeroplanes, and was inclined to beat a hasty retreat.[17] Jim Almonds thought it was a once in a lifetime opportunity for real adventure. Riley saw no undue difficulties. There was an air of unreality about the discussion. Only Lilley appeared to have grasped the implications. But there was no time for any of them to change his mind. They were all accepted and with freedom came a different lifestyle and new challenges.

Number 8 Commando trained at Burnham-on-Crouch where the temporary headquarters of J Troop was a pub called the Welcome Sailor. There were fishing expeditions up the River Crouch, night-training exercises and sailing lessons on the cutter *Playmate*. Almonds took to sailing with an easy assurance. In the pub HQ, he met a newcomer with fair hair, an open face and piercing bright blue eyes.

'Bond, Ernie Bond,' he said shaking hands. 'I'm Scots Guards,' he explained. 'We're part of 8 Commando. I've been in the Army for a few years so the war coming along just means we get a chance to play it for real.'[18]

'Good thing,' said Almonds, 'otherwise you'd go crazy.'

Escape and evasion exercises and water training were treated with deadly seriousness, while the officers dreamed up appropriate challenges. One day, Jellicoe sent them out, tasked to bring back before evening one bowler hat, one ladies' bicycle, a cockerel and a hen, a motor vehicle and various other items. Almonds watched a district nurse go into a telephone box and, while her back was turned, nipped smartly onto the bicycle and peddled away. Meanwhile Bob Lilley waited until the driver of a bus stopped and heaved on the hand-brake, jumped down from his cab and went into a tobacconist's shop. Then Lilley sauntered over and hopped up into the driver's seat. The passengers found themselves being dropped outside the Welcome Sailor.

By now, Almonds was in a milliner's shop. The shop assistant looked admiringly at the tall, smart young man looking for a new hat. He had put on his best suit and was convincingly examining several different kinds of bowlers. He gestured inquiringly towards the door and asked if he could look at the colours in daylight. The assistant readily agreed. 'After all,' he dimpled, 'we wear our hats out of doors, don't we?' The future Commando managed a weak smile in response. He stood for a moment in the doorway examining the bowler at various angles in the daylight, turning it this way and that but watching the salesman out of the corner of his eye. Then, when the assistant was distracted by another customer, he put the hat on his head and forced himself to walk casually down the road. Catching the cockerel and the hen, while dressed in a suit and bowler hat, was by far the more difficult task.[19]

Numbers 6 and 8 Commando went on to Inverary and Loch Fyne where they carried out assault landings on the beaches, training 'schemes' over the hills and forded the Douglas Water. At the end of the summer, they continued their training on the Isle of Arran. Superb fitness was a key objective. As if to make the point, pay parade was held on top of Goat Fell, the highest point on the island and the surrounding area. In the sharpness of early autumn, the view was unparalleled.

Their training involved endurance as well as fitness. Second Lieutenant Collins, their Troop Officer, was an enthusiast.

'Come on now chaps. It's only a bit of rain.' he would say, trotting up and down the sodden column of men. The son of the great publishing family and an England tennis player, he appeared not to mind having to give it all up for the war. One night, at the end of a route march, Riley suggested that they keep going.[20]

'See that hill over there? Let's go in a straight line to it, whatever gets in the way'. The others caught the spirit of the idea. Collins joined them. They linked arms to cross a swollen river and climbed down a twisting funnel in a cliff to reach the hill.

Unwittingly, they had contributed to future special forces training. Collins later told them that he had regaled his CO, Colonel Bob Laycock, with the story and had suggested that Commando discipline should allow for initiative and team spirit. Laycock had seemed convinced. Commando training needed to develop the right sort of initiative and resourcefulness, together with toughness to endure individual as well as shared hardships. The idea of making for an objective across country, surmounting all obstacles on the way, was incorporated into standard Commando training.

In Bristol, meanwhile, the aerodrome at Filton and the munitions factories were enemy targets and the blackout was strictly enforced. In November 1940, at the height of the Blitz, Lockie travelled back to Bristol from Chesterfield. Air Raid Wardens had stopped all traffic because of a raid. Flares hung in the sky and shrapnel was falling from the air defence ack-ack guns, as she carried her two month old baby through the pitch blackness from the station. It was rumoured that food rationing would be stricter in the New Year. The newspaper[21] promised cuts in meat, fruit, bacon and eggs. 'Britain is to live harder from now on', it said. 'Lord Woolton, Minister of Food, announced yesterday that ships now bringing food are to be diverted so that they may take part in a "coming great offensive" against the Italians.' Imports of tinned fruit and all fresh fruit except oranges were to stop at once. 'I am informed on the best scientific authority that the nation can do without them', the Minister explained. But the daily discomforts seemed to bring out the best in everyone. She had even seen a half bombed barber's shop with a sign outside, 'We've had a close shave. Come in and get one yourself.'[22]

Almonds wondered if he would be able to kill a man if he had not first despatched something larger than the snowshoe hare that he occasionally hunted for the pot. One evening, he spent some time working his way round to be directly downwind of a young fallow deer. When he had the heart of the animal in the foresight of the .303 rifle, he gently squeezed the trigger. The crack of the shot echoed around the quiet slopes of the valley. The deer disappeared from view as it was knocked sideways, its legs folding beneath it before it rolled helplessly onto its side. Within a few minutes Almonds had it across his back. Suddenly, he was challenged and realised that he was being sought by the duty picket. Dusk was falling. He instinctively moved up the valley, which became a gully, deeply cut into the solid rock by an ancient water course. The cleft ran almost up into Goat Fell. He estimated that with the weight of the deer he would not be able to get up onto the Fell before his pursuers overtook him. He changed direction. Keeping as high up to one side of the valley as he could, he followed it downstream. The voices grew louder and nearer. When they finally caught up with him, he was standing on a high outcrop of rock, legs astride, with the deer around his neck. The experience taught him that eluding capture requires *total* commitment of all available mental and physical resources. If he had gone uphill, he would have got away.

He was placed under close arrest in the Ormidale Hotel, which somehow rather reduced the heinousness of the crime. Two nights later, he was 'sprung' by Collins and Pat Riley so that the three could go climbing the 'chimneys' of the Sleeping Warrior Ridge. After their night's exercise, the break-out party had more trouble returning him surreptitiously to his 'cell' than they had had in getting him out. During the Orderly Room hearing, nobody wanted to discuss the question of preparation for killing human beings. The case was dismissed.

It was not a good time to go on a cruise. Militarily, the Allies were at their weakest point of the battle for supremacy at sea. After June 1940, the acquisition of bases in Norway and France had allowed German aircraft and submarines a range into the Atlantic which exceeded that provided by cover from any of the allied escort zones. There was no comprehensive convoy system throughout the Atlantic.

In blissful ignorance of these chilling facts, No. 8 Commando prepared to put to sea in the hopeful dawn of January 1941.

Chapter Three

Into the Breach

Number 8 Commando went to Egypt as part of 'Layforce', the newly formed Commando Brigade under Laycock.[1] Riley, Lilley, Bond and Kershaw were on the quayside as Almonds's train pulled in at Gourock on the Clyde. They boarded a transport vessel out to HMS *Glenroy*, a newly refurbished LSI, and set sail for Brodick on the Isle of Arran. Lockie had made him promise to come back. On the first page of a small dun coloured exercise book, he wrote 'RECORD OF TRIP TO NEAR EAST' and above her address a request that if anything happened to him it should be sent to her.[2]

On the evening of 31 January 1941, the troops assembled below decks for a farewell lecture by Admiral Sir Roger Keyes.[3] The two officers of No. 3 Troop, Collins and Jellicoe, sat near their men, together with Captain Griffiths-Jones their Squadron 2IC. Jellicoe talked quickly, making little expressive gestures with his hands. Griffiths-Jones listened impassively. In his mid-thirties, he was their father figure.

At 22.30 on 31January, the *Glenroy* slipped out of harbour south-westwards into the choppy waters of the North Channel, accompanied by HMS *Glengyle* and HMS *Glenearn* carrying Nos. 8 Guard and 11 Commando ('The Scottish'), and a naval escort of one cruiser and four destroyers. A stiff breeze was blowing inshore, but the late evening tide was in their favour. All that could be seen of the land they were leaving was a long low shadowy mass behind their broad wake of tumbling froth.

The 'Glenroy' class of ships, together with their slightly smaller cousin the *Breconshire*, had been built as regular naval storeships. But in April 1940, the Glens were refurbished as LSI conversions.[4] Almonds was interested in everything and toured the decks, testing the limits of the permitted areas. The *Glenroy* had economical 12,000 brake horsepower twin diesel propulsion and an enhanced bunker capacity, giving her an endurance of 15,000 miles at 14 knots, although she could manage 19 knots when really making way. Her armaments consisted of a number of two-pounder pom-poms and 20 mm cannon.

Next morning, the ship was pitching badly in a heavy sea. Many of the crew and soldiers were down with sea-sickness. A huge Guardsman sat embracing a dustbin between his knees, his face set with the studied concentration of those about to throw up. Almonds found he could avoid sea-sickness by staying on deck where he could see the horizon and he volunteered to man the guns whenever possible.[5]

Randolph Churchill, the Prime Minister's son, was on the same ship. He seemed rather insecure and certainly there was no funnier sight than the most famous of their officers taking a turn on deck. He would stand, facing towards the bows, clinging to the railings with his left hand, while holding the other slightly out to the side like a circus tightrope walker. Sliding his hand along the rail, he would make his way forward by jerky little jumps.[6]

They sailed west out into the Atlantic through bitterly cold days of squalls, sleet and snow. Heavy overcast skies brooded over mountains of slate grey water. On their first Sunday at sea, Almonds manned the guns on deck. The ships in the convoy took aboard their paravanes,[7] the depth of the water having removed the danger of mine fields. U-boats remained a hazard but they were unlikely to risk themselves against an escorted convoy when so much unprotected allied shipping offered softer targets. The convoy steamed on at 18 knots, destination still unknown.

David Stirling was a young subaltern in 8 Commando, although Almonds did not meet him until later. For some time before the war, Ernie Bond had been Stirling's Platoon Sergeant.[8] The raw young Second Lieutenant and the newly promoted sergeant were a good partnership. Stirling came from a good Scottish family but was known for his racing and gambling pursuits. He had a strong face, almost square, with a slight cleft in the chin. The mandatory dark moustache was neat, attempting to add gravitas to a demeanour which otherwise hinted of wildness.[9]

Stirling took his turn as officer of the watch, but strained every nerve to avoid administration in any shape or form. He particularly detested writing reports. After each long uneventful duty, he would sit hunched over the Duty Officer's report book struggling to think of anything to write. Bond usually came to his rescue with a reminder about engine room problems or changes of course. His easy pleasant style always made Stirling relax. After offering to 'rough out' the report, Bond usually ended up writing it, while Stirling escaped to a game of cards with Evelyn Waugh and Jellicoe.[10] They would gamble far into the night. Stirling cared nothing for the game itself but the thrill of the chance was everything.[11]

The men on the *Glenroy* spent their days training on the Lewis gun, manning the ship's guns or cleaning their cramped sleeping-cum-eating area. They could soon go on deck without an overcoat. There were clear, beautiful days, fresh like an English spring, but with little puffs of white cloud that looked like snow against the blue sky. The sea was calm and taking on a bluish tinge when they sighted a liner bound for New York. The men leaning over the side of the *Glenroy* waved and the liner blew her whistle. The convoy passed the Azores and changed course, turning southward. Everyone was inoculated against malaria, which provoked fresh speculation about their destination. They sprawled below decks waiting for a practice session on dismantling and reassembling the .303 British Service Bren light machine gun. One of the naval officers gave a lecture on torpedo boats. Only ten days after leaving Scotland, they were walking about in their singlets, turning brown under the heat of the sun.[12]

On 10 February, the *Glenroy* steamed into Freetown, Sierra Leone. Crowds of natives in canoes and little white painted boats came out to sell fruit and dive for pennies thrown from the ship. No-one was allowed ashore because of disease. The harbour was full of shipping and the next day a boat left for England taking with it a letter to Lockie. All their mail was censored by the officers. This certainly had an inhibiting effect on what could be said in a letter home. Fortunately, Almonds was skilled at this kind of writing and his letters were hardly ever touched by the maddeningly irritating black rectangles of the censor's stamp.[13]

They crossed the equator and were issued with lime juice to help guard against scurvy. Day became night quickly in the tropics, with a total absence of twilight. Almonds took to sleeping on deck and would sit, watching the sun inch down the sky, a ball of brilliance which turned the sea and sky alike an incandescent fiery red. His son's precious baby days were passing by and he realised that he would never know them. Still there after dark, he would watch the phosphorescence in the water and huge fish at great depths, flashes of silver in the blue-green fathoms.[14]

In the eastern Mediterranean, British 'planes had bombed the Dodecanese Islands, presently believed by most on board to be their ultimate destination. In an at-sea exercise, a mock German battleship was sighted and the convoy's escort laid a smoke-screen. The Navy and the 'Layforce' convoy ships engaged in gunnery practice. Disconcertingly, they were dive-bombed by aircraft from one of their own carriers, probably some said, HMS *Victorious*. Ernie Bond said that he was always more scared of their own 'planes than those of the enemy.[15]

On 19 February, the *Glenroy* arrived in Cape Town. Stirling and Jellicoe headed down the gangplank with boots and rucksacks, as if they meant business with the hills. Churchill wandered away from the ship on his own, a lonely portly figure. Almonds had been ill and was still groggy. Next morning, he was very impressed by the Table Mountain and tried to get permission to go ashore. Unable to make any impact upon the Medical Officer, he asked Captain Griffiths-Jones to plead his cause and was finally granted leave.

Cape Town turned out to be a fine modern city, run on American lines. He was treated by a doctor who refused to take any money. On the way, a gentleman came up to him and said that he had served in the Coldstream Guards during the First World War. Almonds returned to the ship, feeling better for the exercise and good food, and slept soundly. He awoke early and watched the sunrise. The clouds rolled down over the Table Mountain, just like a tablecloth. The *Glenroy* cast off and soon Cape Town was lost to view. After rounding the Cape that evening, the ship began to roll in the oily swell of the Indian Ocean.[16]

They sailed north-east, destination still unknown. The Captain announced that they would be calling at Durban to pick up a new escort. Later in the day, it was announced that the ship would *not* call at Durban and she set a new course due north. The sea was suddenly alive with flying fish. Again, the loudspeaker informed everyone that the ship would, after all, call at Durban. As if to confirm it, the ship arrived just off the port of Durban. At 17.00 hours another announcement said that the ship would *not* call at Durban. The *Glenroy* was in fact sailing round in circles outside of the harbour. Almonds wrote in his diary:

Wish someone would make up their mind!

They set a course for Mombasa and sailed north accompanied by an albatross. Passing through the Straits of Madagascar, they sighted an oil tanker bound for Durban. It slowly disappeared into the sunset as a bank of dark clouds on the horizon took on their own share of crimson.[17]

The weather grew hotter again under cloudless blue skies. Practice drills, such as 'action stations' were piped and sometimes 'abandon ship'. They were now three hours ahead of UK time. A German raider was seen in the vicinity and there was smoke on the horizon. One of their Troop officers gave a lecture. They practised semaphore signalling and then watched a boxing competition. When he was not writing his diary,

Almonds would sit on the poop deck, thinking of home and the thousands of miles of water which now separated him from Lockie. Then he would sling his hammock and lie there until he fell asleep.[18]

On 2 March, they passed the island of Socotra on the port bow and entered the Gulf of Aden. The loudspeaker announced that they would not call at Aden. The whole area had only recently become safe following the retaking of Eritrea and northern Ethiopia. Since then, most of Italian Somaliland had been reoccupied by the Allies and British and Commonwealth infantry had landed at Berbera in British Somaliland barely a week before. They were all encouraged by this promising turn of events.[19]

They passed through the narrow straits between Djibouti and the Yemen and into the Red Sea. For a while, there was land on both bows. The entire ship's company wished they could believe the loudspeaker when it said that they would arrive at Port Suez in four days. Destroyers took over escort duties from the cruisers HMS *Dorsetshire* and HMS *Glasgow* and gunnery practice began. Almonds tried to estimate the distance to land and one of the crew said that it was about 50 miles. The convoy was 450 miles inside the Red Sea, in known minefields; the paravanes were lowered again. The *Glenroy*'s escort laid a smokescreen and the whole convoy drilled in battle formations. These warlike manoeuvres were carried out against the backdrop of a sunset of unsurpassed beauty.[20]

They passed Mount Sinai and arrived at Port Suez. Crowds of ships were lying at anchor, waiting to go through the Canal. The ship's crew and No. 8 Commando mustered on deck to give three cheers for the Captain, John Padgett, for bringing them safely over 14,000 miles of ocean. No one was allowed ashore. Almonds tried his hand at fishing with a hand line and had lot of excitement with a baby shark. After dark, he leaned over the side watching the riding lights on the ship and the glimmers of civilisation in the distance beyond. Having only ever read about foreign countries in books, he very much wanted to see the inhabitants.

The following morning, the ship weighed anchor and turned back into the Red Sea to find a safer anchorage. Overnight, two ships had been sunk in the Canal and more mines dropped. The enemy was too close for comfort. They learned that following the fall of France and the entry of Italy into the war, the struggle for North Africa had really begun. Along the African coast of the Mediterranean, the Italian forward positions now reached almost midway between Sidi Barrani and Mersuh Matru, along the all-important coast road. Within a few days, they arrived at Gineifa in the Bitter Lakes, so called because of the saltiness of the water.[21]

Almonds thought the Egyptians an untidy race of people but without doubt the biggest pest on shore was the flies. They even clustered over the men's noses and mouths, so that they could hardly speak. No. 8 Commando spent the day unloading ammunition and stores, helped by friendly Italian POWs. Six weeks after they had left the Clyde, Almonds wrote in his diary:

> Today, we packed up our own belongings, left the ship and went under canvas on shore......stopped a passing lorry and had a ride to Port Suez. Very much taken up with the Eastern music in the cafes. It conveys fully to one that mysterious something peculiar to the East.[22]

Next day, they formed a Guard of Honour for General Wavell and Sir John Dill, the Chief of the Imperial General Staff, who spoke to the new arrivals in turn. Wavell's stocky frame gave him an air of invincibility. In spite of his one sightless eye, he managed to make them feel that they were all under detailed observation.[23]

They had their first swim in the Great Bitter Lake and went on a route march to get their land legs back. Having run into a sand storm, they had to spend the remainder of the day in the tent. The sand got *everywhere*. Then the tents blew down. They were given a free issue of cigarettes, which seemed to be used as a morale booster. Almonds made a mental note that when cigarettes were in plentiful supply he could start getting really worried.

The question of their future role began to obsess 8 Commando. They went on punishing route marches up into the hills where chameleons and lizards slithered over oven hot volcanic rocks in short jerky dashes. Almonds, who was the squad right marker, would push the pace, egged on by Riley who said he loved it when the officers couldn't keep up.[24] When they were not proofing the tents against sand, repairing barbed wire fencing or doing PT, they went swimming in the Canal. Almonds instructed the men in reading the compass and took his turn at drilling defaulters. They talked endlessly of home. Kershaw said that what he missed most was 'the sound of the wife peeing in the chamber pot.'[25]

On 9 April, they boarded the *Glenroy* once again and sailed for Port Said, passing three mined ships in the Canal. The enemy was scoring too many hits. Morale in No. 8 Commando reached rock bottom. Crowds of young men sat in the government siding at Port Said railway station singing, '*Why are we way-ayting, why-eye are we waiting?*'

Riley felt sorry for the young officers, Collins and Jellicoe.[26] Whatever administrative mistake had been made, they were powerless to do anything about it. Eventually, a train arrived to take them to Sidi Bishur, Alexandria. It was so crowded that Almonds rode on the platform outside the coach in the cold, clean air. The night was beautiful, with a full moon that lit up the countryside, the most fertile part of the Nile delta. It was refreshing to see green trees and fields of waving corn for the first time since leaving home. At Sidi Bishur they erected double-layered tents to keep out the heat of the sun during the day and the cold at night.[27]

On Easter Sunday, 8 Commando went into Alexandria, Egypt's 'seaside' resort and one of Britain's naval bases. Their return to camp at a very late hour was followed by a night sand storm and they awoke at 02.00 to find that the tents had blown down. Everything was covered with sand and their hair, eyes, nose and ears were choked with it. Almonds noted in his diary:

> Language from the men rather strong!

Mid-April and over 350 miles to the west, Tobruk was now besieged. They packed up all their kit and boarded the destroyer *Decoy*, bound for they knew not where. Early in the morning, boats were lowered and selected men of 8 Commando, including Almonds and Lilley, practised silent rowing. The water was very low and the shore caked thick with crusted salt. After reboarding, the overcrowded ship sailed very fast westwards. They reached Tobruk harbour at midday in the middle of an air raid.[28] A continuous rumble of gunfire came from the shore as the Germans continued their attack. Many ships in the harbour had already been sunk, bombed and run aground, including a British hospital ship. The Royal Navy could be heard exacting revenge. It didn't seem possible that the Axis assault on Tobruk would succeed. The *Decoy* left Tobruk in the evening, sailing further west towards Bomba, their aim being to row ashore silently from the destroyer, get round behind the German lines and cut their supply and communication lines. At last, some real action!

At 22.00 hours the *Decoy* reached Bomba. Almonds could see the lights on shore creeping closer and closer. Then they ran aground across the mouth of the harbour, knocking off their ASDIC in the process.[29] For a while the sea was too rough for them to do anything. With engines going full astern and black smoke and sparks belching out of the funnel, the ship was a sitting target. But gradually, she managed to draw back off the sand bank and put out to sea.

In the face of a rising storm, the *Decoy* set course for Alexandria. Next day, at sea in terrible heavy weather, the decks were awash with water. The ship was behaving like a live thing and all personnel had to use life-lines. Suddenly, with a shuddering crash, the port side deck railing was swept away by a towering sea. A life boat was stove in like match-wood. The ship was at the mercy of the elements and fear of the enemy receded in the grip of this new terror. Then the gale began to blow itself out. In the calm of the evening they arrived back in Alexandria and transferred to the *Glenroy*.[30]

It was on the race track in Cairo that Almonds, Riley and Kershaw met David Stirling for the first time.[31] Riley got a 'hot tip' from Stirling, but when Kershaw later told him that it was not a good horse, Riley hesitated. Torn between his knowledge of Kershaw's betting prowess and the illusion that an officer had to be right about everything, he followed Stirling's tip. Almonds took Honest Dave's advice and collected seventeen piasters when their horse won.[32]

The next day, on 22 April, they caught the train to Amasyria, a tented camp in the desert. By all accounts, a recent British raid on Bardia, east of Tobruk and just behind the front line, had been a success. After a lecture by Brigadier Laycock a few days later on the faults of the raid, it became clear that the bush telegraph had been wrong: the raid had *not* been properly executed.[33] Later that day, they left for Abel Kerdair to protect the Australians and the General Field Hospital. The Australians were all walking about under a huge tent, wearing hats with dangling corks and consuming large quantities of beer. They were very optimistic and friendly.[34]

In early May, a khamsin was blowing hot dry powdery dust when 8 Commando carried out a desert patrol down by the shores of the salt lakes. They trained on Kersing rifles and .303 Bren guns at an air force camp, before spending the night in the desert. As they rolled themselves into their blankets, the air was full of the sound of sand crickets, tinkling bells and the distant howling of dogs.[35]

Number 8 Commando paraded for General Arthur Smith. He was unchanged since Almonds had last seen him in 1932 as CO of the 2nd Battalion Coldstream Guards at the Tower of London. The General was apparently utterly convinced that such a cruel and evil tyranny as Hitler's should and would be defeated.[36] Then came the order to leave for Mersa Matruh in the morning.[37]

The 'Insect' class gunboats were unpromising vessels left over from the First World War.[38] Ugly, flat-bottomed craft, they were the 'large China gunboats', as distinguished from the much smaller, and more lightly armed 'Fly' class 'small China gunboats'. But this was just a device to confuse the enemy because even the 'Insect' class boats were tiny.[39] But, they were powerfully armed for their size. With her one 3-inch and two 6-inch guns and her 14 knot speed, the *Aphis* made a good job of helping to cover the seaward flank of the Western Desert Force, while posing as a harmless wreck whenever she dropped anchor.

From Alexandria docks, 8 Commando were ferried out to the *Aphis* in motor boats. She looked a strange sight with her candy-floss and Neapolitan ice-cream coloured camouflage. Five hundred men were packed on board and she slowly took on the appearance of an overcrowded ferry-boat. They sailed for Mersa Matruh and docked at 10.00 hours. The town was immediately bombed by German 'planes. Having picked up the gunboat, the enemy aircraft came in for the attack but she was so low in the water that the bombs just skimmed the surface and bounced right over her.[40] The soldiers hastily disembarked and camped on the outskirts of Mersa to the sound of the continuing air raid. Next morning, they moved 2 miles out of town and worked until dark to build a new base camp.[41]

Living conditions were much improved when Almonds improvised a cooking range out of petrol cans, half-filled with sand, doused with petrol. Tins of meat and vegetables were heated up together to make an 'all in'. Their menu was augmented by fresh food from the locals who trudged round the camps.[42] This was important because prolonged vitamin shortages began to cause little contusions on the skin. Fortunately, Almonds never suffered badly but other men had sores that gradually became deep and chronic. In severe cases, blood poisoning would set in and unless the victim was evacuated from the Middle East, death usually followed.[43]

With new collapsible paddle boats from the Aphis, 8 Commando began night practices for a raid on a German aerodrome 30 miles west of Tobruk. On 21 May, they set off on a 24 hour trip by sea in the gunboat and were bombed by a formation of eight German 'planes. Skilful manoeuvring by the ship's Captain ensured that the shells fell harmlessly into the sea. Thirty bombs plummeted out of the sky around the ship, sending up huge spouts of water which hung momentarily in the air before falling back with a resounding smack on the surface.

But not everyone took cover. A retired Royal Navy officer, Admiral Cowan, had attached himself to the unit because he wanted to die in action. As soon as the shelling began, he started walking up and down calling out to see if his 'batman'[44] was all right. It was impossible to tell whether he wanted to come under enemy fire or was genuinely concerned for his servant, or both. In any event, he did not get his wish to die at the hands of the enemy.[45] There were no casualties and only superficial damage to the ship's superstructure. But more heavy weather made the planned raid on the aerodrome impossible.[46]

Back at Mersa Matruh, German and Italian prisoners of war had arrived to work in the camp. When Almonds and Riley asked them what they thought about the war, they replied with some spirit that in two months the Fuhrer would be in London. By now, 8 Commando had had so many false alarms to go into action, that the order to 'stand to' no longer caused an adrenaline surge. It seemed almost routine when the Aphis sailed on 27 May to have another go at the aerodrome. Heading along the coast, they passed Halfaya and Sollum, where the 7th Armoured and 22nd Guards Brigades were counter-attacking Rommel's forces. According to Collins and Jellicoe, the Allies were slowly retaking ground but the outcome appeared by no means certain.[47]

The *Aphis* was promptly dive-bombed by Stukas dropping almost vertically out of the sky and delivering their large bombs with unnerving accuracy before pulling sharply away.[48] Things happened quickly. The ship swung round into the wind while the gun crews raced to man the Italian 20mm guns mounted on the ship's superstructure. The powerful 6-inch gun forward was of little use. In its bulky flat-topped housing, it could not be trained up into the sky.[49] But the 20mm Bredas were more than equal to the task.[50] The *Aphis* put up a terrific barrage of anti-aircraft fire, while continuing to manoeuvre skilfully out of the target line. Forced by the flak coming up at them to drop their bombs from a greater height, the enemy began to drop them wide.

One or two aircraft came in lower and one received a direct hit from the ship's Bredas. High over the stern, it exploded in mid-air, in a blinding flash of flame and flying fragments of jagged fuselage and debris. Almonds counted three more spiralling plumes of black oily smoke as other mortally wounded aircraft ditched into the sea. Two more flew off, evidently sobered by the ability of this doubtful looking craft to acquit herself in combat. But the *Aphis* was leaking steam badly where her boilers had been partly ruptured by several near misses. With her engines disabled, she was barely able to steam at 4 knots. Everyone was relieved when the Captain announced that they were now unable to deliver the raiding party to their objective and were returning to Mersa Matruh.[51]

There followed a spontaneous evening's entertainment with the ship's crew and the boys of 8 Commando. But their elation was short-lived. Next day, Brigadier Laycock made clear that Layforce was to be disbanded.[52] They faced being broken up into small special forces troops and raiding parties or staying together and returning to England.[53] Some men were to go to China, others to desert patrol units, or back to their battalion. That night, 'A' and 'C' Companies had a 'breaking up' party in the 8 Commando tent. Almonds, Riley, Bond and Lilley began practice landings along the beach from the gunboats HMS *Gnat* and HMS *Cricket*. Another party underwent wireless instruction, while another began instruction as parachutists.

Off duty, they found a derelict boat on the rocks. It was badly holed but Almonds pronounced it not beyond repair. He and Lilley did some repairs and with a crew of six sailed the skiff round to their camp. A huge turtle basking in the sun awoke startled and dived. They caught some fish with hand grenades before their patched up boat was wrecked on a reef. For a brief interlude the war was forgotten while they had fun working out how to get ashore.[54]

While he was still at Mersa Matruh, Almonds met Jock Lewes and was invited to join him inside Tobruk. Lewes already knew David Stirling, who was still in traction in Alexandria hospital following a parachute accident suffered during the first experimental jump in the Middle East.[55] In the rapidly gathering dusk and without any proper training Stirling and Lewes had jumped with four men from a Vickers Valentia that was used to deliver mail. Lewes was clearly the driving force in the scheme. Having been frustrated in his plans for a sea-borne operation, he wanted to try other methods. The note to Captain Schott[56] on this historic event, signed by Captain T.B. Laughlin for the Major Commanding Special Boat Squadron is instructive:

> ..... I do not know what the intended operations were. For a long time, both Lt. Lewes and Lt. Stirling tried to go by sea but could not get transport so decided to try this way.

Both operations were eventually cancelled, chiefly because the parties were too badly shaken by the practice jumps. *None of the O.R.s (Other Ranks) had even been in a plane before.* [My italics.] The practice took place at a small landing ground about 50 miles inland from Bagush.[57]

Stirling had been the unlucky one. His 'chute was damaged on exit and he had plummeted towards the earth. He had spent a sightless hour lying on the ground in the desert, with an injured spine and his legs partially paralysed, before being carted off to hospital. While confined to bed he came up with the initial idea of the force that would play a major part in winning the war in the Western Desert.[58]

The first thing that Almonds noticed about Jock Lewes during their initial meetings was how keen he was to get on with winning the war. Everything the young Guards officer did focused on striking a successful blow at the enemy. He had a gift for training and was a masterful planner of night operations.

'Just because Tobruk is under siege doesn't mean that we can't go onto the offensive,' he would say as they sat outside in the cool of the evening. He maintained that the surrounding enemy outposts *were* vulnerable. It was only a question of getting up close under cover of darkness, with the element of surprise, and landing a few blows where it hurt most. Silhouetted against the pale blur of the desert, he would thump the back of his hand, encased in a grubby bandage covering his desert sores, on the roughly drawn map of the area around Acroma and El Adem. It was clear that it mattered to Lewes to get his points across. In spite of his rather aloof manner, he wanted a team, with each man taking responsibility for himself and his contribution to the rest. But training was key, until what they *needed* to do came so automatically that they didn't think about it. The brain had to be free to deal with new situations and new problems they could not have been planned for. Discipline did not mean that they were excused thinking.[59]

At night the four men would lie on their camp beds under the dark green triangles of their mosquito nets waiting for the desert night breeze to spring up, flapping the edges of the ground-sheet and softly lifting the ceiling of the tent like a huge bellows. Outside, the occasional muffled, distant pounding of the naval artillery at Tobruk harbour was like a laboured heartbeat. They discussed the prospect of throwing in their lot with Lewes. They had not much to lose. They had been ferried about from pillar to post, loaded on and off ships, trucks and trains, constantly moved camp like a band of gypsies and *all* without seeing any action. Lewes inspired confidence and he appeared to be using his skills and influence as an officer to see what needed to be done and working out how to do it.[60]

Some of the men were undergoing instruction as parachutists and on 14 June they began practise jumping from 2,000 feet. Six men were killed at Tobruk, bringing the total losses of Layforce since leaving England to 570.[61] Almonds had just started to build a boat from driftwood when the order came to leave for another unknown destination. He confided to his diary that this time it was going to be a close call and that many would not return.[62]

Anti-climax. The Operation was postponed for twenty-four hours. It was clear that the British advance, codenamed *Battleaxe* had begun in the Western Desert.[63] British and Australian troops were going forward from Sollum towards Tobruk. The Garrison, which had been cut off for months, was prepared to make a push to meet with the force from Sollum when the right moment occurred. The enemy between these two points was estimated at about 30,000 men. To the south-west of Sollum, the British 7th Armoured Division was heading north-west, towards the front line. Immediately to the east of them, and due south of Sollum, they were supported by the 4th Armoured Brigade, while 22nd Guards Infantry Brigade was on its way. A hastily re-commissioned 8 Commando were to land among the enemy on the coast between Sollum and Tobruk and harass their gun positions and supply columns. About 400 Commandos would be pitted against about 50,000 German troops, among them the well armed and equipped 15th German Panzer Division and behind them the German 5th Light Infantry Division. Since 8 Commando would also lack sufficient air cover, and the Navy was already hopelessly stretched, Almonds thought their chances of return were really rather slight.[64]

Anti-climax again. The Allied advance in the desert was meeting with stiff resistance. Their camp was dive-bombed by Stukas and it was no surprise when they were told that their attack was off. The British advance had been held up and destroyers were bringing the wounded back to Mersa harbour. British forces were, in fact, in retreat. The enemy was too well equipped with tanks and aircraft. Were the Allies going to lose the war?

They returned to route marching and swimming. Almonds did a little to his boat. The craft was taking shape, the challenge of improvising from old crates and packing cases only increasing his satisfaction. At the inter-Troop swimming gala in Mersa Matruh harbour, he took the opportunity to launch it. He had caulked the dinghy well with tar, but unfortunately most of it had not hardened under the hot Egyptian sun and transferred itself to his chest and arms when he manhandled it into the water. Riley and Lilley kept up a steady stream of good-natured teasing until it became clear that their sweaty and tarry comrade was in danger of losing his sense of humour. They gave him and the sticky vessel a wide berth.[65]

Good news. Germany had invaded Russia. The consensus was that Germany had overreached itself and this would bring a speedy end to the war. After packing up at short notice, they left camp by train on 28 June and headed back to Sidi Bishur. The following day, some of the Troop left to join the 3rd Battalion Coldstream Guards at Sollum.

On 6 July, Almonds's group with Bond and Kershaw boarded the Australian naval destroyer *Vendetta* for Tobruk. Another destroyer had been sunk by dive bombers the previous day and they wondered what their luck would be. Landing at Tobruk Harbour, they became part of the garrison of a semicircle of Allied territory containing the besieged city, hemmed in on all sides except for the sea. After bumping over rough country by lorry, the staging camp turned out to be nothing more than a marked-off area of ground in a large wadi running down to the sea with hastily erected ablutions and a medical tent. At 02.00, they took up their positions at the front line. After sleeping among the rocks, they were eating breakfast when a familiar high pitched scream announced a series of Stukas which dive-bombed the entire encampment.[66]

Almonds surveyed his known world from the rim of the deep wide wadi. Like the Avon Gorge, but about a quarter of a mile wide, its wild barren aspect reminded him of the Grand Canyon. They were on the western side of Tobruk, facing towards Gazala and Derna and two mountains whose politer nickname was 'the twin pimples'. To their right, the wadi ran down to the sea a mile and a half away. Across the valley, the outcrop of rocks on the wadi rim shimmered in the heat haze. The Italians were in similar positions and had mounted a large gun between the twin pimples, dominating the Derna road. There was little natural protection. The ground was solid rock after the first six inches and impossible to dig. Almonds wandered about the floor of the wadi, appraising the available building materials and selecting the most suitable rocks. Apart from being comfortable, they needed protection from the regular visitations of Stukas.

With Almonds guiding construction operations, they built two circular sangers just under the skyline against the cliff-like side of the wadi. The dry-stone walls of overlapping grey rocks came up to shoulder height, providing a perfectly blended camouflage against the backdrop of the valley wall. Having taken advantage of a natural dip in the ground, Almonds and Riley were able to step down into their sanger and have a little more headroom. There was just enough space for two to lie out, with a small living space in the middle. Almonds made himself at home and put up his greatest treasure, his photograph of Lockie. The extent of his culpability for their situation was an issue he constantly pondered and he still poured out his feelings in the diary. To the left, barely a 100 yards away, a beautiful bay marked the lower end of the wadi. To the right stood a group of swaying date palms and fig trees, next to two fresh water wells. When returning from their sorties, the sanger began to look almost welcoming.

They were not short of armaments. Blakeney and Lilley found an old machine gun, a Schwarzlose. It was probably left over from Italian war reparations after 1918. There was plenty of ammunition. They quickly set it up outside the sanger so that they could take a crack at the enemy. Before long, Almonds and Riley had perfected the art of thoroughly annoying the Italians by firing off two belts on the machine-gun in the middle of siesta time and then beating it up the hill for a cup of tea.[67]

Before all the disaster, it must have been a prosperous little valley. Everywhere there were visible signs of the ravages of war. The ground was strewn with smashed up lorries, Italian equipment of all kinds, rifles, guns and ammunition. Someone had even left a brand new Moto Guzzi motorbike. Several large cartons of tinned food seemed to have been opened at once, as if the retreating occupants had engaged in a last minute orgy of gluttony. There were even boxes of cigars, of which Almonds's section had a good share and were soon strutting about like a lot of budding Churchills.[68]

There were no civilians left in the area. Their abandoned animals had attached themselves to the soldiers. Almonds befriended one of the donkeys, whom he nick-named 'the moke', and amused him by singing 'Wanderers of the Wasteland' in a falsetto warble. The song mentioned a lop-eared mule, which might have been such another as this forlorn, flea-bitten and sand-blasted creature.

They were visited by friendly soldiers of the 43rd Australian Battalion. They had already been out on quite a few patrols, mainly with the aim of getting a prisoner for interrogation but had not reckoned with the Italians' skill at holing themselves up in the solid rock.

'It's like tryin' a git a dingo out of a hole,' said one. But friendship with the Australians had to proceed with caution because somewhere in Riley's past he had fallen out with their antipodean allies.[69]

Tobruk had successfully withstood the siege for the three months. It seemed clear that the garrison would continue to hold off the enemy until relieved by a British advance from Sollum. When the men were not manning their positions, the daily routine was dominated by the ubiquitous camp duties. They took turns to go into Tobruk in twos to get the rations: tins of 'bully' beef, tinned 'M and V' (meat and vegetables), soup and tea.

Air raids continued day and night. One morning a dive bomber, returning from Tobruk harbour, crippled and flying very low, passed over their post.[70] Without compunction, they let him have it with their commandeered machine gun, but failed to bring him down. In the evening a small artillery piece known as 'Little Audrey' arrived at the top of the wadi and opened up a bombardment which received an immediate reply from the enemy. Shells fell thickly all around their position but no one was injured. They continued to sit out the heat, worried by monster flies out of all proportion to English ones, and at night by a very large, savage species of sand fly.[71]

Two golden eagles were seen soaring high over the wadi, apparently not in the least frightened by all the noise going on around their once calm and peaceful retreat. When there was no firing, the valley was unbelievably tranquil, with an immense calm grandeur. Then the illusion would be shattered by a sudden burst of gunfire, crashing and rolling down the valley and echoing up the side canyons. There was usually slight artillery and machine-gun activity after stand-to at dawn. 'Little Audrey' would create quite a disturbance but often failed to get a reply from the other side. Almonds always had one ear open to detect the whistle of an approaching shell. He was now practised at telling almost exactly where they would drop.[72]

Before long, Lewes Almonds and Riley began to go out into no man's land at night to reconnoitre enemy positions along the front line. It was risky because they had to go at moonrise, otherwise they would not see anything at all. They learned a lot about the enemy's routines and defences. On one occasion, another British foot patrol on the same site engaged the enemy throughout the night, unintentionally giving them noise cover. Artillery and machine-gun activity continued during the daylight hours, with 'Little Audrey' doing her share. Shells went on falling around their position and at night the air raids would take over. But they remained unharmed. The worst of their wounded was Blakeney, in a surprisingly bad condition from the effects of a scorpion sting.[73]

They decided to test their skill in no man's land during the day. Almonds and Lilley left at 04.00 hours and hid themselves not far from the enemy's lines. By sunrise, they were already cramped up among the rocks, afraid to move for fear of being seen. Soon they were eaten alive by the flies, their lips cracked and blistered. Baked by the sun, their water supply was all gone by mid afternoon. But there was nothing for it but to wait for darkness and make a dash for home. They returned late that night, exhausted and desperate for a gallon of purified sea water.[74]

Almonds was fascinated by the enemy's fundamentally different approach to war and impressed by the Italians' skill as engineers. Experts at excavation, they clearly intended to be there for some time and had made elaborate ground preparations. Huge holes, with steps down into them were hewn out of the solid rock. It was all biased towards the defensive, though the enemy never seemed to expect it when 8 Commando turned up and casually dropped a hand grenade down the hole.

Very heavy shelling forced the posting of sentries on front line positions throughout the day. At night the bombing of Tobruk harbour continued. Lewes announced a night operation to take a prisoner for interrogation, deciding to take only Almonds and Riley with him. Almonds sensed that Lewes had to work himself up to tell them this. It did not come naturally to him to be at ease with the men under his command. He was a good leader and they respected him. But he seemed to struggle to find the right touch with the British 'squaddie'. He lacked the easy assurance of David Stirling or George Jellicoe. It was partly due to natural shyness but it led to a reserve which at times bordered on aloofness.[75]

It was time to go. They had darkened their faces with brown boot polish, before starting out between the Australian and Indian sectors. Each carried a .303 rifle, two hand grenades and bayonets. Lewes had the private purchase Zbrojovka Brno[76] shotgun he always carried and his officer's pistol. They kept close to the Aussie patrol, who knew what they were up to. At first, inky blackness, until their eyes got used to the dark. Then, towards Derna, they made out the 'twin pimples' against the starry sky, still faintly suffused with lingering rosy light. The warm humid air carried sickly-sweet Middle East smells of rubbish, overripe fruit and exotic foods, mingled with wood smoke and oil fumes from a hundred primitive cooking stoves and lamps. Occasionally, they caught the smell of the sea, borne in on the night breeze from the bay. The bombardment of Tobruk thumped periodically.

'Watch our wire! Watch our wire!' They had come within a few yards of the Australian night patrol. The Australian officer kept repeating his territorial war cry and Lewes vanished momentarily to reassure him. Then, with a sweep of his arm, he motioned to Almonds and Riley to give them a wide berth.[77]

In spite of his size, Almonds could move noiselessly through the rocks and tussocks of wiry grass. He was truly in his natural element. They kept looking for the Australian's wire which would enable them to swing right across towards the India sector. Then they froze at the sound of German voices. Two tiny comets of red marked the traces of cigarettes being tossed into the desert. The voices retreated into the distance.[78]

They cut across and entered the Indian sector. After two hours, they saw a bouncing red point of light in front of them. It vanished and they heard the splattering of someone relieving himself, then long shuddering groans followed by little gasps of expelled breath. After the last satisfied grunt, cold steel connected with bare flesh as Lewes stuck his pistol into the exposed small of the man's back. Almonds and Riley were immediately on either side.

'Jim. What's the Italian for 'pull your trousers up'?' whispered Riley.[79] Lewes motioned to the man to pull up his shorts and they got him moving, clutching his clothing with one hand, the other on his head. They handed him over to the Indians who had Italian interpreters. The Indians had shown themselves gentle and friendly but he suspected there was another side to them.

They probably had better ways of getting the prisoner to talk than 8 Commando.

Chapter Four

The 'Tobruk Four'

Lewes's section began to prepare for a night raid on the Italian positions around the Derna road. The objective was to knock out the enemy machine-guns and mortar posts which dominated the road and the 'twin pimples'. A small band of sappers joined them for the purpose of spiking the guns in a frontal attack. Lewes and his party of about thirty were then to move in and finish off. Almonds committed his feelings to his diary:

> Well darling, it is the King's will and the country's wish and I go to do my best. But not for one moment will I forget you or little John. Don't forget, do the best for yourselves and get all the happiness out of life that you can ……. Anything which brings you happiness kid has my full approval.[1]

'Down! Keep down!' Lewes whispered fiercely over his shoulder as they belly-crawled forward through the now familiar terrain of rocks and gullies. Almonds rolled his wrist over so that he could see his watch on the inside. It was 01.13.[2] Suddenly, at about 50 yards away from the Italian position, the encircling British sections opened fire simultaneously. They went in at once with fixed bayonets, firing as they advanced. The noise was deafening. Reverberating off the rocks, it made the whole ground shake beneath their feet and ten minutes later the occupants of the Italian positions, twenty or more or them, were dead. Only one prisoner was taken and he was more dead than alive, pierced right through the middle with a bayonet. Apart from a few shrapnel splinters in the arms and legs, Almonds was unharmed.

But two of their men were wounded. One had a bullet through the neck, which they bound up with a handkerchief. The other, 'Scoffer' Marden, had been shot through the thigh and through the upper arm, which had been broken. He was in terrible pain. Almonds and a medical orderly tried to make him comfortable under a fig tree while they waited for the field ambulance to arrive. Then Lewes asked my father to take the wounded man back. He and Lilley helped to bring Scoffer back to their own lines.

The journey was a nightmare. The Italians from other positions had opened fire and shells, bombs and bullets were flying everywhere. Whenever a star shell or bomb burst near them, and they were seen from the enemy lines, a perfect hail of ordnance had to be dodged. Tracer shells from the Italians' Breda guns kept coming across like strings of Chinese lanterns while incendiary and explosive bullets from the machine-guns cracked and popped all around them. By the time they arrived at the big wadi, Marden was exhausted. It was 05.00 hours. They rested a while and Almonds loosened the tourniquet around Marden's arm, then re-bandaged the stricken man. The moon had now risen and by its light they got down the side of the wadi and lay at the bottom, as shells were bursting over their positions. Mortar bombs falling down into the wadi bottom covered them with sand and stones, but sheltered in a hollow, they escaped the worst of the blast and splinters.

A stretcher finally arrived from the first aid post and with the help of an Indian Major and his men they got Scoffer fixed up. They helped the stretcher party up the hill with another wounded man called Maynard. He was in a bad way, shot through the body, just below the heart. Still cheerful, he was clearly a dying man. After a while, he died bravely. It had a profound effect on everyone. Late that night, Almonds wrote in his diary:

> England gets what she expects. Her men still do their duty. Our crowd are awesome fighters; no wonder the enemy fear us.[3]

Morning dawned bright and clear. Back in their front line positions, 8 Commando were highly recommended on the results of their raid: enemy guns, mortars and ammunition dumps had all successfully been blown up. An enemy attempt to raid the British positions was repulsed with more losses to the Italians. An assault of artillery and mortar fire had to be endured in the process and an enemy tank was seen in position behind their front line.[4] Forward lookout posts were shelled relentlessly by the enemy. But Almonds did not care because had received a letter from Lockie, which made the fleas, flies and barren countryside seem like one huge bed of roses. For a man who had just collected his first battle honours, his thoughts were less than patriotic:

> I hope this accursed war ends soon, so that I can get back home to them all again. Even the police force will be a wonderful job after this![5]

In London, the long summer evenings had reduced the enemy's air raid hours to a minimum and the Joe Loss orchestra was already optimistically playing the Victory Waltz. The sound drifted in through the open windows where Whitehall civil servants still laboured. On 18 July 1941, a badly typed 'C in C Middle East' cable winged its way from Cairo to 'Troopers'.[6] The cable sought approval for a post-Layforce unit to operate in four-man sections, behind enemy lines with parachutes.[7] The submission was approved and the seed of the SAS was sown. According to notes of a lecture given after December 1941, the basic idea for this 60-man detachment was night landings by parachute, well in rear of enemy forward troops, of small parties of expert saboteurs who would destroy aircraft at aerodromes by night, dumps, petrol stores and any other suitable installations.[8] Stirling had bid for a unit of 200 good men from the disbandment of Layforce but this optimistic figure had allowed for it to be cut down.

In late July, the shelling of the Derna road was accompanied by German aircraft bombing raids, day and night, on Tobruk harbour. The boiling hot days, characterised by afternoon machine-gun activity, were spent on reconnaissance patrols. The enemy carried out a heavy air raid on Tobruk harbour. The 'Tobruk Four' were now an item: Almonds, Riley, Lilley and Blakeney patrolled into enemy territory with Lewes and captured another prisoner for interrogation.[9] There was a sharp fight between the Indians and Italians and a number of the enemy were killed. Enemy shells and machine-guns bombarded their positions all that night.

At last, on Sunday 28 July, they were able to leave the front line to go to a rest camp that sprawled in the sun beside a beautiful little inlet, nicknamed 'Rest and be thankful Bay' by battle-weary soldiers. Almonds had a wash and shave and a swim, the first for a fortnight. But respite was all too brief. The next day, Lewes and his party left for a new position on the escarpment to bolster the 23rd Australians on the Palestrino front of Tobruk. It was a terrible bleak and open place, with the enemy lines barely a thousand yards away. Machine-gun fire and mortar activity were incessant. The ground was not too hard and Almonds immediately built himself a comfortable dug-out and settled in.[10]

A hot desert wind began to whip up clouds of sand and powdered fine dust into huge clouds of swirling brown and yellow grime. It got in their eyes, up their noses and down their throats. In the excessive heat and with no shade, the water shortage was acute. Even when they had something to drink, the desert got there first. Opinion varied as to whether it was better to try and skim the sand off the top of a mug of tea, or stir it in, let it sink and avoid drinking to the bottom. Then the issue became academic because they ran out of water all together. Almonds was so dry that his throat rasped when he tried to swallow and his skin was chafed raw by the stinging, flying sand.[11]

On 1 August patrols went out into enemy territory in an attempt to reconnoitre the land for 8 Commando's attack the following day. Morale was high and they were hopeful of taking the enemy salient to the west of Tobruk. The aim was to 'straighten out' the bulge in the front line which the enemy had pushed into the Allies' territory. This would remove his advantage of angles from which to fire into ground held by the Allies while at the same time reducing the length of front line to be defended. The following morning, Saturday 2 August, three German aircraft flew low over their positions and appeared to be searching the ground. Almonds wondered if they suspected something. He sat in his dugout with the diary on his knees.

Well darling, going out tonight and if all goes well, I shall put the night's activities under tomorrow's heading. Have just had information about the job. May be away for two days. Sounds pretty stiff and the going hard and difficult. Will do my best, however, and will be thinking of you all the while. Goodnight darling, xx.

Another raid in support of the Australians. Lewes inched forward. Without looking back, he slowly raised his right arm and then motioned them forward. From their prone positions, the four could just make out the signal, silhouetted against the pale night sky. Slowly, they made their way across the rocky ground towards a natural dip about 150 yards in front of the centre of the salient. The thump of mortars and the whine of the shelling became more intense. Suddenly, the enemy let fly with everything they had. The earth and air trembled and rocked to the concussion of bursting shells and mortar bombs, some of which exploded only a few feet from their position. Almonds threw himself behind a low stone wall, the remains of an out-post position, and almost immediately a bomb burst on the other side. Had it not been for that wall this story would have ended here.

It was almost as though the enemy had been able to see them coming. Pinned down by the heavy shelling, the Commandos waited. Under such a barrage, the element of surprise was lost and there was no chance of

RAID ON THE ENEMY SALIENT TO THE WEST OF TOBRUK

Mediterranean Sea

Front line — Enemy salient 13 — Front line
German minefields — German minefields
NO MAN'S LAND
AUSTRALIANS — INDIANS
Position held by Lewes and my father

them creeping up on the enemy positions and knocking them out. Then on either side of them, they heard the charge of the Australians. The primeval roar was enough to make the blood run cold. But the pitch-black night swallowed up every glimmer of light and they could see nothing. Unable to make a move, Almonds studied his immediate surroundings and realised that the other walls of the former outpost position in which he was sitting were made entirely of tins of bully beef. Never one to miss an opportunity, he decided to open one and sat eating his way through it while he waited.

At 04.00 hours, Lewes decided that they would have to start the hazardous trip back, as they could leave it no later. Just after dawn, the awful truth was revealed. The attack had been a total disaster. The Australians had lost 100 men killed and wounded out of their company of 120.[12] Almonds was appalled. Many of them he had known well, fine young men all of them, loyal, and courageous. The enemy had also suffered a considerable number of casualties. To everyone's amazement, a truce was arranged so that both sides could go out to collect their dead and wounded. At this stage of the war, the Germans still honoured the normal conventions of battle, accepting as prisoners those men who surrendered and looking after the wounded.[13]

That afternoon, Almonds lay on his camp bed, scribbling furiously.

> My God Lockie, it was an exciting night. It looks as though our attack failed because we were expected. There has since been some talk of 'fifth column' activity by the men, although I doubt the truth of it. I doubt that the enemy is brave enough, or clever enough for that matter, to infiltrate our lines to gather it. But while the truce was on Gerry proved himself a gentleman. He assisted with our wounded and was full of praise for their bravery. He also gave tea to the injured men and stretcher bearers. But immediately after the truce deadline had expired, a large formation of Stuka dive-bombers came over and blew the hell out of our artillery positions![14]

The 4 August Bank Holiday Monday. It was hardly a holiday back in their positions. Living like a colony of rabbits or desert rats, as Lord Haw-Haw called them, they were eaten alive by flies and fleas and covered all over with bits of sticking plaster and bandages. Their enforced diet of tinned food and the fact that they could not wash meant that every little scratch or cut turned into a desert sore which would not heal. Almonds dreamed of a long shower, green vegetables and fresh fruit.

The day before his twenty-seventh birthday Almonds was again nearly killed.[15] Together with Riley and Blakeney, he went on a mission with Lewes. Nothing was left to chance; everything that could and should be thought about in advance had been systematically considered and checked. Lewes had spent some time planning the operation, researching the known facts about the area, the enemy's strengths and armaments, the likely weather conditions, estimated moonrise, the timings, any concurrent operations and a million other details which could possibly have a bearing on the success of the operation. The pale discus of the moon hung, semi-translucent above the desert horizon as they went out, into no man's land.

No one realised the danger until Lilley caught his foot in the trip-wire. They felt, as well as heard, the murderous blast of the land mine several feet away at the end of the wire. They were all blown off their feet and lay in the dirt, each man motionless, mentally exploring his body. Lewes made them report alphabetically.

Amazingly, they were all unhurt. Then, even lying flat on the deck, Lewes went into lecture mode. They were in a minefield, he said, but it was impossible to tell how far they had gone inside it. They would need to check for mines all the way back until they knew that they were clear. That was a long way and it would take until sunrise. The devices needed a fair amount of pressure to make them explode, so the four just had to explore the ground lightly in front of them. These were probably German 'S' mines. There were two charges inside each mine: one to get it going and one to blow it outwards. They were sometimes set to go off when trodden on. About tea-plate size with three pins projecting just above the ground, they were designed to jump up to waist height and then explode.

'As high as that?' said Lilley. 'That's considerate of them.'

Blakeney asked how they would find the mines and Lewes explained that while it was still dark they would have to feel for them. Later the devices could probably also be seen. They needed to be careful of booby-traps as well. When there was no particular beaten track to lay mines on, such as the area they were now in, mines were often connected to a trip-wire to increase the chances of scoring a hit. But that could mean that the damage inflicted was less direct. Fortunately for the four of them, they had been some distance away from the one that had gone off

They began to crawl slowly back the way they had come, taking turns to be first to go forward, two abreast, the others following exactly in their tracks. They inched along the treacherous ground, feeling carefully in front of them for the mines. Almonds found one and felt around the cool hard circumference barely covered with loose dirt. Working in towards its centre, his finger tips found the evil little prongs. The four men continued, grovelling agonisingly slowly on their stomachs as the minutes turned into hours and the strain on their minds and bodies mounted. It was terrifying to go first. But it was even worse following behind, wondering if the man in front was checking properly.[16]

On the way back, they discovered several more mines which had been individually laid and some trip-wire booby traps. Once found, avoiding the hazard took up more time while they checked the surrounding ground for trailing wires and additional mines before they could crawl past. As the first faint streaks of dawn glowed across the sky, they began to see the telltale smoothed lines in the sand around the mines. Fortunately, the minefield had been only recently laid and the sandstorms had not covered the tracks of the mine layers. They wondered how on earth they had managed to get so far on the way out without setting one off. Then they were spotted and the Germans began to amuse themselves at their expense with machine-gun fire. They lay dead flat on the ground and wondered if it was possible to crawl without lifting their heads up at all. Lewes had been right; they arrived back at dawn. After this terrible encounter with the enemy's minefields, Almonds for ever after automatically searched the ground of enemy territory for mines.[17] Later in the war it was to save his life.

Down by the sea on the Indian sector the blue-green kaleidoscope waters of the Mediterranean were a pleasing sight after so much rock and stone. Just beyond the gently breaking waves, the sunlight danced through the crystal clear water to the white sands beneath, ribbed by the pattern of the swell. Almonds's section had packed up and left the Palestrino sector at midnight for some brief rest and recuperation in a nearby wadi. The parched valley bottom was covered with a kind of small green prickly bush which was also a welcome change for the eyes. He sniffed the vegetation, trying to overcome as many sensory deprivations as possible. To satisfy his creative urges he built a new home, using some of the bushes to put up a screen of protection from the blistering sun. He went swimming and floated languorously on his back, his body cradled by the surface, gently rocked by the ebb and flow of the waves which broke on the perfect long white beach. How could such an idyllic place could be so close to war?[18]

At Tobruk, everything happened in the early hours of the morning. During the siege, entry and exit to the town, every item of stores, food, water, spares, medicines, POL (petrol, oil and lubricants) and ammunition had to take place under cover of darkness. Relief troops went to the front at night. Even the one hot cooked meal a day of tinned stew and Army tea fit to stand the spoon up in, went to the forward positions in the moonlight. Almonds watched the Indian sepoys swarming over the boats, working frantically to unload the stores in a race against the dawn. Shells splashed into the harbour among the numerous wrecked hulks and enemy mines and he wondered how any boat managed to make it in and out.[19]

At about this time, David Stirling came to see Lewes to talk over his ideas about setting up a special unit of highly trained men to operate behind enemy lines. He was fairly sure that GHQ Cairo were about to give in to his request to be allowed to lead such a unit. Since they had last spoken in Alexandria hospital, Stirling had managed to get to see the DCGS (Deputy Chief of the General Staff), Neil Ritchie, the man put in by Auchinleck to replace Cunningham.[20]

Modest about his own contribution, Stirling was always full of praise for other people's achievements and he genuinely appreciated Lewes's ideas. Nevertheless, Lewes seems to have remained circumspect, perhaps doubting whether the scheme wasn't just some harebrained flash in the pan destined for disaster in which he wished to play no part. He was much less extrovert than Stirling and shared none of his exuberant social life or gambling pursuits.[21] That was why Stirling went to see him. He wanted Lewes very badly, for his leadership qualities and for his ability to organise training and weld a new bunch of men together. Lewes's experience of active service and of operating behind enemy lines with the 'Tobruk Four' was also invaluable. Stirling himself had yet to fire a shot in action.[22]

When time and bombardments permitted, Almonds did a little 'housekeeping'. The photograph of Lockie was beginning to look a little ragged so he trimmed, cleaned and then reframed it, putting the screws right through the edges of the picture to ensure that it stayed put under its perspex cover. He found a piece of wood and began to carve it carefully into a desk ink stand shaped like the centre of a propeller.[23] Next came swimming and laundry. He wrote in the diary:

> Getting quite a dab hand at this kind of thing, though anyone can tell by looking at my 'whites' that I do not use Persil!

Up in the morning at dawn, he and Riley went fishing, Commando style, with a box of hand-grenades. They returned 'home', 'mashed' some tea, made some batter, cleaned and fried the fish and had a first rate breakfast. Then their brief interlude of peace was rudely shattered. A large formation of Stuka dive-bombers came over and bombed the hell out of Tobruk harbour.[24]

> It is a marvel how the garrison here stands up to such treatment, cut off from the outside world, bombed day and night, continually shelled and yet life goes on. The chaps will go almost crazy when they are once again free men.[25]

They packed up and left the wadi for fresh positions in the salient hot spot. Riley returned from a run into Tobruk for rations and the latest rumours. The other three crowded into the shade of the sanger, eager for condensed milk and news. Riley said the word was that they were going to make a raid on some of the enemy front line positions. But there was something else, something more interesting.

'Oh yes? What?' they all chorused. The sailors appeared to have got wind of some new 'do or die' unit that was being formed.

'*What* "do or die" unit?' they all chorused again. 'Come on Rat (they often called him Rat Piley). But, having whetted their appetites, and to their immense frustration, Riley was unable to deliver. He had not been able to pick up any further details. But despite the paucity of information, their imagination had been well fired up.[26]

At the new positions, they discovered that their particular sector of the line was known as the Fig Tree, although there were no signs of trees anywhere. Almonds and Riley built themselves another new home of rocks, for protection against bullets and shell splinters. They lay inside while enemy ordnance whistled and spattered all around. On 12 August, Almonds received two birthday cards, one from Lockie and the first one from his son.

'Bless them', he wrote in the diary, 'they have not forgotten me.'

On 18 August, the Prime Minister ordered the Commandos to be reconstituted. The days were marked by continuous artillery activity and heavy bombing raids by formations of Stukas. At night, machine-gun fire rattled and ricocheted around the rocks. It was worse in the mornings and evenings when visibility was at its best. The stunt that Lewes and his men had come to the front to carry out was cancelled. The loss of life, they were told, would have been enormous and the new positions, even if taken, not worth the price. German bombers continued to carry out murderous raids, during which they were almost blinded, covered with flying sand and half gassed by cordite fumes. Nobody was hurt. The time spent building the sanger had not been wasted.

Day after day began to seem the same. Hot sunny days nearly roasted them alive. Beautiful starlit nights were heavy with dew. Almonds lay in the sanger talking to Lockie's photograph while enemy shells burst all around. At night, he listened to the air raids over Tobruk harbour. Occasionally, they went out on patrol in the evening to recce enemy positions. Then one evening, at the end of a sweltering afternoon, Lilley skidded into the sanger sending up a shower of sand and small stones. Almonds was patiently sanding his propeller ink stand, pausing every now and then to smooth away the fine particles of sawdust. Lewes wanted to seem them all at 18.00 hours.

Lewes got the four of them together and began rather formally. He was pleased to be able to tell them, he said, that on the basis of his recommendation, Captain Stirling had invited all four of them to join his new unit. They were sitting on the low stone wall outside the sanger. An ochre sun dappled a parchment sky. The calm that comes in the Middle East just before nightfall was broken only by the faint squawks and flappings of roosting birds as they jostled for possession of the few available perches. This time there was no doubt about it – they *were* being asked to volunteer.

The basic idea sounded good. But then Lewes knew how to put ideas across. They were all stirred at the thought of parachuting and landing by night as small groups of expert saboteurs, well behind enemy lines. Never in all his wildest dreams of *Boy's Own Paper* adventures had Almonds ever imagined anything like this, the reality.

'So, how about it? Lewes ended, spreading out his diseased hands like a salesman setting out his wares. It was now or never. Nobody thought about the risks.

Lewes made clear that he was on for it himself and would be leaving immediately after their next rest leave. That added a new factor into the reckoning. The status quo wasn't an option. Lewes would no longer be there. They had grown to trust him, in spite of his distant manner. He never asked anyone to do anything he could not do himself. They did not fancy going out on night patrols under anyone else's leadership.

It was 'make your mind up time'. One by one they all bought in.[27]

Lewes continued to organise recces in groups of four with the aim of taking more prisoners for intelligence purposes. Monotonous artillery and machine-gun activity punctuated their days. Behind enemy lines after dark, they lay outside the Italian positions listening to them talking and watched as an enemy working party started making new positions. They deliberated over the ideal time to raid them. Getting ready for the attack, Almonds could think only of Lockie.

Keep your fingers crossed darling. xx. Remember that I loved you always.

They squirmed their way perilously right up to the enemy positions and listened to them talking. Once again, the Italians were clearly expecting the raid.

'*Now how on earth can they know about it*'? Almonds fumed silently. He thought of the posters he had seen before leaving the UK: 'CARELESS TALK COSTS LIVES'. It certainly nearly had here. Since they were in the middle of another of the enemy's minefields, they decided that discretion was the better part of valour.[28] Slowly, silently, the group withdrew and arrived back at their own position in the morning. They were punished by a very heavy shelling by the enemy.

At the end of August, the remnants of 8 Commando were relieved from Tobruk. Right to the end, it was touch and go. The enemy's parting shot was to bombard the destroyer HMS *Hasty* as she slipped out of Tobruk harbour at midnight.[29]

The Nile flowed dirty brown and uninviting through Cairo. Thankful to be alive and in one piece, Almonds and Riley enjoyed the simple luxuries of being able to wash and sleep in a bed with sheets. They visited the Pyramids, King Farouk's palace and the School of Hygiene. Almonds looked round the souk in the Khan Al-Khalili but in spite of having been paid his back pay, could not afford to buy anything for Lockie.[30]

On 3 September, the 'Tobruk Four' caught the midday train for Ismailia. The enemy greeted them at the station with an air raid and bombs fell thickly all around the platforms. After a long delay, they caught another train and arrived in Geneifa at 03.00.[31]

The next day, they left by lorry for Kabrit to join the Special Air Service.

Part II

The SAS desert raids, capture at Benghazi and two escapes from Italian prisoner of war camps
November 1941–December 1943

Chapter Five

Reserves of Courage

On 17 October, the 'plane returned from having its fittings modified and practice jumping resumed. Almonds welcomed the distraction from worrying about Lockie and his son, of whom he still had no news. 'L' Detachment was in serious training for night operations, for which the parachuting was only a means to the end. For this reason it was carried out separately from the Commandos and was much more positive.[1]

The Bristol Bombay, one of five kept on the RAF aerodrome opposite the camp at Kabrit[2] took off with a stick of blokes mostly making their first jump. The 'veterans', with one jump behind them, were full of well-meant jokes and back thumping as the novices, grim-faced but resolute, climbed into the old twin-engined troop-carrier. The drone of the engines and the vibration of the aircraft made conversation impossible as the plane climbed into the sky over Kabrit and circled out over the Great Bitter Lake. Ernie Bond watched as the dispatcher worked his way around the aircraft checking the attachment of the static line from each parachute to the fittings inside the aircraft's fuselage. They would ensure that the weight of the man's falling body pulled the rip cord so that the parachute opened automatically.[3]

The Bombay dropped one wing and veered round to come in over the drop zone (DZ). Through the opening in the side of the fuselage, dizzying glimpses of lake and desert slanted away far below. Men with even and odd numbers stood on either side of the aperture. The drop zone was coming up.

'Ready number one!' mouthed the dispatcher. Warburton, a young man from the Seaforth Highlanders and a gifted pianist, nodded and half lifted his hand in acknowledgement. He had an honest open face and a determined expression.

'Go!' shouted the dispatcher. For a moment, the body hung, suspended in the opening out to the sky, and was then snatched violently away.

'Ready number two!'

Ernie Bond saw the eyes of the second man, Joe Duffy, a close friend of the first who had jumped, look from the edge of the exit, to the static line fixture, and then back again.

'Go!' shouted the dispatcher. The trooper hesitated. Again his eyes went to the edge of the opening. He half turned away from it and pointed up towards the static line fixtures, a questioning look on his face. There were shouts of encouragement from the pent-up men still waiting to jump.

'Get on with it man!'

'Come on, stop pissing about!'

'Go!' shouted the dispatcher again. But he made no move to touch the reluctant parachutist. With a half sigh of resignation, the man jumped. Then the dispatcher looked down and saw that his parachute had not opened.[4]

In the Bristol Royal Infirmary, Lockie was visiting John every day but was not allowed into the ward.[5] The doctors said that his condition was undiagnosed but he must be protected from any stray infections. She would watch through glass doors as two young probationer nurses pushed a trolley of baby foods along the ward and passed by her son because he was too ill to eat. As if being separated and having to worry about Jim were not enough, now their baby was dying.

Out walking, miserable because she had no pram to push, she met a woman she hardly knew and found herself pouring out her problem. Her son had stopped eating and there was nothing she could do but watch him die. The woman listened quietly. Then told her that there was one thing she could do. That was to go home, shut the door and pray. Lockie did pray and felt that she had an answer. She should take John out of the hospital. Her father told her to go straight to the hospital and not to come back without the baby. Perhaps he was thinking back to when his first wife had died in childbirth in the Bristol Royal Infirmary.[6]

Lockie went back to the hospital and demanded to see the doctor. He was aghast at her request to discharge John. But the baby was receiving no treatment for his unknown illness. If he was not eating and going to die, his mother pointed out, he might as well die at home with his family who loved him. The doctor said it was unthinkable, adding that even if the baby lived, he would 'Always be a weakling'. After an age of form filling and signing, Lockie discharged the desperately ill baby from hospital and took him home, haunted by the doctors last words. Twenty years later, the 'weakling' went on to pass the SAS selection course and command one of the SAS Squadrons at Hereford.

On Thursday, 17 October 1941, Almonds wrote in his diary:

Plane arrived again. More parachute descents. Decided with plane fittings [sic]. Two of the boys killed. Chutes never had a chance to open. Brought them back across the Canal by boat. Route march at night, 14 miles. Still no news of Lockie.

Then he looked back to the diary of 7 October, 'Fittings on the plane scrapped. Inadequate to stand up to the job.' The lads had had no chance. Their static lines had ripped completely away from the inside of the aircraft and since there was no pressure to pull on their parachutes they did not open. Fortunately, the dispatcher had spotted the problem before any more had jumped. The men in the other planes had all jumped successfully. Almonds had more than a passing interest – he was due to make his first jump the next day.

Ernie Bond explained[7] that that day they had been experimenting with a new attachment clip. They all filed into the aircraft. When they attached their static lines there was a new arrangement into which they had to slot the metal ring on the end of the line attached to the parachute. Usually there were shackles on a long steel bar that ran down the centre of the 'plane. Each shackle had a screw which had to be undone and the ring slipped into it before it was screwed up again. But this time instead there was a U-shaped clip. It was a large hook with a spring release clip, rather like that on the end of a watch chain. It was a lot quicker hooking on because the man just held it open, slipped his ring in and let it spring back to close. But it wasn't strong enough. When Warburton went out, his whole static line went with him. But worst of all, Duffy must have realised it because there was no line trailing over the edge of the exit. So he would have known that his mate's 'chute hadn't opened. He had tried to point it out. But then, with incredible courage, he jumped anyway.

Jimmie Storie went out with Bond to pick the boys up and bring them back across the canal by boat.[8] Even after jumping, Duffy hadn't stopped thinking. When they found him, it was obvious that he had tried to pull out his parachute himself. If they'd been jumping from higher up, he might even have managed it. The most remarkable thing of all was that the two close friends were found lying exactly side by side, head to head and toe to toe. 'If you'd wanted to lay them out for burial,' said Bond, 'you couldn't have done it any better.'[9]

After the funerals, it was Almonds's turn to jump. He had thought that he could not cope with any more pressure. He was wrong.

Plane arrived again. Jumping in the morning. Hope to God the 'chutes work this time, for your and the baby's sake. Goodnight darling.

That evening, Stirling addressed them all. They had had some very bad luck, he said, which had resulted in a terrible accident. But they knew what had caused it and the problem had been rectified. Tomorrow, they would all jump together. Then he wished them good night and good luck.[10]

Morning came too soon. They climbed aboard. They had all been issued with fifty cigarettes and the fingers fumbling with the jumping harnesses were dark brown with nicotine stains. By Almonds's self-devised indicator, he knew that the chips must be well and truly down. As in every situation where danger threatened, his mind was a fever of activity. He rehearsed mentally all the training he had had on exiting, descent and landing. Then he leaned against the fuselage of the Bombay, closed his eyes and prayed.

High over the DZ, David Stirling jumped first without a moment's hesitation. He was without doubt one of the bravest men my father ever knew. The rest of the stick followed quickly and efficiently, eager to get it over with and lay aside their comrades' deaths with honour. Almonds accomplished the task more easily than he had anticipated.

> Made first parachute descent from one thousand feet. Feelings hard to describe, as you hurl yourself out through the door in the 'plane's side. Men must be absolutely crazy creatures to do and think of doing such things. After a fall of about a hundred feet, your 'chute opens and you glide gracefully and comfortably towards earth. The last fifty feet, the ground rushes up to meet you and you prepare yourself for a jar, and then roll up into a ball, collapse your chute and remove the harness. Jumping again tomorrow morning, will be thinking of you. Writing out application tonight to return home. Terribly worried, still no news from you.[11]

The next day he jumped again, this time from 1,500 feet. He experienced the same sensations as before but this time was able to keep full control of the parachute. His diary entry was optimistic:

> No news from Lockie. Application handed in. Finished with training and pending liberation to return to England.

But it was not that easy to escape from his task of bogus Garrison Engineer. Work on the jumping towers was now completed. Next came the assembly of the wire steadying guys needed to accommodate the 4-inch convex camber that he had built into the line between the two main towers for reinforcement and extra safety. The structure was well anchored by a heavy sleeper let into a tee-shaped trench. The job of building in the parachute rings through which parachutists would simulate exiting from an aircraft still remained. Almonds threw himself into the task in an explosion of energy, partly to numb the pain of worrying about Lockie and partly because the equipment was badly needed to improve and speed up SAS parachute training. While continuing on the rigging, the rings he had ordered arrived. Their construction was too heavy and he was unable to use them. He would have to make do by adapting some old rings from Kabrit aerodrome. Lewes made it clear that he still wanted him to concentrate on the task, pointing out to Almonds that he had proved he could jump without any problems. He could navigate and was fitter than most, so his time was better spent on the construction.[12]

Almonds did not know whether Mayne knew about his son's illness, but the Irishman was particularly solicitous at this time.

'Here,' he said one day as the 'bogus engineer' was working on some designs, 'this might prove very handy for you.' He held out a set of drawing instruments, neatly packed in their own case.[13]

On Friday 24 October, Almonds received 'a wire' from Lockie to say that at last John's health was improving. He was immensely relieved. The rest of the men went away on a weekend leave but he did not, preferring to keep himself hard at work to make the time pass quickly. By the time they returned, he had fitted the parachute rings to the towers.[14]

Being in camp did not mean any reduction in pressure. Stirling had a very subtle way of making demands so that he never appeared to be ordering anyone about. His charm alone made people want to deliver their all for him. One day he appeared as Almonds was hand-sawing a length of timber spread between two home-made trestles. A khamsin had just blown itself out and nearby the half finished jumping rig rose like a giant piece of Meccano against the dull pewter sky. Everything was slowly returning to normal and a cloud of flies had already returned to torment Almonds as he worked.

Stirling was in an open bush jacket and khaki shorts, plus the inevitable dark glasses. Almonds, wearing only a white singlet and his navy blue PT shorts, suddenly felt dishevelled. But his CO waved away his apologies and told him that he was 'doing a damned fine job'. He did not underestimate the amount of work involved, he said, and they all appreciated it very much. Immediately, Almonds felt that he could have gone on to build the Forth Bridge. What a little encouragement can do.

They walked round the structure, discussing all the possible ways that it could be used in training. Then Stirling asked him how things were at home now and whether he still needed leave. He seemed sincere, but slightly less at ease discussing the problems of married men. Almonds, desperately wanting to minimise his personal problems, said there had been a slight improvement, but that he wanted to let the application stand for the time being. Stirling said that was fine and asked to be kept informed.

He lingered, his gaze wandering over the huge framework of metal and wooden girders, down to the ground and then turning round towards the Great Bitter Lake.

'I've been wondering,' he said. 'Do you think you could possibly build us a boat?' As if to dull the shock of such a stupendous demand, he hurried on to explain that they really did need one because they dropped the chaps over the other side in the desert and then they had the most dashed awful problem bringing them back. He smiled appealingly, as though his request were the most natural in the world. Too late, Almonds realised that he should have seen it coming. He wanted to say that he was not sure, that it was not possible, that anyway it was ridiculous and totally unreasonable to expect one man to build a motor launch, for that was clearly what was needed, out here in the desert without the right tools and materials. But he dared not. He knew that if he did, he would feel churlish, unpatriotic and disloyal. It depended, he began cautiously, on what sort of craft Stirling had in mind and where the materials were coming from. A decent launch would need at least a 50 horsepower engine. Stirling was immediately all largesse. Almonds was just to let him know what was needed and he would get it for him, even the wood. There were masses of packing cases available from all the aircraft being shipped in from America.

The man *was* absolutely impossible to refuse.[15]

General Sir Claude Auchinleck, Commander-in-Chief, was another man who usually got his own way. He had spent much of his time since taking up post in July 1941 stiffening the backbones of his generals before making inevitable changes. He was obsessed by the idea that if one didn't go forward one was almost certainly pushed back. Standing still simply wasn't an option with an opponent like Rommel. The 'Auk's' first aim therefore was to relieve Tobruk and his second was to push Rommel back out of Cyrenaica (which is now Western Libya). He badly needed to grab hold of some airfields so that Allied convoy ships to and from Malta could have air cover. But if he couldn't get to use himself, then he definitely wanted to deny them to the enemy.

The coastal strip was crucial. To the west of beleaguered Tobruk, right on the coast, below the escarpment which ran parallel to the sea, lay the airfields around Gazala, at the northern end of the Gazala line, and El Timimi. These airfields were much closer to Tobruk than the Derna and Mekili aerodromes further west and would be easier to consolidate with any retaken ground around the relieved city. The Auk and Ritchie, his Deputy Chief of General Staff, had approved Stirling's plan for a small but strategic operational unit to be deployed when the new offensive was ready. They had thought it worthwhile letting Stirling set up a unit to start training some of the Commandos who were now surplus to requirement. If it worked, they would be invaluable in infiltrating behind enemy lines to destroy aircraft on the ground. If it didn't, they would not have lost very much.[16] The offensive was to be ready for mid-November; the question was, would Stirling and his men?

By the beginning of November, Almonds had made a good start on building Stirling's launch. It was to be twenty-three feet in length and have a Ford V.8 engine.[17] On the edge of the Great Bitter Lake, he erected some stocks on which to build the boat and brought the workbench and such tools as he had down onto the beach. He was pleased with his canoe which was a light and seaworthy little craft, capable of carrying four. He had even gone night fishing in it and caught enough crabs for a meal for the Sergeants' Mess. Then a post card arrived from home. It seemed to be preparing him for the worst. He would have risked anything to get home quickly. Lockie dominated every waking moment. But he could not feel any relief from constant anxiety about the baby unless pressing himself hard. Work was an opiate. He could not even manage to write a letter. Only writing up his diary partially relieved the terrible dread of their son's imminent death.

> What *is* wrong with John? Cablegram received by CO said meningitis. Cannot seem to keep my mind and hands working together. Mind races on at a great pace. Hands seems foolishly slow and stupid – inadequate to the task set before them. I can no longer continue. Packed up my tools and stopped work like someone in a dream.[18]

Then he began to think that the wire from Lockie with 'health improving' may have been sent after the postcard. He prayed that this meant the little chap was well on the way to recovery.

While he continued on the completion of the towers and the launch, the Squadron made a night jump. On one drop, two 'chutes were ripped leaving the plane. They went up the following morning to throw out some dummies. He also took on the task of putting in a proper floor for the Sergeants' Mess by lamplight. There was still no news of his application to go home. Knowing that things at home were really bad, Stirling suggested that Almonds should not go on the imminent first raid.

'That way,' he said, 'you'll be here to receive any news that comes and you'll be able to send a wire or write a letter.' He too, Almonds noted, seemed to expect that the baby would die. But his kindness was not entirely altruistic.

'And,' he added, 'While, you're waiting, you'll be able to get on with the work here.'[19]

In spite of the constant application to his tasks, inwardly Almonds was distraught and desperate.

> Sometimes, I even feel like deserting and making my own way home. Realise that such action would be silly. Also, too tired! No news from Lockie. A note to say that John was better and she was happy would have meant so much to me.[20]

On Sunday 16 November the whole squadron – 54 men – left early in the morning for the forward airfield at Bagoush. From there they would carry out the planned parachute raid on the Gazala and Timimi aerodromes in the Western Desert. The objective was the destruction of as many German fighter aircraft as possible whilst on the ground before they could participate in the main battle. It was estimated that 300 aircraft were based on three aerodromes around Gazala and two at Timimi. All five were to be attacked simultaneously on the night of 17 November. The five parties would then be picked up by the Long Range Desert Group (LRDG) at an RV track junction 38 miles south of Timimi on the night of 20 November. Success depended upon pinpoint serial navigation so that the parachutists were dropped in their correct locations.[21]

Almonds watched the raiders embark and the planes take off. A light desert breeze flapped at the jeep awnings as pale oblongs of sunlight stole across the cool grey tarmac. The weather report over the DZ was appalling, with a wind-speed and visibility that would turn parachuting into a death defying game of Russian roulette. He waited until the 'planes became distant specks in the glimmering sky.

Suddenly, he was alone.

Chapter Six

First Strike and Regroup

At Bagoush, the RAF regarded the 'L' Detachment raiders as little short of a suicide squad.[1] The chances of landing anywhere near the target without being badly injured were indeed low. But they all cheered when, after consultation with his officers, Stirling decided that the attack still would still go ahead. He was under several pressures from above and below. The assault was important in its own right. If successful, it would support Operation Crusader[2] by crippling the enemy's air capability. If it were postponed, it would miss that opportunity and MEHQ would jump at the chance to put the boot in on the viability of the unit. In addition, Stirling knew only too well what cancellation would do to morale. The men had joined 'L' Detachment because they were sick of the many aborted raids of the Layforce days and expected something better. The raid had to go ahead.

The decision had been made and the raiders were in fine fettle. Jimmie Storie was with the group about to go into action the following night. How were they to pass the time until then?[3] Dave Kershaw said that there was no point in a few hands of cards because none of them had been paid. That meant that they couldn't have a drink either. Blakeney said that he was dying for a pint. There were shouts of agreement. They thought the 'crabs' (the RAF) must have some somewhere.

Emboldened by perceived moral self justification and the safety of collective offending, they made their way round to the back of the RAF Officers' Mess tent. It was Sunday evening and it had closed early. Since the 'bar' consisted essentially of a plywood cupboard, it was not difficult to cut the back out of it and transport the contents back to their own tent. They had been tanking it up for some time before the fly sheets were whipped aside by a huge man with handlebar moustaches. There was a momentary pause while they squinted blearily at the newcomer. Then Kershaw, with all the bonhomie of one scattering largesse that is not his own, offered the man a drink. The potential fellow carouser asked what they though they were doing. When they explained that they were just having a few drinks before they went into action, the big man bristled.

'Yes, and with our booze as well! I'm the Camp Commander.'[4]

The next morning, a grim-faced Lewes had them all on parade.[5] He was furious and embarrassed but even he could see the funny side of the situation. The row of men stood at attention, staring straight ahead. A long moment passed. He told them all that they were 'an absolute shower'. Silence. Then, in spite of himself, he burst out laughing and rolled his eyes heavenward.

'Oh, for heaven's sake,' he said. 'You're either habitual criminals or a bunch of congenital idiots!'

At any moment, Almonds expected to be leaving for his son's funeral. Yet his duty was also to remain with 'L' Detachment. On 16 November he wrote:

> They are a fine crowd of lads. How many will I see again? Left alone in camp. Wandered around from tent to tent – all empty and yet so full of hope and faith. Photos of sweethearts, wives and mothers on the walls, awaiting their return. May they none of them be disappointed. Did nothing all day; just aimlessly wandered about.[6]

He tried to start work but gave it up as a bad job. His thoughts were constantly with the men now 230 miles inside enemy territory, hiding in the sand waiting for darkness before beginning their reign of terror and destruction.

> After the massacre is over and the enemy's planes blown up or burned, there remains that terrible march back through the desert. No one who is sick or wounded could possibly make it and no one can afford to help. The weight already carried by each man is as much as he can bear; great supplies of water and food are so essential to such a trek. I am not there. I sit back here in the safety of the camp and wish I were with them. One more would have made the load lighter. A few words of encouragement when hard pressed go a long way. In action before when we've been up against it, I've managed to get a smile or a joke out of them, which has helped a lot along the way. Anyway, had I been with them, at least I could have tried. Reality beats fiction for sheer, cold, calculating courage. Some of these lads cannot be beaten. Films and books of daring and adventure fall far short of this, the real thing. More will be heard from the SAS, should this raid go through as planned. The war in northern Africa should soon be brought to a successful conclusion.[7]

He drove himself to work. But concentration on the tasks in hand eluded him. He wandered around camp again. He thought that he must have been overdoing the work. Whatever it was, his own reaction frightened him. He had no interest in doing anything, not even things that he used to like most.[8]

> Had a letter from home. Dad wrote about a page, extracts from the Bible. Enjoyed reading it so much. Wish I had a Bible.[9]

He continued for several miserable days, unable to work and without news of Lockie or the raiders. He wandered around the accommodation. Late at night, he prayed for her, the baby and his friends somewhere in enemy territory. In his own tent, Bond's photograph on the locker gazed calmly across the empty bed-spaces. Then on 19 November came bad news. The 'plane his section had gone off in was missing.[10]

> Poor devils. They need all the luck possible. In this tent there will be Mrs Bond and two children waiting for Ernie, Mrs Stone and son waiting for Barney, Mrs Quinton waiting for Spike. May it please God that they don't wait in vain. Had it not been for John's illness, Mrs Almonds and son would be waiting for Jim. I should have been with that 'plane. The turns of fate are past all understanding. Wrote a letter to my darling Lockie. Wish I could hear from her, if only a few lines.

By now my father had finally acquired a nickname – 'Gentleman Jim' – because he did not swear and was always courteous. He was also sometimes known as 'the quiet man' because, according to Jimmie Storie, 'he wasn't like a lot of the Guards, always shouting the odds'.[11]

A newspaper brought back from Suez revealed that Allied troops had advanced 50 miles from Sollum towards Tripoli.

> According to this progress, Tobruk should be relieved in another two days. God, will this happen? Will they find our boys safely hiding up there somewhere? Each night I say my prayers for Lockie and John and all the boys.[12]

At the end of an anxious week, he received a letter from home, although not a recent one. The advance in the desert continued; the Allies were only 10 miles from Tobruk. A week from the day they had left, he heard that twenty-one of the men had been picked up out in the desert by the Long Range Desert Group patrol and would be back shortly.[13] He was immensely pleased and relieved. At last he found he could work again. But there was still no news from home. He could not stop worrying. Not knowing was the worst agony of all.

On Wednesday, 26 November, the remnants of the SAS returned, twenty-one as rumoured.[14] They had been recovered by the LRDG and taken back to their HQ at Siwa Oasis, just to the north of the Great Sand Sea. To Almonds's enormous relief, Pat Riley was among them. But one of the 'planes was missing and Blakeney too. Blakeney, intelligent, courageous and uncomplaining, was always willing to take on any job and deliver to the finish. His disappearance was a terrible blow.[15] Bond had not returned either.[16] The diary entry for 26 November says it all:

> In our tent, the beds remain empty and their personal effects lie strewn where they left them. I do not have the heart to alter things. I still cannot give them up as lost, even though the Government has. What happened to that 'plane, no one knows. Was it shot down? Anyway, I will keep the hope for another month. May their wives never know of this. Twenty-one out of fifty-four; nearly half. I suppose one must not expect too much.[17]

Back at Kabrit, Pat Riley eventually started to talk about the raid and Almonds wrote it all down in his diary.[18] They had taken off from the forward area at 19.00 hours. All went well until they were approaching the objective, the aerodrome beyond Tobruk. Then they had to pass through the anti-aircraft barrage. Their 'plane was hit several times. Once, while they were in the full glare of a searchlight, it was so bright that they could even read a newspaper. Tracer shells and 'flaming onions' kept leaving the ground and coming up towards them. They carried on and evaded the searchlight. Then came the time to jump. They all left the 'plane in quick succession. Jock Cheyne was the second to last to go.[19] He was a good bloke, according to Riley, 'full of quaint Scots humour'. But he was never seen again. They thought his 'chute may have been damaged by the anti-aircraft fire or perhaps it failed to open. Riley was worried about that because he and Cheyne had just swapped 'chutes for a better fit – he was even bigger than Riley. They had searched for him for a while couldn't find him.

The landing was really rough. A 30-mile-per-hour wind was blowing and they were dragged quite a long way over awful rough ground before they could release themselves from their harnesses. Then they folded up their chutes and buried them – £80-worth of pure silk. Then, incredibly, an electric storm that had threatened for some time finally broke and within minutes they were knee deep in water. They had no supplies or explosives because their supply parachutes had got caught on the tail of the 'plane. There was nothing for it but to try and make it back to their own lines.

The following ten days and nights consisted of marching across the desert, still in enemy territory. Twice they were bombed and strafed by low-flying enemy aircraft. Eventually, they met up with their own desert patrol and came back en bloc, except for two members of LP section. They had broken ankles from the rough landing and had to be left behind, together with Jock Cheyne. It was the worst nightmare of the desert soldier.

The next day, Almonds was able to establish that the story, as told by Pat Riley, was the same for the other 'plane.[20] Of the total four aircraft, one air-crew from 'B' Troop got back safely, as well as one 'plane from 'A' Troop, with the exception of a few casualties. The other 'A' Troop 'plane had dropped its cargo complete. According to an Air Force report, the crew of that 'plane had accounted for 40 enemy aircraft but they were still missing. The other 'B' Troop 'plane had been lost. Although there were theories as to what had happened to it, no one really knew.[21]

Out of the five raiding parties, two had failed to reach their objectives at all, owing to the appalling weather which had led to inaccurate estimations of their positions. The third party (with Pat Riley) reached the vicinity of their objective and had seen aircraft on their aerodrome but heavy rain had made their bombs ineffective. The aircraft carrying the fourth party (with Ernie Bond) had been unable to navigate in the storm and had force-landed in the desert, inside enemy territory.[22] After a short fight with an Italian position, they took one prisoner back to the 'plane. When the weather conditions improved, they took off again, short of fuel, intending to make for home. But the pilot's call to the aerodrome at Bagoush was intercepted by the more powerful German wireless at Gazala. The aircraft was guided in to land there and all personnel were captured. The RAF file note, which had been compiled from conversations with Captain Stirling, OC 'L' Detachment, stated optimistically that he was expected to submit a report himself but this was unlikely to arrive for several weeks.[23] It never did.

Almonds was fascinated by the resilience of the human spirit.

> It is difficult to get a story out of these people. They are a tight-lipped lot and never go into detail. But from their appearance on arrival back in camp, the last ten days in the desert must have been hell. Today the lads who returned to fight again another day went on leave to Cairo for a weekend. Left of the old Commando, sixty-two men raided part of the coast between Tobruk and Bardia from submarines during the beginning of the week. Three have returned; the rest are reported killed or missing. Why I tell you all these things I don't know Lockie but they were my friends, comrades in arms. Left of our troop, 3 Troop when we were in England, are only Pat Riley, Lilley and myself.[24]

He felt that somehow his diary entry was a kind of tribute and memorial to them.

On 2 December, David Stirling asked the 'L' Detachment remnants to go on a new operation.[25] Before departure, the men took advantage of their last chance to go to the aerodrome cinema. The SAS was supposed to be highly secret so they were amazed to see a Pathe News film about themselves. 'That's quite a good show', Almonds confided to his diary, 'for a unit that's supposed to be "hush, hush".'

The next day, they left by Douglas airliner from Kabrit Aerodrome via Bagoush for Jalo Oasis to start the new 'adventure'. All they knew was that they could be away for one or two weeks. Almonds had heard nothing more from home but felt increasingly certain that no news was good news. He signed off in the diary. It had already seen enemy action and the back cover was holed from shrapnel in the sanger at the Fig Tree sector, Tobruk. Whenever he went on a raid, he kept up the entries on scribbled bits of paper.

> Goodbye, Lockie darling. Shall be thinking of you and Sonny and the boat I am to catch to return to you when I come back off this trip.[26]

After the failure of the first raid, David Stirling kept a low profile. Contact with Headquarters was the last thing he sought until he had delivered a success. But Ritchie sent for him and he had to make an oral report. The most he had been able to offer was information on enemy strengths and troop movements. He had not enjoyed the experience.[27]

Before long, it was realised that the SAS needed the LRDG to run 'tug patrols' to take them in near the target and recover them afterwards. Rommel had counter-attacked brilliantly and Auchinleck wanted blood. It was rumoured that both Cunningham and Ritchie were likely to 'get the chop'. Stirling had forged a strong link with Denys Reid, a brigadier who had just recaptured Jalo Oasis. It was about 200 miles south of the coast, equidistant from Tobruk and Benghazi, just to the north-west of the Great Sand Sea. This would be just the spot for nipping out and giving Jerry a bloody nose, too far out to attract unwelcome attention from HQ in Cairo and yet offering the delights of the Oasis whenever they returned from their dastardly deeds.

On 7 December, the SAS arrived at Jalo. It was all Almonds had ever imagined an oasis to be and quite a contrast after a miserable day's delay sitting in the tent at Bagoush while a sandstorm raged outside. About 7 miles long by 2 miles wide and abundant with water and waving palm trees, it had its fair share of desert heat and flies. But the luxuriant greenery and running water seemed to make them more bearable. The wooden fort set in the middle looked just like a child's toy. Only the model soldiers of the old French Foreign Legion with their blue kepis and white cross-belted uniforms were missing. The people were friendly and considerably more sociable than the bad-tempered camels that plodded by with supercilious expressions on their scabrous faces.

Three days before, on 7 December, Jalo had been in Italian hands. Now it was the SAS base, a quick change-over for local inhabitants accustomed to the slow-moving pace of Middle East life. From the spoils of war, 'L' Detachment immediately procured for themselves two Italian Lancia Trente Quatro lorries, enormous great things that had to be cranked into life by winding the fly-wheel until the engine started. Long poles were used to unstick the double rear wheels. Mounted in the back was a 20mm automatic Breda cannon. The Lancias were ten-tonners that ran on diesel but had solid tyres which shook them to bits among the desert boulders. They were not a terribly good idea in the desert because when a Lancia broke down it meant that ten tons of supplies were delayed.[28]

When they had settled in, David Stirling addressed the remnants of his unit in a pool of shade under clumps of ancient, thickened date palms. Tethered donkeys twitched at the flies and small children trekked back and forth in tattered outsized clothing carrying water from the wells in a strange assortment of receptacles. In spite of their initial failure, Stirling was relaxed and confident. The small groups of men listened attentively. This time, he told them, they would not be going in by parachute. But that did not mean they wouldn't in future. Instead, they would be using 'tug patrols' from the Long Range Desert Group to take them in near the target and pick them up afterwards. He thought they would find the LRDG very much kindred spirits. Although their main aim was reconnaissance – and what they didn't know about desert patrols wasn't worth knowing – they had absolutely no compunction about landing one on the enemy whenever they could. He concluded by saying that he hoped they would take the opportunity to learn from the LRDG because they never knew when the additional skills might come in handy. The group broke up, humming with speculation about the forthcoming raids.

The LRDG were indeed like-minded partners in crime. Their unit was split up into various patrols, each with very fast all-metal 20cwt trucks, fitted with special machine-guns and four-wheel drive. They operated and patrolled vast expanses of the Western Desert. At the beginning of the desert war, the Allies had done badly. But, as the memos on file bore witness, they were not too proud to admit it. There had been lots of experimentation; cynics called the results 'private armies'. The LRDG was an early success. The SAS is one of the few that still exists. It was the LRDG who had had the experience, skill and self-discipline to obtain the necessary information to help the Allies improve their performance. 'An army marches on its stomach' was the old adage. Well, the LRDG gathered detailed data about what was going into enemy stomachs and a whole lot more: troop movements, what sort of stores, fuel, water, equipment and munitions were moving where and in what quantities. The enemy was forced to make trade-offs between men and other resources and the results of his deliberations were infinitely interesting to Auchinleck and MEHQ.[29]

Almonds was immediately intrigued by this new science and its proponents. A young LRDG Sergeant called Mike Sadler was detailed to brief them all on the field of LRDG operations.[30] Sadler was in his early twenties, quietly intelligent with a droll sense of humour and a perceptive wit. He had an open pleasant face and a shock of thick light brown hair. Most things seemed to amuse him and his face often creased into a slow smile while he was talking. He had left England before the war to farm in Rhodesia, then joined the Rhodesian Artillery and Anti-tank Battery, where he trained as an anti-tank gunner. They had driven up from Rhodesia, via Mombassa and Abyssinia, in flat-backed 'portés'. Designed and built in the railway workshops in Nairobi, these vehicles were fitted out with anti-tank guns and had led the advance into Italian Somaliland. With this set of skills and experience, the LRDG had immediately fancied Sadler, only to discover that he also had an interest in, and undeniable aptitude for, navigation. His uncanny skill had attracted Stirling's attention and earned him an enviable reputation.

According to Sadler, the most valuable LRDG operation was the road watch. It gave a rather fascinating insight into the arithmetic of war. Each road watch patrol did a two-week stint. Every night, they would go down in twos to a point on the main coastal road behind enemy lines and stay for 24 hours. They would lie up close to it and watch the traffic passing in both directions and record every vehicle. They were usually relieved late on the second night, without ever seeing their replacements. And then, *provided* they had checked everything carefully, and handed in an accurate report back at the truck, some very useful information got radioed through to Cairo. When it was put together with a whole lot of other, he emphasised, *accurate* reports, it could lead to some very useful information indeed. It might even be possible to tell whether Rommel was planning a new assault, or an outing to the sea, or even that he was so short of fuel that he was finding it difficult to move at all. The point about the road watch was that it was continuous, a bit like watching blood circulate. It measured the enemy's pulse and was a good indicator of his general health. If he didn't have a good strong pulse, he was probably feeling rather seedy.[31]

Sadler made it all sound so logical. Some of the men asked him why it was that so many people seemed to go wrong when navigating in the desert. But he was far too well brought up to agree with a statement couched in such terms. He explained that it was always difficult to avoid running into some problems. Day or night, they went by dead reckoning.[32] The desert was anything but flat, so having set a course they would be driving on a bearing of a shadow on a sun compass and as the vehicle lurched and tipped, some margin of error was bound to occur. It was a question of recognising that and knowing how to compensate. The LRDG were using the Bagnold compass, designed by the chap who founded the LRDG. Sadler thought it pretty good and rather better than the British Army compass which was covered in azimuths and almost impossible to read.[33]

Sometimes they had to correct as often as every eight minutes. Occasionally, the navigator had to take noon sightings for latitude – usually when everybody else was enjoying a brew up. At night, he had to stay up late with the wireless operator and get a time signal from a Cairo broadcast. That was needed to work out the difference between their theoretical position from dead reckoning and their actual position. They would set up the tripod and theodolite, an instrument about the size of a kettle, and get a position line at right angles to a star and then to two more stars. That gave them what they called a 'cocked hat', a tiny triangle on the map, and that was where they were. Of course if was cloudy, there was more messing about. You would have to aim at where they thought the star ought to be. Then when the cloud cleared for a moment, they would take a sighting. But people sometimes came to grief simply through lack of faith. It was important to make a conscious decision to believe in the reading and act on it, and not be distracted into putting trust in something else. Most people who went wrong in the desert either hadn't corrected for the errors of the day or, if they had, didn't hang onto their faith in the calculations.[34]

After moving to Jalo, the SAS planned the first raid. Stirling and Mayne were to be dropped by the LRDG near Sirte, further along the coast to the west of Agheila on the Gulf of Sidra. Lewes was to take his usual group, including Almonds and Lilley, in the Lancia Trente Quatro lorries, to have a go at Agheila airfield.[35] The party was minus Blakeney and Bond. By now it was known that they were 'in the bag' and probably on their way to an Italian or German POW camp. Both raids were timed for the night of 14 December. Bill Fraser, a Lieutenant in the Gordon Highlanders, was to make an assault on Agedabia aerodrome, again on the Gulf of Sidra but to the east of Agheila where the coast ran directly north up to Benghazi. Another airfield, Nofilia, lay between the two.

Almonds's party left Jalo and headed north east, deep into enemy territory.[36] All day they saw nothing but sand, without even a large stone to break the monotony. Alone on the great ocean of the desert, under the bowl of a cloudless, but grey winter sky, they could see clear to the horizon in every direction. By nightfall they had covered 120 miles and were in a position about 75 miles south-east of Benghazi, some 200 miles behind the German and Italian front lines at Tobruk.[37]

Next morning, they started away early, travelling east by north. The country began to change. Deep wadis and escarpments gradually replaced the level sand and in the wadi bottoms a sparse growth of shrub sprouted. Progress was much slower and the negotiating of steep hills and rocky ridges very dangerous. Lewes mounted a sharp lookout all day for enemy aircraft. On the second day, they continued through very rough wild country. The only signs of life were occasional gazelles and herds of wild camels. They crossed the Italian road that ran south from Agheila, on the southern-most point of the Gulf of Sidra, to Marauder and camped barely 13 miles from their target. Bob Lilley was in high spirits and thought it would be like old times going out on patrol again with Lewes and Almonds.

Later that evening, Lewes was as exacting as ever. He still addressed them as if they were a public meeting. Their objective, he said, was to destroy the aerodrome at Agheila. They would proceed to the target, and attack by placing bombs in the aircraft and destroying all ammunition dumps and petrol supplies they could find. They would begin that night by watching the traffic on the Tripoli main road. The other party had headed off to Sirte. They were carrying out the same operation in preparation for their own assault. Lewes's party checked their navigational equipment, ammunition and water and ran over the preparations. Then, at dusk, they moved into the fast freeze of the desert night.

Compared to the LRDG, the 'L' Detachment men were novices in the skill of the roadwatch. But they were keen and learned fast. Lewes, Almonds and Lilley spent some time watching Italian vehicles plying back and forth along the coast road between Tripoli and the Axis's front line to the east.[38] The enemy was now stretched to the limit of his supply-line, hence the potential for maximum aggravation at minimum input from the SAS. After noting the enemy's strengths and apparent state of unreadiness, the three returned to camp and camouflaged the lorries. Almonds and Lilley took charge of the camp, while Lewes left with about ten men for Agheila aerodrome.[39]

Lewes's party approached to within sight of it and found to their great disappointment, that it was deserted.[40] Undaunted, they searched around and found some lorries full of 'ammo' which they blew up, together with a good mile of telegraph lines along the main Tripoli road. In spite of the dearth of machines to destroy, they ran into a platoon of one of the Italian native regiments. These were hardly made of fighting stuff and Lewes captured the platoon corporal, who was promptly nicknamed 'Sambo'. He was 'as black as ink, a good sort of chap and very friendly towards his captors'. Except for these most un-warlike soldiers, they encountered no one. Corporal Sambo's entire platoon laid down their arms and all wanted to be taken prisoner. They were very disappointed when only the corporal was taken.[41]

Back at base, Almonds was awoken early by a slight noise. He stole towards the edge of the camp, slowly working his way round to where the sound had come from. A small skinny Arab was creeping through the low scrub towards their camp. Without even a struggle, Almonds quickly captured him and held him prisoner by fastening his legs together with the tow chain of the lorry! They looked after him well but could take no chances of allowing him to escape. A slip-up at that point could have proved fatal.[42] Several times during the day, they sighted enemy trucks, none of which passed close enough to see them and, much more threatening, enemy aircraft overhead.

14 December. Nightfall. The whole party left camp and drove along to the main Tripoli road. They halted 200 yards from the road while a large German convoy passed. Then they lit up cigarettes and started off along the coast road. Soon they were bowling along to the north-east in the direction of Mersa Brega and Agedabia. The Italians had made good roads and it was a pleasant change to travel on one after so much rough country. Everyone was in the best of spirits and waved to the soldiers coming in the opposite direction as they passed by in the continual streams of German and Italian lorries.[43] The SAS were in ebullient mood, the sight of all the tanks and petrol wagons being enough to make any enemy's mouth water.

Arriving at Mersa Brega, the raiders saw the lights of a large roadhouse and a fort. It was clearly some sort of staging post for enemy supply convoys and probably used by top enemy brass for operational planning meetings. Disappointed at having drawn the short straw at the airfield, they were suddenly itching for action. But why go to the trouble of ambushing the enemy on the road when they could get them there like sitting ducks?

They pulled in to the side of the road and parked their lorry, the captured Italian Lancia Trente Quatro, among a lot of Italian and German trucks.[44] Right beside them was a lorry just like their own. The driver had no matches. Seeing them with cigarettes in their mouths and suddenly desirous of a smoke, he fished in his pocket, stuck a weedy brown cigarette between his lips and got out for a light.[45] They all sat motionless. Lewes grinned in a friendly fashion. He got out. Still without saying anything, he offered the enemy a light. The flare of the match lit up a small sallow, unshaven face. While the Italian was bending over, cupping his hands around the tiny flame, Lewes struck. With his right hand, he grabbed their enemy's right arm, spun him round and twisted it half way up his back, while at the same time putting a throat lock on him with his left. Then he hustled his half choking victim round to the back of the truck which opened hastily to receive him.

Lewes gave him a helping shove, jumped in behind him and slammed the door. Inside, silence. The precipitately introduced occupants surveyed each other in the confined space. The kidnap victim was speechless. His eyes panned all the way left, then right, then back again. Suddenly, he let out a torrent of voluble and indignant Italian. When he got no response, the Italian shouted with increasing desperation. Lewes continued to listen with mock patience, his head sympathetically on one side while the prisoner kept up a stream of invective which gradually degenerated into a low-level whine. From what they could make of it, he gave them to understand that this sort of treatment was just was 'not done' and went to considerable pains to explain to his abductors that *he* was Italian, whereupon Lewes told him that *they* were English and *he* was a prisoner. Another stunned silence in the back of the truck. The captive, open mouthed, looked from one face to another. Slowly, realisation dawned that they were not Germans. His face crumpled and he broke down and cried like a baby. Then he started bawling for help. In the front, Almonds was aware of other Italians strolling around the car park. They needed to keep the man quiet or he would give the game away. Lilley clapped his hand over the Italian's mouth to prevent him from spoiling the show.[46]

Having bound and gagged their prisoner, it was time to go in for the kill. Lilley got out and wound the fly-wheel to crank up the lorry until the engine started. It kicked into life and they drove for about 50 yards to give Almonds enough room to operate the Breda cannon. They intended to destroy the lorries and the fort.

'Come on, come on!' Lewes hissed low and urgently. 'If we don't get on with it or move off we'll attract attention.' Almonds struggled with the weapon, muttering softly under his breath. Although he'd checked it out and fired it off earlier, right then the thing just would not function. It was no good. It was so cold that the oil had congealed and the mechanism was fouled up with sand.

Lewes quickly decided that they would go in and attack the place on foot. They had sub-machine guns, revolvers and bombs and would make them count. Lewes and Almonds strolled across to the far end of the car park. Then they worked fast placing bombs, conscious that the shortest time pencil was only 7 minutes. And all the time, German and Italian lorries were pulling in and out of the car park.

'That's it!' shouted Lewes as the first bomb went off. They ducked for cover behind another huge Lancia Trente Quatro.[47]

After the occupants of the roadhouse had recovered from their initial surprise, a sharp fight ensued. But it soon became apparent that the enemy had withdrawn to take shelter in the fort, closing and barricading the gates behind them. Without more weapons and equipment, it was impossible to get at them. At first frustrated, Lewes and Almonds quickly turned their attention back to the unprotected enemy vehicles. There was now no one to stop them from getting on with placing more bombs on the lorries. The 'defenders' were all hiding inside the fort. Lewes and Almonds set to work again. The fire coming from the ensconced enemy was so poor and erratic that they were able to ignore it. However, there remained the continual risk of more enemy vehicles pulling into the road house. So, after accounting for all the lorries in the car park, they moved on down the road for about 2 miles. There they stopped, made a thorough job of mining the road, and set charges on the telegraph poles. A bit further on, they passed a brightly painted truck and trailer. Small, pale faces peeped out from the windows in the back. It was a travelling brothel. Lewes wrinkled up his nose in disgust. The end of Almonds's diary entry for 24 December captures their mood:

> We left the road here and headed out into the desert and towards Jalo. After going a very short distance, we heard the mines go off and we knew that someone was in trouble again. Then a series of bangs told us that another half mile of communications between German and Italian Headquarters at Tripoli and the front had been destroyed. Two nights ago, the remainder of the Unit with Captain Stirling were playing similar games 60 miles further down the road. Enemy Headquarters must be very wroth and almost ignore the telephone as a means of communication![48]

After driving all night, they stopped 25 miles from the main road for breakfast, camouflaged the lorries, posted a lookout, and lay down to sleep. There was no sign of pursuit or enemy aircraft. They pressed on and crossed the Marauder road. The going was bad, through rocky country with patches of very soft sand and they spent much of their time digging the lorries out of the large drifts. At last, the rough country was left behind and they regained the flat hard surface before camping about 50 miles from home base.

Jalo at midday on 18 December was balmy and unbelievably welcoming. Back at the oasis, Lewes's party handed over their prisoners and met the rest of the crowd who had been back a few days. They had given up Almonds's party as lost. Stirling's main raid on Sirte had been observed from the air and they had been heavily bombed. The element of surprise was lost and in any case there were very few aircraft on the aerodrome. Paddy Mayne had discovered a new landing ground near the main road 18 miles west of Sirte and had decided to attack it. Mayne had also stormed the door of an unguarded hut and machine-gunned the occupants, mostly waiting pilots and Officers' Mess staff. The whole landing ground area had been totally unguarded. Almonds's diary for 18 December records grimly:

> They succeeded in destroying 24 enemy aircraft, besides the bomb dumps, petrol dumps etc. and shot the staff, pilots etc. in the Officers' quarters – no prisoners taken.

The successful raids were celebrated by an issue rum and lime party. The Italian prisoner taken at the roadhouse seemed to have regained his sense of humour and joined in the sing-song with great gusto. In the end, they had their work cut out to shut him up.

For him there were no doubt advantages in finishing out the war as a POW.

Chapter Seven

Engaging the Enemy

On 20 December 1941, the SAS lay sprawled under the shade of the swaying palms of Jalo Oasis. High up, sunlight glinted through the long ragged fronds, flickering dappled patterns over their prostrate bodies. All was still. Occasionally a sun tanned arm swatted idly at the flies, sending up tiny incensed hordes. The SAS had become like a gang of outlawed bandits from a wild west film, riding out and swooping down on the unsuspecting countryside to carry out their dastardly deeds and then return to lie up in the hills, dusting off their weapons and planning the next raid. How many times in their lives would they be paid to do that? Suddenly, there were shouts from the lookouts.

'Enemy aircraft coming in from four o'clock!' They scrambled up and ran for cover.[1]

Almonds and his party were awaiting the return of the other raiders before heading back to Kabrit for Christmas. Although in many ways idyllic, Jalo lacked certain basic amenities. They were living in mud huts with roofs made from straw. The holes in the walls meant that they shared them with scorpions which scuttled in and out, which was not conducive to sleeping very soundly. There were two large cisterns, about 15 feet across that they could swim in. But they had not been able to wash or shave properly since leaving Kabrit and Almonds disliked feeling rather rough and dirty.[2]

On 22 December several more SAS parties returned, including Bill Fraser's.[3] The news was good: 37 enemy aircraft had been destroyed in the raid on Agedabia, as well as the usual aerodrome installations. But sadness marred the success. Two more of their number had been lost by way of accident – LRDG Rhodesian boys killed by 'friendly' aircraft fire. In spite of having laid out the correct ground recognition signals, their party had been attacked on the way back, while they were having tea, by two Allied 'planes. Operating so deep behind enemy lines, there was always a risk of being attacked from the air by their own side, as well as the enemy. Lilley soberly reminded them that Bond had always said that it was the RAF they should be afraid of, not enemy 'planes.

A few days later, their situation changed quite dramatically. Lilley, who was a walking Part I Orders, said he had heard that they were not going back to Kabrit. They were to do another raid: four aerodromes this time.⁴ Almonds mentally relinquished all thoughts of a shower.

The next day, he watched Stirling go off with half the party, heading for Sirte, before supervising the loading of the lorries, ready for an early start in the morning. Lieutenant Bill Fraser with a party of five also left to attack the aerodrome at 'Arae Philenorum', nicknamed 'Marble Arch' by the soldiers. The arch itself was an incredible edifice erected by Mussolini to mark the border of Tripolitania and Libya and the height of *Il Duce*'s self-aggrandisement. Having just returned from a raid, Fraser had not exactly volunteered to go out yet again but when Stirling had idly wondered if it wouldn't be a good crack to have a go at Marble Arch, the young Lieutenant had succumbed to their CO's charm.⁵

On Christmas Day, Lewes's party, consisting of Almonds and Lilley, a chap called Chalky White⁶ and Jimmie Storie, were also away early, heading for the aerodrome at Nofilia.⁷ They had a dinner of stew that night in enemy territory. Almonds lay rolled up in his blanket in the 'fish fish' – the very fine dust that lies at the bottom of the desert valleys – thinking of Lockie as he gazed up at the canopy of stars.

> What a Christmas, Lockie. You think I am in a training job somewhere. I feel a terrible cad to be hoodwinking you like this but if I told you the truth, well, you would only worry.⁸

They crossed the Marauder road again in the evening and the day after Boxing Day, were still heading north-east.

By precise navigation, Lewes's party arrived in a position 12 miles south of Marble Arch and just 10 feet off from Fraser's Section!⁹ He had with him Sergeants Bob Tait and Geoff Duvivier and Troopers Byrne and Philips. Together, the two SAS patrols watched formations of German Stuka dive-bombers landing and taking off from the aerodrome. They arranged to RV three to five days later; then Fraser's party left them, taking six days' rations. Lewes's group set off towards Nofilia. The next day, they left the lorries to march to the aerodrome. 'Eighteen miles to go if our maps and calculations are correct,' Almonds noted in the diary. He was in charge of the navigation, direction and distance, while Lewes looked after the time-keeping. By 02.00 the following morning my father reckoned that they were a few miles from the aerodrome.

'OK. We'll rest up,' Lewes decided. There were several encampments of troops round about and they had to make several detours to avoid them. They hid, not very comfortably, in a fissure in the ground and covered themselves with sand and shrubs. Almonds saw the funny side of their situation:

> I hope we don't wake up to find ourselves on someone's barrack square!

He was awakened by the roar of aircraft engines as the planes warmed up on the aerodrome.[10] His concealment was good, so that presently when a flight of brand new brightly yellow-painted Stukas came over he was able to appreciate their beauty. They were Junkers Ju 87B-2s. He could see the distinctive sharp angle of their wings and the black crosses outlined with white on the side of each machine. As they got closer, the swastikas on their tails were clearly visible. It was a stirring sight.

> If it were not for the war, it must be glorious to soar over the desert on a morning like this.[11]

He and Lewes left the remainder in hiding and went out to have a look around. In the distance, they could see the sand rising behind a hill and guessed that the landing ground lay beyond it. It was a beautiful day and the blue waters of the Mediterranean looked very tempting. But they were there for business, not pleasure. They turned their backs on the sea and made towards the landing ground, covering about 8 miles before they were in a position to observe the aerodrome.[12]

Yes, it was a fine sight. They counted 43 aircraft on the aerodrome, with troops camped around it and several large dumps of supplies.[13] They sat, watching all the activity, and planned their campaign for the night, marking out about 18 target aircraft.[14] The moon would be almost full and it would not set until about 02.30 so they would not have much time to do their work and get away before daylight. Where they were sitting, just out of sight of the airfield, there was a bir, a large underground water storage cistern like the one on the Fig Tree front at Tobruk. It was safe and quite dry inside. That evening, Almonds and Lewes went back to fetch Bob Lilley, Chalky White and Jimmie Storie.[15] Then they all settled down to rest until the moon set, and their attack could begin.

There was nothing to do except think. And Almonds thought a lot. On the floor of the cavern was a wizened carcass of bones and fur, still recognisable as a desert fox that had either gone, or fallen, into the bir. Unable to get out, it had perished of thirst and hunger. It was a gruesome spectacle. Perhaps curiosity had lured it down there, from which there had been no way out. Almonds saw the parallel with his own circumstances. Was there a way out for him? Or did death wait on the aerodrome? The moon went down and away they went.

The first 'plane was easy to find because they had noted its exact location.[16] Guards had been posted not too far away, but they were asleep. Lewes crept forward. Without disturbing them, he sealed one of his bombs onto the machine. There was a gentle kissing sound as the two surfaces made contact. From there, it was easy to make their way to the second 'plane. Almonds delicately fixed one of his bombs to the wing. It was a shame to destroy such a beautiful piece of aeronautics. At least there would be no people involved. That machine was unguarded. Then, disaster overtook them. There were no more aircraft. The enemy had clearly moved all but two that were probably non-operational.

'Why did we not hear them take off?' With the super alertness of proximity to danger, the thought flashed through Almonds's mind. *'If the noise of the engines was loud enough to wake us up this morning, why didn't we hear them during the day, when we were already awake? Did they tow them away? Perhaps the wind direction changed or, being down in the bir, the noise just didn't reach us.'*[17]

They began to search frantically, zig-zagging to and fro across the airfield. After twenty minutes, the bomb went off and then the second. But the 'planes did not catch fire because their fuel tanks were empty, so it was very disappointing.[18] However, the whole show was aroused and after watching the activity for a while, they decided to make their getaway. A mile from the aerodrome, they placed all their explosives in a heap and, leaving a time delay to explode them, they set off on a back bearing towards the trucks about 25 miles away. As before, Almonds took responsibility for their direction while Lewes kept the time. With the daylight, enraged Nazi aircraft began a search, but still the party marched on. They arrived back at camp after nightfall. The five LRDG trucks manned by the New Zealanders of T1 Patrol immediately got under way and they covered a further 20 miles.

New Year's Eve, 1941. They were on the move early, travelling northwest to pick up Fraser and his party.[19] At 10.00 hours they sighted a lone scouting twin-engined Messerschmitt 110 fighter 'plane heading their way. All they could do was stop and keep still, in the hope that he would not see them. He passed right overhead to take a look at them. He seemed to be going away, everyone breathing a sigh of relief, when suddenly one wing tilted and round he came.

'He's coming back!' Almonds shouted. On sighting him, the trucks immediately drove apart. But the desert was like a flat table and there was no cover. The other four vehicles headed off towards a group of large rocks about a couple of miles away at eleven o'clock, taking Chalky White with them. The 'plane circled once, very low, and then came round again, in for the kill from seven o'clock with the sun in the east behind him. He attacked hard, with four machine guns forward and two cannons. The noise was deafening and he gave them hell, not to mention the gunner in his tail. A sharp fight followed as Almonds quickly manned the Bren guns and gave him as good as they got.[20] His second burst got their truck but did not hurt anyone or set it on fire.

It soon became obvious that if they stayed in the truck it was only a matter of time before they were all killed. Lewes was still in the front. Almonds and Lilley both shouted to Lewes to take cover as grabbing the Bren gun, they leapt clear. Lewes was still in the front.

'*Dear God*,' Almonds thought, '*he's fiddling about with some papers.*'

The fleeing men were joined by three of the New Zealanders of the LRDG, one of whom was Alan Nutt.[21]

They raced for a rock knoll about half a mile away at three o'clock. It was every man for himself. The 'plane turned its attention to them and for a while the five of them played a deadly game of 'ring a ring of roses' with it round the rock. The knoll was only about head height and barely gave them the cover they needed. But they quickly realised that they had the Messerschmitt beaten. It took him some minutes to get round the rock but they could do it in a few strides. In the intervals, Almonds and Lilley took turns with the Bren gun. Before long, the Messerschmitt's cannons went quiet.

'I reckon you got him!' shouted one of the New Zealanders. 'Or maybe he's out of ammo.' Either for that reason, or out of concern for his stricken rear gunner, the 'plane flew off back to its base. They immediately set off and ran back towards the truck, anxious to get as far away from the scene as possible before the enemy aircraft returned.

On returning to where they had left Lewes, the vehicle appeared to have been moved from where they had last seen it.[22] One or two LRDG were in the vicinity. Lewes was nowhere to be seen. Almonds quickly assessed the damage to the truck. He was staggered to discover that the drive shaft had been riddled right through from side to side.²³ The Messerschmitt must have come in at an incredibly low angle, in fact dangerously low, in the hope of killing the occupants. Inspecting it closely, he could see that the angle of the shot meant that it must have been fired from some distance away, and as the aircraft was rising. Amazingly, the 40-gallon steel drum of water standing in the back of the truck and the jerry cans of petrol had escaped damage.

As quickly as they could, the five made off south, constantly watching the skies for more aircraft.²⁴ However, the fun was not over. The Stukas kept reappearing and shooting up the sand. Jerry did not do things by half. Almonds knew, as everyone must have known, what was to come. They had covered about 7 miles when two tiny specks were suddenly visible in the sky.

'Stukas! Heading our way!' he shouted. 'Take cover! We can't dodge them like the Messerschmitt.' He quickly grabbed what rations he could and four bottles of water, before spreading the camouflage net over the truck and dashing for cover.²⁵ Their only chance was to hide in the sand. As the first planes arrived, they spotted the truck straight away and the first burst from their guns set it on fire. The five SAS men and the LRDG patrolmen sprinted towards some sparse low scrub. Lilley immediately went to ground at about three o'clock. Almonds went further round at two o'clock and dropped to the ground. Sprawling out in the most unnatural shape he could think of, he scooped handfuls of sand into his hair and onto his clothes to break up the outline of his body. Half out in the open, he felt like an ostrich with his head stuck in a tiny shrub. Heart pounding, he lay like some bizarre desert flower. Bullets spurted in the sand all around him as the enemy machine-gunned all large groups of bushes and rocks in the hope of getting their quarry. Showers of hot dust and grit flailed his sweating skin. It took all his self-control not to flinch. Even if he took the risk of trying to give himself up, he knew he would be gunned down. He waited. Had they really missed him? He lay still. At last, he knew that they had gone after the other LRDG trucks.

Watching the 'planes start to circle over some invisible objects in the distance, he surmised that they had been spotted. Then the explosion of bombs and machine gun fire across the desert silence left no doubt. T1 Patrol had been found. One by one, four ominous columns of foul oily black smoke twisted up into the sky. Time passed. Slowly, the fugitives emerged from hiding and began to drift back together. They gazed at the spiralling plumes of black smoke.

'That's four trucks gone and it's a long way to Jalo,' said one of the New Zealand patrolmen flatly.

Almonds, Lilley and a patrolman started away from their smouldering truck towards the other burning debris but had not gone far before the Stukas reappeared and the horrific game of hiding began all over again. Time and time again, Almonds thought it was all over as the 'planes skimmed low over his back to machine-gun some dark patch in the sand. He braced himself. What if he were only badly wounded? He pushed the thought away. And so the deadly sport was kept up all that long hot day. The enemy was replacing the Stukas in pairs, so that they could keep the SAS men constantly strafed.

But by 16.00 hours, all was quiet and they broke cover again. Almonds left Lilley and the patrolman in hiding and went to look for any survivors. He was concerned to render first aid to anyone who was wounded. After walking to the top of a hill of dunes he saw in the distance two figures walking. He fired his revolver. The sound disappeared into the great expanse. But the two men heard it, stopped, and then started making towards him. Long before they were within earshot, he sighted an aircraft approaching and did the customary dive for cover. This time, it was a spotter 'plane, a German Fieseler Fi 156 *Storch*, a highly efficient and slow-flying reconnaissance aircraft. He lay on his side. Peeping up at it through his fingers, he could see three crewmen, plainly visible in their blue uniforms, inspecting the damage. After circling several times, the 'plane went away. He hurried on and two LRDG New Zealanders came into sight.

'G'day.' The cheery greeting was music to his ears. Almonds said that he was not sure there was much good about it, but he was glad they were all right. The patrolman grinned and said it would take more than Jerry having a few pot-shots to get them out. Then his expression changed and he said that he was really sorry about Lewes. Apparently, he had been shot by the Messerschmitt. Almonds felt a shock wave travel right through him. Yet his first reaction was coldly logical.

'The only one to be killed and it had to be him. If the enemy only knew the loss to the SAS.'[26]

The other patrolman took up the story. They hadn't actually seen what happened but one of the SAS men[27] had said that Lewes had been wounded in the leg while still on the truck and then was seen by the enemy pilot as he tried to make for cover.[28] As he got behind a bush, he was caught full in the back by a burst from the enemy's guns and must have died very quickly. After recovering from this bad news, the survivors began to discuss their predicament. The patrolman said that one of their vehicles was still in workable order. It had obviously been knocked about a bit, he said, and was minus two tyres but it was nothing that could not be fixed. The water and petrol, without which they would have been finished, had also miraculously been saved.

They were about to start on the practical task in hand, when there came again the notorious scream of their favourite dive-bomber. 'Hello, yes, it's those Stukas again!'[29] They dived for cover as the job of hiding began all over again. The Stukas circled around again for a few minutes that seemed like hours. Then, apparently satisfied, they left them alone.

Suddenly exhausted from the physical stresses of the day, Almonds had to summon up the energy to go back for Lilley and the other patrolman. Then, together, they set off to help with the repairs of the one now priceless truck. Their number was depressingly small. The three SAS included Almonds, Lilley and Storie. Lewes was dead and Chalky White had gone with the rest of the LRDG patrol who not having any vehicles, had decided to strike out for the Marauder Road. The four New Zealanders, including

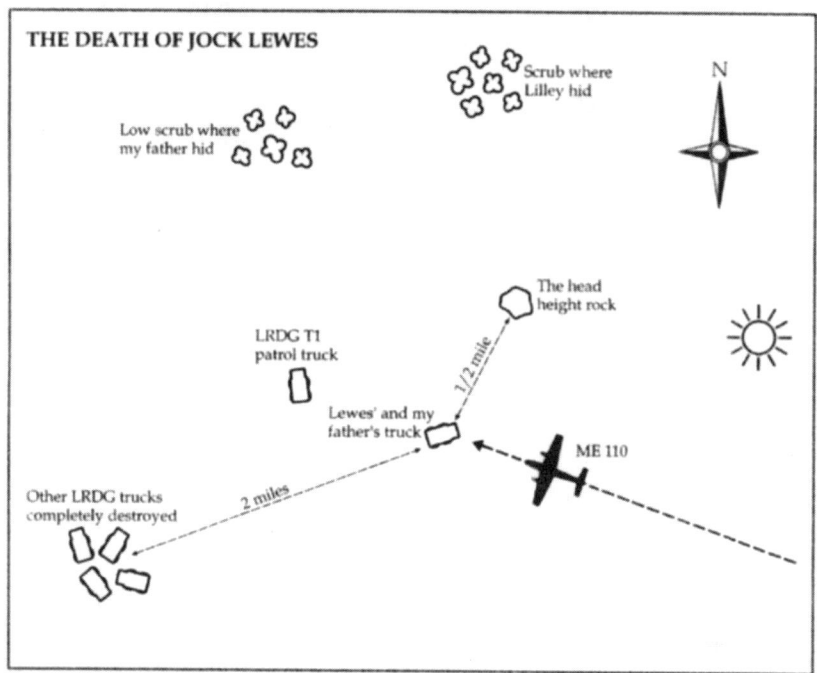

Alan Nutt, made Almonds's party seven. Being now the senior one and therefore in charge, he decided that the best thing to do was to hide until dark, scour the area with the truck for further survivors and then make a non-stop run back to Jalo. Then they found Morris, the LRDG New Zealand officer, and another man, bringing their number to nine.

Waiting for the safety of darkness, the group talked quietly, trying to piece together the violent events of the day. Perhaps because of the trauma, they found that they already had slightly different impressions of what had actually happened. They concentrated on planning their next move. Morris thought that they should presume that the rest were dead. He was keen to collect his men together and put as much distance between them and any Jerry 'planes as possible. Almonds made it twelve men altogether. But they wondered about Fraser's party. Perhaps they too were already dead or in the bag. The events of the day had given them a new awareness of their own mortality. Almonds thought that it was hard to tell, but the enemy could have been waiting for Fraser and his group to pick them up on arrival. In which case, they may already have been captured or killed. Anyway, they could not assume it. They needed to leave some water. Morris said that that would be difficult. There were no spare water tanks left and they would be lucky if we could leave them more than a teaspoon each.[30] After leaving as much by way of supplies as they could, they set off on the long run home.

Midnight. Crossing the Marauder road, they passed through wild desolate country, with deep gorges and huge rocks, shining gauntly grotesque and ghostly in the moonlight. White chalk cliffs alternated with precipices of black volcanic rock. The New Zealand patrolman drove with an uncanny skill, as if he had eyes that could see through the thick desert night. Often they came to a shuddering halt, at the very brink of a hundred foot drop. Time and again they found themselves hemmed in by towering walls of rock and had to turn back and go round another way.

'How on *earth* do you do it?' Lilley said to their driver. 'Have you got some sort of special equipment in that head of yours? You're a real 'Sensor box'. All through that long night, Sensor box stayed hunched over the wheel, his staring eyes trained on the formidable terrain ahead. The others were silent, dozing fitfully as they jolted against the hard inside of the truck.

Almonds stared into the darkness. The Stukas hadn't bothered with their truck but instead had concentrated on the other group of LRDG vehicles.[31] The Messerschmitt had already attacked it earlier, which was when Jock must have been killed. He must have been fleeing from the vehicle because there had been no trace of any blood inside it. Then the aircraft had followed them to the bizarre game at the rock before finally flying off. So Jock had already been buried by the time they got back to the truck, in the interval before the Stukas arrived. That must have been why the vehicle had been moved, so that they could bury him where he had fallen. Almonds had stood by the grave, a mound covered with small rocks. As he lingered there, he had composed the words that he would write in his diary by way of an epitaph. Would Jock's contribution ever be fully recognised? Although the raid itself would not count as a success, Lewes had done something for the SAS that no other man, not even Stirling, could have done. He had developed and tested out a new operational mode, carried it into the SAS, and then translated it into an effective training philosophy.

The desolate landscape flashed past. Then Almonds remembered the beautiful private rifle that Jock always carried with him. It was the Czech-made Brno that he used to take out with him when they were inside Tobruk, about .275 calibre, usually used for shooting game but anyway a beautiful piece. It had not been there when they went back to the truck. Jock couldn't have got far from the vehicle before he was killed. Surely the rifle had not been buried with him? Then it became too painful to think any more. Later, he wrote in his diary:

> Yes, in many homes the Old Year is being watched die and new hopes rise with the prospect of the New Year. Lockie, I thought of you and wished on the New Year. Also I thought of Jock, one of the bravest men I have ever met, an officer and a gentleman, lying out in the desert barely covered with sand. No one will ever stop by his grave or pay homage to a brave heart that has ceased to beat. Not even a stone marks the spot.[32]

New Year's Day, 1942. Daylight came. They continued travelling south-east through better country. Daylight was giving way to darkness again when Almonds saw in the distance a dim, dark outline, like a shadow on the ground – the Oasis Jalo. 'A hot meal, roll up in a borrowed blanket and Goodnight Lockie'. It had taken them 48 weary hours to get back to Jalo.[33]

The next morning, Stirling sent for him. He had not even had time to part with his beard, which he noted in his diary had attained a remarkable length, very curly and of a fine texture. Stirling was waiting for him, spotless in khaki shorts and bush jacket. Suddenly, Almonds felt like a ruffian. He gave the best account he could of Lewes's death and whereabouts he was buried, supported by fragments of scribbled entries for the diary. He explained to Stirling that when they had left the truck they had scattered in different directions. Riley thought that Jock must have been incapacitated in some way.[34] Lilley certainly believed that Lewes had been shot in the leg, making it difficult for him to run,[35] and died in about four minutes. If so, it must have happened in the few moments after the others had dashed away from the vehicle. Then according to Storie, Jock had caught it full in the back from the Messerschmitt's cannons.[36]

Stirling was still visibly shaken from the news of the loss. It was hard to believe that Lewes was gone. Lewes, so methodical, almost clinical. Stirling comforted himself with the fact that, in the end, Lewes had joined 'L' Detachment.[37] He had believed in the idea which he himself had then helped to make work by successfully translating his ideas into practice. Of Lewes and his four, only Almonds, Pat Riley and Bob Lilley were left. But, as ever, Stirling was quick to mask one emotion by overtly displaying another. It was all about bolstering morale, he said. It was vital that they learned from the incident. It was clear that he was in planning mode again. They had to train for this sort of thing. And they must recruit and train fresh men. Then he was brought up short because it was Jock who had prepared and delivered all the training. So Stirling's next task was to find someone else to handle the recruitment and training. Lewes had left no notes on his selection and training ideas. They realised that they had never really known Lewes at all.

The CO's concern for recruitment and training was not entirely due to Lewes's death. He had lost too many good men and now had only one experienced officer – Paddy Mayne. And there was some evidence that MEHQ still did not understand the role of the SAS and were aiming to 'clip his wings'. On Christmas Day, Brigadier J. F. M. Whiteley, the DDO, had written to brief the new DCGS, A. S. Smith, on his predecessor's decision to establish the Middle East Commandos under a Lt Col Graham:

> Some unit commanders, such as STIRLING, want to be absolutely independent and directly under GHQ. Our experience in the past has proved this very unsatisfactory.[38]

Smith's reply, written on Boxing Day, concurred. 'Yes. I agree. It is of course quite wrong to have a number of little private armies, each under

GHQ,' adding as a hand-written after-thought, 'I think Stirling deserves to have charge (under Graham) of the parachute wing [handwritten].'[39]

Denys Reid came to talk to the group.[40] It was clear that he wanted to salute their efforts and do what he could for morale. On their last night in Jalo, there was a party with an issue of rum and lime juice. Someone even made fritters. Corporal Sambo, who had become a personal friend of everybody's, joined in. He was going back with them to Kabrit, although it was unclear in what capacity: POW or unofficial servant to the SAS.

Almonds and Lilley went on leave to Cairo. The high-pitched whine of the truck wheels on the smooth metalled road drummed the same note as they sped through the frizzled Egyptian landscape. In the back, Almonds and Lilley looked at each other like long-lost friends. New clothes, a bath and a shave had separated them from the desert life. Just to have a roof, three good meals a day and a hot bath before going to bed – a bed with springs and sheets – was paradise. Pat Riley was not with them; he was away on the Bouerat scheme.[41] When he returned, he was to be IC training. Almonds was to be IC just about everything else, beginning with building a new set of parachute swings for training the recruits.[42] The job required considerable amounts of materials and manpower but the deal with Stirling, as before, was that he would get whatever it took, as long as Almonds made it all happen. 'All' included building a new canteen for the men who were to be inveigled out of MEHQ, as well as two new jumping stands, and responsibility for the Sergeants' Mess. Stirling certainly believed in horses for courses.

In Cairo, Almonds went round to the New Zealand Club to enquire after the members of the LRDG. There was no news. He strolled back to his hotel through the Marde suburb of the city. The green grass and trees reminded him of a small English town. By now, he had been away for over a year. A whole year of his young married life was gone. His son was now sixteen months old. He did not know what a sixteen month-old was like. Even if they met again tomorrow, they would not know each other. Time was passing quickly and the number of places he had been made it seem like a decade. He bought some books and lay on his bed at the hotel reading between meals.

The next day he recorded in his diary that he had 'met a party of ghosts!'[43] Right in the middle of Cairo he found the LRDG New Zealanders left for dead in the desert casually wandering round the bazaar like tourists. They grinned lazily and said they were doing a bit of sightseeing. When he pressed them about what had happened and how they had got back with no vehicle or water, they admitted that it had been 'a bit of walk'. Together they ducked into a mataam,[44] and a white-aproned walid[45] wearing a red fez appeared with tiny cups of turkish coffee and glasses of iced water. When they had quenched their thirst, Almonds got them to tell their story.

It had taken eight gruelling and painful days for the six men to make the 210 miles back to Jalo. With Dennis Bassett in charge, they made their way using the hand compass that he always carried. After a few days they ran out of water and then after a few more days they began to hallucinate. As they reached the outer end of the oasis, Bassett collapsed and sent the others on with the compass. A huge sandstorm blew up and he crawled into one of the black oil drums that were set up to mark out the road across the desert and passed out. When he came too, all he could do was crawl. He kept going and still on his hands and knees, he crawled into the oasis the next day, where he was found by some Arabs. They took him back to their family who fed him dates mashed in camel's milk for an hour or two until he recovered. One of the Arabs then went on his donkey to tell the SAS. The other LRDG men meanwhile had gone back to good old western food straight away and had become very sick so that they had to be hospitalised.[46]

Almonds was amazed but relieved. Then he remembered the SAS man, Chalky White, who had been with the LRDG and asked what had happened to him. They looked at each other as if surprised that he did not know. Chalky hadn't wanted to go any further with them, they said, because his feet were really bad from his previous march. He said he'd had enough and wouldn't be able to make it. He probably didn't fancy their chances anyway with such a distance to cover. So he decided to stay at the Marauder road where he could wait and hold up a German truck. He had some water and a revolver. But nobody had heard anything of him since.[47]

Next day in town Almonds and Bob Lilley met yet another party of 'ghosts': Fraser's party, the Gordon Highlanders, were clearly bent on letting their hair down. This time, Almonds was less amazed than interested in the technicalities. He asked how on earth they had made it back. Everyone thought they had been captured.

'Far from it, laddie,' they said. They were not captured – they did the capturing – and by commandeering a series of German and Italian transport vehicles, good old fashioned 'hold-up style', less masks, they had arrived back safely in their own lines.[48] Their story was interesting. Marble Arch aerodrome had turned out to be almost empty at night, suggesting that it was being used largely to land reinforcements or as a refuelling point.[49] After waiting six days, they had left the RV on 2 January. They spent the next day distilling water from the salt marshes but this was insufficient so they went to the road to look for derelict trucks with the intention of draining their radiators. By this time, they were half crippled by sickness and bowel disorders caused by drinking the semi-salt water they had distilled. But they held up a German truck and got hold of three days' supply of water. Sandstorms and enemy traffic on the Aghelia to Marauda road meant that they made slow progress before reaching Maaten Becleibat and the Wadi Farag.[50]

During the night, Italian troops moved in. Several times, the section was nearly discovered, the closest being when a party of twelve men advanced in line towards their position from about two hundred yards. Fraser successfully withdrew his party and when he returned later he found that a telephone line had been laid right over their former position. Since their food and water supplies were exhausted, he marked out for attack a truck that had been stationary all day. That evening, they moved in and took the unguarded truck by surprise. The occupants were all sleeping and became hysterical when captured. For some time they remained under the impression that Fraser and his men were Germans and kept insisting that they were not 'Inglezi' but were comrades of the German soldiers. Once again, the enemy's total unawareness of SAS operating tactics meant that they could not even envisage that their attackers might be their enemy. Without particularly bothering to sort out this misunderstanding, Fraser and his men helped themselves to food and drained the radiator for water. The Italians were very anxious to be taken prisoner but Fraser got them to understand that two British Divisions were just around the wadi and that if they did not raise the alarm they could surrender the next day. Their somewhat disappointed foe went back to bed while Fraser's party marched due north to the salt marsh two miles south of Mersa Brega.[51]

A few nights later on 8 January, they attacked a German truck near the 13 kilometre stone from Mersa. They forced the driver to head eastwards to the 11 kilometre stone, left the road and drove south for 7 miles before the vehicle stuck fast in a salt marsh. They then marched on a bearing to the south of Agedabia, about 50 miles away. After 2 miles, they were challenged by a sentry, whom they evaded, only to come upon a strong enemy position running along a ridge north to south, 3 miles further on. The section tried to circle the enemy to the south, but on discovering that the position curved back westwards, they tried to walk through. It was a moonlit night and they were seen by the sentries who opened fire. That woke up the whole camp. After crawling for a quarter of a mile, they found the net closing in on them. The nearest enemy was not more than 20 yards away, so they rose to their feet and just started walking, intending to shoot their way out when the time came. To their amazement, nobody interfered with them and they were able to walk out of the lines and across the minefield in front. Simply by remaining calm and not running, they had given the enemy the slip.

This intrepid party then covered a further 12 miles before dawn, which came just in time to prevent them from entering another enemy position. They continued to make slow but steady progress, in spite of being inconvenienced by enemy transport and lookout posts. On the night of 10 January, they met some friendly Senussi at El Gtafia who gave them dates and water and the next day they made contact with KDG (King's Dragoon Guards) patrols south of Agedabia. Eventually, the entire section had been flown to 8th Army HQ where Fraser had reported personally to General Ritchie and the Intelligence Branch. The final words of Fraser's report, sums up this remarkable episode in the spirit of the times:

> The NCOs and men under my command behaved admirably during both these operations and made the task much easier by their cheerfulness and ready obedience to orders. Particularly noticeable was their determination not to be captured under any circumstances.
> The section was composed of:-
>
> | 2885693 | L/Sgt. | Tait R. | MM The Gordon Highlanders |
> | 2885910 | " | DuVivier J. | " " " |
> | 2060658 | Pct. | Byrne J. | " " " |
> | 5107891 | " | Phillips A. | The Royal Warwickshire Regiment |
>
> [signed] W. Fraser, Lieut.
> Gordon Highlanders[52]

Back at Kabrit, the camp was gradually changing. It was taking on more the air of a 'proper' base for selection and training of the SAS. Bob Tait's design of the flaming sword Excalibur and the motto 'Who Dares Wins' had become official.[53] The SAS now had a sand-coloured beret. When they met up in Cairo, Almonds and Alan Nutt had their photograph taken together with Bob Lilley, 'Snowy' McCulloch and the remarkable 'Sensor box'. The two SAS were wearing their early white SAS berets, which were so often a cause for 'Mickey taking' when they were out in the town. The soldiers of other regiments would attract their attention from across the street by putting the backs of their hands on their hips, taking little mincing wiggling steps and pursing up their lips. Inevitably they had to be 'sorted out' and a 'punch-up' usually ensued.[54] In the end, the white beret had to be withdrawn because its colour was not very practical and replaced with the new sand-coloured one.

Stirling had made it clear that all aggression was to be saved for the enemy. He was generally economical with the resources he had to work so hard to squeeze out of his superiors so he did not want any time or effort wasted on aspects which did not contribute to advancing the operational effectiveness of the SAS. In keeping with this general philosophy, he also wanted to limit the demands he made on MEHQ to those items that he simply could not get from any other source, mainly men, vehicles and rations. He told Almonds, when they were discussing his new tasks, that every single request had to be made to count.[55] Asking for things like training equipment and new accommodation would be a waste of shots because the materials would have to be ordered from the UK. He said that this was a dashed shame because the chaps really needed these things and they deserved them too and he wondered if they couldn't be a little more self-sufficient and independent. Whenever he talked like this, Almonds would begin to tense up, half expecting what was coming next. Stirling always had a way of making it impossible to refuse any request without feeling as though one was letting the side down.

Stirling made it clear that they needed to do their own thing. They could do that by making better use of their available pool of talents. On one occasion, he told Almonds that it was most important that each man had more than one set of skills. In his, Almonds's, case, he already had an extra gift which could be put to excellent use, along with some materials that he thought he could lay his hands on. By this time, Almonds was getting ready for another demand and pointed out that there were a number of forthcoming raids and he was not sure how much he was going to be around. But Stirling would have none of it. Nothing, he said was more important at that time than getting the new men trained up to the right levels of fitness and skill. They may not be parachuting right then but they needed to keep the capability. Certainly they needed to select on that basis. And they must have a reasonable level of basic facilities.

'You're replaceable out there', he said. 'You're not replaceable here.'[56] Almonds considered his new challenges.

'*They might not be as dangerous as going on raids,*' he thought, '*but they're testing all right.*' The first task was Stirling's new set of parachute swings. They needed several platforms about 30 feet high from which the trainees could swing in jumping harnesses and practise their landing techniques. That would mean two main towers of about 40 feet high, connected by metal girders and anchored by steel guys well bedded in 6 feet below ground level. When completed, the girders alone would weigh 2 tons. Each tower would need to be weighted down with 2 tons of sandbags. As with the first set of towers, he planned in a 4 inch camber for safety so that the force of the weight of men suspended in the centre would be thrown outwards. He supervised the start of work on dismantling the old towers and soon had eight 'L' Detachment men and twenty-four Italian prisoners employed on the job.[57]

Next came the construction of a new canteen. Having received Stirling's not very explicit instructions, he drew up the plans, chose the site and marked out the ground for foundations of 41 feet, by 20 feet, by 4 feet 5 inches. He set another party of men to work digging out the foundations and laying down narrow gauge lines for trucks to remove the bulk of surplus soil from the excavation. While they toiled, he sat down to work out the indents for the necessary materials. He had no illusions. Most of the used timber would need to be hauled with two lorries from the DCRE's dump at Gineifa. Suddenly, a sand storm blew up and life almost ceased before the blinding clouds of fine sand. Incredibly, it was followed by a thunder storm and heavy fall of rain. But there was more in store. On 1 February the diary records:

> Took over the running of the Sergeants' Mess. Spent the evening puzzling over the accounts!

At the beginning of February, Riley returned from the Bouerat Operation. The raiders had been 500 miles behind the enemy's front lines and done considerable damage to transport and installations. Everyone got back safely but they had been ambushed by ground forces, machine-gunned and bombed from the air. The story, as told by Pat Riley, was similar to Almonds's own experience at Nofilia.

The construction work was progressing well. The workforce, with varying degrees of willingness, started to concrete in the foundations of the canteen and its floor. Soon, the brickwork was almost completed and the steps to canteen were being built. He put in for some Italian carpenters from the prison camp to work on the internal fitting of the doors and the bar. Then he went to Suez with a lorry to fetch a load of building materials for the swings. More ferrying about in the lorries, picking up materials off dumps. To fill in the time, he had the men erect a set of parallel bars and some bolting and heaving stands for use in training new recruits. After finishing off the stands, they laid out a quoits and tennis court. Just to make sure that nobody got bored, he supervised the construction of two extra jumping stands, made of steel with wooden platforms at heights of 4 feet, 6 feet, 8 feet, 10 feet and 12 feet. They had a wooden framework for the top with a sliding centre section and a ladder for the victims. Several times a week he requisitioned lorries to collect timber or bricks from Fanara or to scavenge other items from the dumps.[58]

He went on a borrowed Norton motor-cycle on a quest to the Garrison Engineer's because the couplings for the tower girders were unsatisfactory, only to find that couplings of the type required were not available. Well, he would improvise or make the necessary parts himself. Gradually, the tower base was completed and the towers rose to 30 feet high with temporary guys in position. By the end of February, they had completed the two towers and work began on the girders. Helped by another party of twelve Royal Engineers, they started to erect the stands for the towers. Then came a setback. While raising the first girder into position with sets of pulley blocks, the first tower broke in two. Thirty pairs of eyes looked at Almonds.

'*O ye of little faith*' he thought. '*It's the same whenever I build a boat. They never believe it's going to float until they see it in the water.*' But he was infinitely patient. He seemed to hear his father's voice.

'*So far, your engine building seems to have been all failure but you have one consolation: you are not the only one who has met with disappointment. I too have been up that street and many before me. Look how James Watt and Matthew Boulton were nearly broken with disappointment before success came with the improved beam engine ...*'[59]

They began to rebuild the first tower. The guys were placed into position and the central platform completed. Almonds applied for two sailors to splice the wire ropes and they fitted the harness to the swings. With some satisfaction, he put the Royal Engineers to work laying the track for the jumping trolley and building the stocks for the line. But there was a personal opportunity cost. Riley went away on another scheme with the rest of the lads. Being engineer and works foreman, Almonds could not go. Work on the towers, canteen and stands was nearing completion when Stirling asked him to build several more constructions, including a further set of towers![60] At the end of March, he confided to the diary:

> Four and a half tons of scaffolding to fetch from Fanara and four tons from Barrage, Cairo. Sergeants' Mess and Canteen to restock from Suez Depot. No prisoners today. No Royal Engineers. Spare time supervising the canteen, relaying railway track, stocktaking for the Sergeants' Mess. In short, am acting Quarter-Master, acting Sergeant-Major and Sergeants' Mess caterer!

Chapter Eight

SAS to the Rescue

The struggle for control of the SAS intensified. While 'L' Detachment strove simultaneously to carry out raids and act as its own recruitment and training centre, MEHQ deliberated about special forces operational questions in general, and who was Stirling's boss in particular. On 10 March, Major General Arthur Smith replied to a letter from Lieutenant General Ritchie:

My Dear Neil,
  You asked me under whose command was Stirling's detachment. Please see CRME/1679/G(O) of 22 February 1942, which makes clear that they are at present under your command but revert to GHQ on completion of current operations.
  I have heard that Stirling is planning an operation against shipping in Benghazi. I don't know the details of the plan as it is, of course, an 8th Army operation, but I would like to stress the point that Stirling's chief value is that of commanding a parachute force. We are, therefore, anxious that he should not be thrown away in some other role and I hope that any plan he has made will be carefully examined so as to ensure, as far as possible, that he does not do something foolhardy.
  As if the writer had still not got the matter of his chest, below the signature he added a hand-written sentence.

PS He needs restraining, and we can't afford to throw him away.[1]

Even so, Stirling had managed to arrange that 'L' Detachment would come under GHQ and not, like the Commandos, under the new Ministry of Economic Warfare. This had been created following the visit of the Middle East Mission of the new Ministry of Economic Warfare (i.e. Special Operations Executive – SOE) in early January.[2] The downside was that by 8 April, the SAS were expected to be back at parachute training work and by 1 May their future role and training was supposed to be as parachutists. But Stirling had other ideas. On 3 May, he wrote to GHQ on the subject of 'L' Detachment's future. He was down to twenty men and they risked being used to train the Indian parachute battalions. He set out the doctrine of raiding on the basis of a high level of skills, making use of the element of surprise, claiming once again that 'L' Detachment were not just parachutists.[3] In fact, it was to be Rommel's success in moving eastward that was to assure the continued existence of the SAS.

The Gazala Line stretched, awkward and unlovely, like a stringy necklace of sparse empty wooden beads, from its namesake on the north coast, to Bir Hakeim at its southern end. From east to west, mid-way between the Gulf of Sirte and the Libyan plateau, the Gazala Line was like a half-way mark on the ground in the great 'tug-of-war' over Cyrenaica. The northern end of the line ran into the sea. But at the southern end in the desert, there was always the possibility that one protagonist could whip round and attack the other from the flank. In any case, this was no normal battlefield front line. For a start, it was not continuous. The Allies had laid 35 miles of heavy minefields along it but then had established all their ground troops inside half a dozen 'boxes' spread out along the line, each about 2 miles square. It was the 'square' used at the Battle of the Boyne and Waterloo, all over again. It did not matter if the Axis forces got through the front line minefield and headed eastwards. The desert itself was not worth fighting over.

The point about the 'boxes', Gazala, Knightsbridge, El Adem, Bir Hakeim and, slightly further east along the coast, the box of Tobruk open on one side to the sea, was that they prevented the enemy from getting past them and making any *worthwhile* advances. The armaments in the boxes faced out in all directions so that they were well defended. As soon as the enemy came level with them, or even if they got through, the Allied troops would come out and attack them in the flank or from behind. In addition, there were always several tank brigades prowling about looking for trouble. It was along this slender line that the Eighth Army aimed to prevent Rommel from advancing towards Egypt.[4]

In late April, eschewing the small office afforded him at MEHQ, Stirling had decamped to his brother Peter's flat in Cairo. There he could run things his way. Close to the British Embassy, the apartment was a hedonist's delight, shared by the other Stirling brother, Bill, not to mention various occasional, usually well-connected, passers by. 'Sahib-like' and spacious, its drawing room exuded a glorious bachelor disarray of apparel, books, papers and assorted artefacts as fittingly adorn the male abode. Tools, sports equipment, the odd revolver, rifle cartridges, old shell cases, generous supplies of liquid beverages and tins of Three Nuns tobacco and Players Navy Cut cigarettes adorned every available horizontal surface. A pair of pictures of the King and Queen hung deliberately askew, so as to hide the effects of impromptu shooting competitions reminiscent of Sherlock Holmes. The place bore signs of heavy occupation by young men. The gracious pre-war dark oak furniture was scratched and ringed by the beer glasses of many nights' carousing and the edges of the side tables and the square of pale Berber carpet randomly patterned by the burn marks of many inadequately extinguished cigarettes. Life's more boring essentials, shopping, cooking, cleaning and laundry were taken care of by the Stirlings' Egyptian sofragi[5] Mo, who presided over the chaos with cheerful magnanimity.[6]

It was here that Mike Sadler used to attend some of Stirling's planning meetings.[7] Even during the day, the room was always dark. Squinting through the pall of smoke from Stirling's pipe, amid the acrid aroma of Dark Empire Shag, they would study the map of Cyrenaica spread out in front of them across the dining-table. Piles of intelligence reports and aerial photographs with 'PI [Photographic Interpretation] – MOST SECRET' stamped across them spilled over onto the edges of the map. From time to time during their deliberations, Mo would suddenly appear noiselessly in the doorway to the hall to offer them drinks. He would then return and thump the mugs down on the map, leaving a series of large wet rings all the way from the Qattara Depression to the Jebel Akhdar.[8]

Along with Sadler, Pat Riley, now IC Training, Johnny Cooper and Reg Seekings were other regular attendees. The officers were Paddy Mayne and Robin Gurdon, an outstandingly able and confident LRDG Lieutenant. They were all good reliable men who were trusted and respected. This was not always the case with Stirling's choice of officers. He had a slight weakness for involving the well-heeled with the right old school tie.[9] In his drive to recruit officers of the right calibre, he had been tempted to take on one or two whose suitability some thought questionable. Randolph Churchill perhaps fitted into that category. But by now the SAS knew Stirling well enough to accept that he must have his reasons. No doubt political influence through the Prime Minister's son would further the cause of the unit.

But not all of the aristocracy were a liability: some were quite the opposite. The swashbuckling Lieutenant Sir Fitzroy Hew Maclean, destined to become 15th Hereditary Keeper and Captain of Dunconnel, was courageous and able, and hugely popular with the men. After living dangerously as a diplomat in Stalinist Russia, he had had to get himself adopted as an MP in order to get out of the Diplomatic Service and enlist as a private in the Cameron Highlanders. The tough and sardonic George Jellicoe had also joined and was busy setting his own cracking pace. My father, Riley and Lilley of course remembered him from the Guards and the Commando training days at Burnham-on-Crouch. Most of the men knew that he was related to the famous Admiral of the Fleet Earl Jellicoe who had successfully commanded the British fleet during the critical Battle of Jutland in 1916. His arrival had been seen as a huge vote of confidence.[10]

In spite of the early disasters, MEHQ seemed pleased with 1 SAS. In the New Year Stirling had been promoted to Major and had persuaded the 'Auk' to grant him up to six more officers and forty men. He and Mayne had also both received the Distinguished Service Order. Prior to the Bouerat raid, Paddy had been left in charge of the base with orders to train up the new recruits. But the achievements of the raid were marred by the disgraceful state of affairs that Stirling found on his return to Kabrit. A sulking, morose and mostly off-duty Mayne had led to sloppy administration and zero progress on the training, in spite of the fact that the necessary equipment and facilities had been built for him by Almonds. It was immediately clear to Stirling that someone other than Mayne had to take over the training. Riley had had the right combination of outgoing enthusiasm and discipline.

It was fairly common knowledge that Stirling did not think of Mayne as a 2IC for the SAS. Mayne probably found this hard to accept because in terms of successful raids and numbers of enemy aircraft destroyed he far outstripped everyone. He had immense charisma and the leadership skills to match. Men would follow him anywhere, in spite of the fact that he maintained strict standards of discipline. But he did not have Stirling's social graces and polished easy style with important people: people who had power over resources. And out on the raids, Stirling was always several jumps ahead. He was always very optimistic, overly so on occasions.[11] Paddy was immensely practical and always knew who was where, doing what. He had both physical and intellectual aggression, whereas Stirling had a more academic approach. Both were respected by the men for their different abilities. But while Stirling's portrait hangs in the Officers' Mess at Credenhill, it is Mayne's grim countenance that adorns the walls of the Sergeants' Mess.[12]

The next raid was scheduled for the middle of May. The SAS had the element of surprise and, since they had attempted to raid Benghazi before in March, they had a good idea of the lie of the land. On that occasion, they got right down to the harbour front with the intention of assembling an SBS boat before loading it with bombs and setting off to plant them on key ships and installations. But rough weather and damage to the boat had scotched the operation.[13] This time, they would use two rather more robust inflatable craft and limpet mines, for which the expansive Bill Cumper, their new ballistics and explosives expert, provided the training. Relations between Stirling and Paddy Mayne were still slightly strained. In any case, Stirling counted on taking Maclean with him again. His language skills, particularly Italian, had already proved useful. When challenged by a Somali Italian sentry on the Benghazi waterfront, Maclean had even had the nerve to pretend to lose his temper and bawl the chap out in Italian. It worked and the humiliated *caporale* had stalked off in disgust.

The Bouerat raid had deprived Rommel of large quantities of his precious fuel supplies, with minimal losses to the SAS. But it had not stopped Rommel from launching a massive counter-attack in mid January. Since then, he had been having things far too much his own way. The enemy had retaken Jalo and by mid-March the Allies were dug in along the Gazala line. It was vital that they were not forced to retreat any further. The SAS had shown that the LRDG could take them closer to the target, more accurately and, more importantly with more bombs than if they were dropped in. But Stirling believed that they had nowhere near reached their potential. According to intelligence sources, Rommel was massing in the west and it was expected that before long he would launch another offensive, even bigger than his push in January, to try and break through to Egypt.[14] The question was where could they hurt him most?

As they pored over the maps, all roads seem to lead to Benghazi. Bouerat had shown that it was perfectly possible to get into a harbour and wreak havoc in a very short space of time. Stirling knew that the port of Benghazi was Rommel's most vulnerable spot. If it were seriously crippled, he would not be able to extend himself much further than Tobruk, never mind get as far as the Egyptian border. Having established the objectives and 'roughed out' the operational timetable, neither Stirling nor Mayne could cope with the sort of planning that involved administrative details or logistics. As soon as the talk turned to mileage, stores requisitioning and POL (petrol, oil and lubricants), Stirling's eyes would begin to glaze over. He loathed administration of any kind.

'Well if that route doesn't work because the trucks can only do five miles to the gallon,' he would say testily, 'maybe it's possible to make them do six miles to the gallon.' His NCOs would exchange glances and suggest, tactfully, that that was not actually possible and so it might be necessary to consider changing the route.

'There's not a great deal of flexibility about the route,' Sadler would say pleasantly, smiling as he spoke, as if he were enjoying some private joke. He had a unique way of being able to deliver unwelcome news which Stirling rather preferred to ignore with an ease that nobody else would have been able to get away with.

'If we deviate too much from it, we'll have to make further detours to avoid sinking sand and other obstacles. That means carrying more food and supplies and we're back to the petrol problem. It's not an insurmountable problem, but it needs some careful working out.' Stirling would groan, look as if he was going to say something and then glance at his watch.

'Good Lord! Is that the time? I'm due at the Shepheard's Hotel for dinner in ten minutes. Must dash. Carry on will you? Mo will see you out.'[15]

In the end, the Gazala line had not been able to stop Rommel and the Allies were pushed back to El Alamein. On 21 June Tobruk finally fell. The South African General Klopper was up against impossible odds and was forced to surrender. But a group of Coldstreamers refused to be taken prisoner and fought their way out eastwards back to the British lines.[16] In camp at Kabrit, Almonds watched British warships slowly passing through the Great Bitter Lake as they retreated back down the Suez Canal and into the Red Sea. It was a sombre sight. The sailors leaning over the sides of the vessels waved slowly to the soldiers on the canal bank, as if sending a final farewell signal. Although largely unspoken, there was a tangible sense of fear that the enemy would push right through to Cairo. If that happened, the way to India and the Far East would then lie open to them.

But Rommel's breakthrough also provided a real opportunity for the SAS. The Axis needed to bring up their supplies but since they were now at the end of a long supply-line, there were many more miles of it exposed and to Stirling's mind 'just begging' to be cut. It was a case of 'SAS to the rescue'.[17] Their new objective was to go round behind the enemy's front line and cause as much trouble as possible. This new role was accompanied by a marked change in the SAS style of operations. The second raid on

Almonds in the
Coldstream Guards,
Tower of London, 1932

Almonds, 'L' Detachment, 1 SAS, Kabrit,
1941

Jock Lewes, hand bandaged
from desert sores, Kabrit, 1941

Three of the 'Tobruk Four': (*l-r*) Jim Blakeney, Almonds, Bob Lilley, Cairo, 1941

Pat Riley, who described Almonds as 'one of my best pals', Kabrit, 1941

SAS training: jumps and rolls from trucks at 30 mph, Kabrit, 1941

'Paddy' Blair Mayne, when still with 11 Commando, 'The Scottish', at Lamlash, Isle of Arran, 1940

Almonds off on one of the first SAS raids, Kabrit, late 1941 – the slight lean forward is due to the weight on his back

Almonds building Stirling's boat

The boat taking shape, Kabrit Point, 1941

Almonds (*top right*), with two Italian POWs, building the parachute training rig, Kabrit, 1941

The finished parachute training rig Almonds built for Stirling, Kabrit, 1941

Survivors of the Nofilia raid: (*back l-r*) Alan Nutt, LRDG, Brown, LRDG ('Sensor Box'), 'Snowy' McCulloch, LRDG; (*front l-r*) Almonds, Bob Lilley, 'L' Detachment, SAS. Note the early white SAS berets

Weapon cleaning before a raid: (*l-r*) O'Dowd, Rose and Storie who took part in the attack on Nofilia aerodrome

Dennis Basset, LRDG, immediately after leading the marathon walk from Jalo. Merlyn Craw said, 'He looks all in, doesn't he?'

An LRDG patrol at Howard's Cairn, a rare landmark in the Great Sand Sea

SAS jeep north of Kufra Oasis

David Stirling, south of Marauder, 1942

Mike Sadler, England, 1944

LRDG truck with anti-tank gun in the Wadi Tamet area

The Road Watch: Frank White, NZ LRDG, observes enemy convoys on the Trig el Abd road

Merlyn Craw, NZ LRDG, 1942

Johann Folscher, British South African Police, a member of the 'Empire Effort' first escape from Italian POW camp, Italy, 1943

The ketch *Kumasi*, Almonds designed and memorised in solitary confinement in the Italian POW camp in 1943. He later built her by hand in Ghana and sailed her back to England in 1961.

Almonds, six months after 'the Italian picnic', with John, Bristol, spring 1944

'Paddy' Blair Mayne, CO, 1 SAS Regiment, Scotland, spring 1944

Georges Poulard, the Frenchman who met Almonds at the DZ France, June 1944

The chateau at Chailleurs-aux-Bois where Troopers Ion and Packman were murdered

Almonds with 'Monsieur le garagiste', Antoine Krutchelnitski, a member of the French Resistance

Almonds at the Vickers-K with his section behind enemy lines in the Forest of Orléans, July 1944

Cartoon by Ian Fenwick who was ambushed and killed in the Forest of Orléans on 8 August 1944

Almonds, aged 84, visiting the New Zealand SAS in January 1998

Benghazi had not been a success in meeting its planned objectives – this time they had had mechanical problems with their truck – but it had proved that they could remain for some time behind enemy lines and move around more or less unmolested. So Stirling decided that trekking in and out over long distances to get behind enemy lines, just to carry out one raid, was a waste of time and resources. They might as well set up a base deep in enemy territory. The SAS moved to using jeeps, Willys Bantams, fitted with mounted Vickers-K machine guns, so that they could adopt a new method of motorized attack. They also acquired some three-tonners, again, appropriately armed. Almonds was immediately involved in redesigning the jeeps to add the necessary sun compass mountings, winches, long range fuel tanks, extra water carriers and sand channels for digging the vehicles out when they got stuck. Condensers fitted to the front of the vehicles meant that the water they used was recycled, cutting down the amount that had to be carried. It was at this time that he collected some permanent dark patches of skin on the backs of his fingers from abrasions caused by holding the twin Vickers K machine guns – his only wounds of the war. The SAS then began to carry out operations during the moonlit nights of the month.[18]

The additional resources meant that every SAS operation could provide maximum support to other major operations if timed in conjunction with them. Instead of parties operating on foot, the heavily armed and specially modified long-range jeeps could take the raiders as far as 600 miles into enemy held territory. There they would mine roads, blow up supply trains, cut signal and phone communications, strafe road convoys, carry out night attacks on camps and laagers, while all the time sending back valuable information about the enemy's dispositions by wireless. The jeeps enabled them to travel through parts of the desert that were previously unknown, even through areas marked as impassable and, more importantly, which the enemy thought *were* impassable. These changes in tactical operations also required more self-sufficiency in navigation, in the form of the LRDG. With their skills came their greatest resource, their men.

One of the first was Mike Sadler. Apart from his fabled navigational ability, Sadler had made his name through an incident that happened while he was out on patrol in preparation for a raid on Derna airfield in June. Together with his Patrol leader, Gus Holliman, formerly of the Royal Rhodesian Tank Corps, Sadler had gone up onto the Jebel Akhdar to help with preparations for the raid. Each was carrying about 50 pounds of Lewes bombs in his rucksack and after being taken in as far as possible by an LRDG truck, they were forced to make a long march to the RV on foot, including the long climb up the Jebel.

They were not expecting company and just over the top of the Jebel, they rested 'absolutely knackered', a little way below the summit on the other side. Suddenly, as they were munching some biscuits, they became aware of a man standing on the ridge above, staring down at them. He was an Italian native 'levy' and things began to look decidedly uncomfortable. Holliman's pistol was at the bottom of one of the rucksacks. As the soldier made his way towards them, his rifle still slung over his shoulder, Sadler and Holliman quickly agreed tactics. While they both kept him chatting, Holliman started unpacking his bombs, one by one. When he got to the bottom of the rucksack, he unpacked his pistol, pointed it at the enemy and told him that he was now their prisoner! Then they marched him off, at a fair old speed to make the RV, at which treatment he was most unhappy. On the way back, having run out of water, they found an old Roman cistern. It had water but the surface was covered with goat droppings. They swept these aside and drank their fill, without any apparent ill effects.[19]

Tempted away from the LRDG by Stirling, Sadler joined the SAS and was later commissioned in the field. Unfortunately, Stirling's aversion to administration meant that he forgot to arrange for the appropriate Part II Order authorising the commission (and the pay!) to be published. Consequently, the RAPC (Royal Army Pay Corps) knew nothing about it. It was only long after Stirling had been captured and was languishing in far-away Colditz that questions were asked about why a somewhat embarrassed Mike Sadler was running round 'masquerading' as an officer.[20]

When the LRDG had been founded, by Brigadier Ralph Bagnold in June 1940, he had used New Zealanders. When he wanted to enlarge it, he recruited some Scots Guards to create 'G' patrol, which was about thirty-six strong. 'Y' patrol consisted of mainly English Yeomanry, while 'R' patrol was made up of Rhodesians, from which came Mike Sadler.[21] On one occasion, Stirling had gone out on patrol with the Scots Guards. On returning he had met up with T1 patrol whereupon his eyes lit up at the sight of their jeeps. He then used their radio to 'order up' some jeeps of his own from Cairo. They did not believe that he could possibly get any but he went off saying

'I'll be back with my own jeeps!' Before long he had reappeared at the head of about twenty Willys Bantams.[22]

Almonds had already got to know the LRDG men well the year before and felt very comfortable operating alongside them. His friendship with one of them, Alan Nutt, had been cemented by the deadly game of 'ring-a-ring-of-roses' with the Messerschmitt 110 after the Nofilia raid and the long dangerous journey back to Kabrit. For a while, the LRDG had been based at Siwa Oasis, between the Qattara Depression and the north of the Great Sand Sea. Nutt could remember an evening when a big clumsy 'plane had lumbered in and a whole lot of SAS men had piled out. They began to intermingle and after they had done a few night operations together, as Nutt said, 'Then you sort yourselves out.' He had been called up on the outbreak of war in 1939 and had had to leave his beautiful farm at "Lakelands", Motukarara in the South Island of New Zealand. He immediately volunteered for the LRDG and ended up in T2 Patrol.[23]

Another LRDG New Zealander Almonds got to know well at this time was Merlyn Craw. Unusually, he had joined the LRDG T1 Patrol direct, without first joining a parent Army unit. The desert had always fascinated him. In 1930, while still at school during the Depression everyone had a school end of term prize. He had asked for *Seven Pillars of Wisdom* by T.E. Lawrence. The headmaster gave him the edited version of the work, *Revolt in the Desert*, and this had a profound impression on his life. He was equally captivated by the notion of blowing up trains. So the combined operations of the LRDG and the SAS were for him a happy marriage of both his key interests.[24]

However, the New Zealanders were often perplexed by what they saw of the British class system. In particular, they could not understand the deference which British Other Ranks showed to their officers and which they believed was woefully misplaced. Sometimes, the cultures and anachronisms clashed. On one occasion, towards the end of 1941, Merlyn Craw's patrol was supporting the Scots Guards at Jalo Oasis. At the time, Rommel was withdrawing from Cyrenaica to an area between Agedabia and Agheila and they were therefore not very far from the front line. Merlyn went with his driver, a man called Gerry Gerrard, to collect from the Scots Guards the password of the day, which was changed every 24 hours. Gerrard was an older man with a stained beard and false teeth, which should have debarred him from joining the LRDG. This artificial dentition had become broken and chipped on the hard biscuits they had to eat. Unfortunately, the desert was no place for carrying out running repairs to dentures and this left Gerrard somewhat incapacitated in the eating and speaking department. On arriving at the Scots Guards' lines, the two LRDG men discovered that only the Colonel knew the password. They were taken to his tent where they found two Guardsmen marching up and down as if they were outside Buckingham Palace. Gerrard got past these but in no time at all he emerged from the tent in a huff, followed by the Colonel with a pained expression on his face.

'I say, don't you fellows *ever* salute an officer?' said the ruffled guardee. 'And what the deuce do you want anyway?'

'Oh well,' said Gerrard, shrugging his shoulders and thoroughly annoyed, 'if you're going to be like that about it …' And he stomped off in a fit of pique. So Merlyn had to go in and get the password himself, which being the sergeant he probably should have done in the first place.[25]

At around this time, the SAS also acquired their own Medical Officer, Malcolm Pleydell. He and Almonds got on very well together and used to spend many hours of enforced idleness when they were lying up at 'L' Detachment's desert rendezvous discussing rock formations or the provenance of the many shells and fossils that are to be found in the desert. On one occasion, Almonds found some pottery fragments which Pleydell later dated as second century B.C. They had in common an insatiable curiosity about their environment and would spend hours watching the wildlife that is surprisingly plentiful in the desert to anyone who will stay quiet and observant for a while.[26] In 1945, immediately after the war, Pleydell, writing under the name of Malcolm James, wrote the first book about the SAS, *Born of the Desert*. For my money it is the best of them all, capturing the flavour, the humour and the spirit of the time. In it, Pleydell described Almonds as 'a finely built man and more sensible and intelligent than the average officer' (which betrays a certain attitude of the times, as if intelligence were restricted to rank) and a 'fine disciplinarian over his water consumption' who 'never used his water-bottle, sufficing himself simply with the ration at mealtimes'.[27]

It was at about this time too that Stirling actually got around to doing some 'admin'. He wrote Almonds up for an immediate Military Medal and told him that he was being recommended for a Commission. This was for his part in the raids on Agheila and the roadhouse at Mersa Briga, for destroying five enemy heavy MT (motor transport) and for taking command after the raid on Nofilia and extricating the party with the one patched-up truck.[28] All this Jock Lewes had sadly not lived to report.

By now Almonds was wearing 'operational' parachute qualification wings. These wings in white and two tones of light and dark 'Pompadour' blue were awarded to every man after seven successful parachute jumps.

In addition, after three raids on active service behind enemy lines, they were permitted to wear them on the left breast. The Army Council stopped this practice after the war so that only the Army Air Corps and Glider Pilot Regiment could wear breast wings. SAS wings worn on the breast therefore denote very early and distinguished service in the regiment and are now very rare.[29]

On 3 July, he was glad to be heading out once more into the desert, his construction and administration tasks for Stirling finally finished.[30] The camp at Kabrit was coming to the end of its normal working day when he set off with the rest of the SAS raiding party. New volunteers paused on their way back from training to watch as the trucks rumbled out, sending up clouds of dust into the late evening sunshine. Instruction had become even more specialised and every new arrival was faced with a daunting array of training for which brawn alone would never suffice. Apart from the parachute training and jumping, the men had to become proficient in navigation, demolition, languages, specialist weapons, foreign weapons, special boating, motor transport, wireless use and many other areas of competence.

There were also many refinements on the simple practice of self denial. Full-scale operational exercises and extensive 'schemes' were carried out on foot in the desert. Some of these consisted of forced marches over difficult country with a full operational load for distances in excess of a hundred miles. The only water available was what a man could carry for himself, which was never enough. Inevitably, they suffered, but in their suffering they learned. And yet every man was still a volunteer. More and more came forward, eager to join if they could pass the torturous training.

This time, the SAS targets were the aircraft on the enemy's forward landing fields at El Daba, Fuka and beyond. But 'L' Detachment had not hitherto been motorised and had only four days to prepare fifteen jeeps with special equipment and load twenty 3-ton lorries. This involved crews and drivers in working some seventy-two hours without a break prior to departure.[31]

They set out, heading ever deeper into enemy territory.

Chapter Nine

Partners in Crime

Almonds was assigned to the raid furthest behind the enemy's front line at Sidi Barrani, led by Captain R. P. Schott. The whole convoy headed north to Alexandria, ever closer to the advancing German Army. There they contacted the LRDG, under command of Robin Gurdon, and met up with David Stirling at Eighth Army HQ at Amaria on 4 July.[1] They left all together the same day, their route being to slip through the southern end of the line unobserved. This meant they had to go south west, squeezing between the northern edge of the perilous Qattara Depression and the bottom of the El Alamein line.

This line northwards from the Depression to the sea marked the 30 June limit of the Axis advance.[2] The Depression itself had to be one of the most godforsaken places on earth. It was a vast sunken area of plain, several hundred feet deep with salt lakes and quicksands, surrounded by towering, jagged escarpments. It was because it was so impenetrable that it formed the southern tip of the new line. They took until the afternoon of 6 July to crawl cautiously round the rim of the Depression, ever conscious of the blistering vault stretching away below them. After carefully negotiating their way around this giant-sized death-trap, the SAS crossed through first the Allied positions and then the enemy lines.

Throughout this journey they were exposed to the threat of disaster from several quarters. The encircling, slightly proud lip of the Depression was fissured by rocky gullies and channels which ran back up into it. The terrain was an appalling test for vehicles. The engines groaned and strained as the wheels bounced and the trucks thudded up and down over the jagged rocks. Mechanical breakdowns and running repairs were a constant problem. But they had to keep moving. Without any cover, they were perpetually at risk of being attacked from the air. This danger was intensified as they sneaked round between the edge of the Depression and the southern ends of both the Axis and Allied front lines. Even their own side did not know of their presence. They were supposed to take the track from the edge of the Depression to Mersa Matruh and then follow a zigzag track to Siwa. But they found that they had gone so far up towards Mersa that they could not make use of the track.³

At approximately just over half way between Mersa Matruh and Siwa, and east of the Mersa to Siwa track, they made their rendezvous with three further LRDG patrols. This spot had the advantage of some caves where they could lie up during the days as a respite from the heat and the flies. After a day and a half spent settling into what was to become their new base, sorting out stores and making final arrangements for the various parties' objectives, Stirling called them all together for their final briefing. Even with a few days' growth of beard, he still managed to look impeccable. *'Like an English sea captain or a robber baron,'* Almonds thought.⁴

'L' Detachment's operations were designed to cooperate with General Auchinleck's own attacks on the area. On 5 July, a New Zealand column got round the enemy's position and destroyed 40 aircraft on one of the Fuka aerodromes, while the 9th Australian Division and 1st South African Division took objectives at Tel el Eisa and Tel el Makh Khad.⁵

Each party was allocated to its LRDG patrol and given its own instructions. Jellicoe had been tasked with El Daba to the north-east and was to strafe the coast road, blowing up dumps and communications lines and anything else he could find. Stirling, Mayne and Robin Gurdon with the LRDG were to take the second party, heading almost due north to Fuka, to raid the Bagoush and Fuka airfields on the coastal plain. Bill Fraser and the doctor were also in this contingent.

Saving his detailed instructions for his own party until later, Stirling turned to the Sidi Barrani party, including Almonds, who were to operate furthest west and would therefore be the deepest behind Rommel's front line. They were to be under command of Captain Alistair Timpson, LRDG G2 Patrol, he said, until they were dropped for offensive operations. Until that time, they were to remain in wireless communication with HQ LRDG. The SAS personnel included Captains Schott and Warr, Almonds, Sergeant W Brough, Corporals H White and C Baird, Parachutists Thompson, Meyer and Ridler and Driver Hope.

After telling them that their objectives were Landing Grounds (LG) 121 and 05, Stirling was at pains to stress that they were not to attack these LGs unless at least twelve aircraft could be destroyed. Almonds wondered if the Nofilia raid and the death of Jock Lewes were in Stirling's mind. The CO went on to say that he knew it would be tempting after going all that way, not to say frustrating, but they were not, he repeated, not to engage in any action for less than this number of enemy transport. He told them that in any case intelligence understood that these airfields were mainly used for refuelling and so they might not get an opportunity to do much damage. But their observations alone would be invaluable and they were to keep on the lookout. The group murmured assent. With a last cheerful 'Good luck!' he strode away without a backward glance.[6]

After all the parties and stores had been divided up, they departed from the RV in their different directions. Nevertheless, Almonds's party started out with a severe shortage of petrol and water. After several days, they feared that it might even be necessary to wireless for aircraft to drop supplies. Apart from that constantly worrying situation, their progress from the time when they left the main body until the day of their planned attack was fairly uneventful. They had one or two very narrow escapes from enemy aircraft, which appeared suddenly overhead but which fortunately failed to observe them.[7]

Then the water situation became desperate. For the first time in his life, Almonds was confronted with the terrors of death by thirst. Apart from the physical discomfort, each man experienced the mental anguish of knowing that in reality they were very unlikely to find any water. This mental suffering was for the most part entirely unspoken. This was to some extent due to the fact that speech became non-existent. Every time a man opened his mouth it meant giving away vital life fluid. But order prevailed. The same disciplines were observed over the sharing out of one teaspoon of water per man, per day, as had been observed when it was more plentiful. Then the water ran out altogether. After three days without anything to drink at all, it was pure serendipity when they came to a petrol and rations dump on the way to Sidi Barrani. They helped themselves, slaking their thirst and filling up every available container and water bottle as well as their petrol cans and reserve tanks. From then on, the petrol rations and water situation was solved. The more sobering fact was that these dumps had all been left by their own side's forces as they retreated to El Alamein.[8]

Their first lying up base was in some wadis south of Sidi Barrani. It was depressing to see so much abandoned Allied equipment lying around, reminding my father of the Fig Tree wadi near Tobruk that had been littered with abandoned Italian equipment and stores. Once again, the east to west ebb and flow of the tide of war had left its grubby tide mark of human detritus. Since separating from the main party, Schott had been slightly ill, Timpson was suffering from extensive desert sores and the

LRDG sergeant had bad jaundice and was running a very high temperature. The remainder of the party, including Almonds were in high spirits.⁹

The attacks on the airfields were duly carried out as ordered on the night of 12/13 July. They divided into two parties, one led by Warr, consisting of Almonds and Parchutists Meyer and Ridler aiming for the objective at LG 05. The other led by Schott, consisting of Brough, White, Baird and Thompson, was to attack LG 121. Warr's party was to be dropped by the LRDG about 4 miles from their objective at '23.59 hours' – the Army's more precise expression for 'midnight'. Unfortunately, due to errors on the maps, the Warr party found themselves 10 miles from their target while Schott's group were 3 miles away from theirs. After about two hours' sleep that night, Almonds's party moved to a lying up point. They found an excellent OP (observation post) but Schott's party was not so lucky. Before they had even reached a point from which they could observe their LG, they quite unexpectedly came across a six-man German patrol with an LMG (light machine gun) and a dog. After this unfortunate encounter, at which they were sure they had been seen, they decided to take up an all round defensive position on a bir and fight it out when the inevitable recce party arrived.¹⁰

Expecting the enemy to attack, Schott's group lay up the entire next day. Eventually, when no attack came, they realised to their relief that they had not been seen after all. But the time was not wasted because they could see enemy aircraft arriving at LG 05 and were able to make accurate plots of their courses on the maps. They were also able to ascertain that LG 121 was not being used by enemy aircraft but was only being used as a decoy at night when Allied bombers flew over. Baird confirmed this after a further recce. In fact the same practice was being carried out at night at Almonds's objective, LG 05. All the aircraft were being flown off in the evening in a westerly direction, leaving the LG empty except for one crashed Ju-87. The LGs were being kept empty at night so that there was no question of them suffering from clandestine enemy attack. In addition, the SAS men noted that all enemy transport on roads west of Mersa stopped from dusk until dawn. The enemy was beginning to learn!

On the night of 13 July, Schott's party was picked up by Captain Timpson at 11.30 hours but Warr's party failed to make the rendezvous with the LRDG. Schott's party had no choice but to proceed back without them because the base had been changed during the day when the LRDG were chased out of the wadi by armoured cars and aircraft. A new lying up position was established 35 miles to the south. As Schott and his men made their way to it, they left water for Warr's party at the old RV. Still concerned, Schott sent out a recce party the following night to see if they had appeared, but there was still no sign of them. In the meantime, Schott and Timpson made plans to strafe the road at 'Bug Bug' (Buq Buq) on the night of 15/16 July. They set out to put this into effect and as they passed through the old RV there they found Warr, Almonds and the rest of the party, very weak and exhausted from another four days' lack of food and water. But they had gathered important information about enemy transport aircraft and this was then swiftly 'wirelessed' back to LRDG HQ. Timpson then decided to go off and strafe the road at Kilo 86 between Sidi Barrani and Mersa. This time, Almonds stayed with Schott, Thompson and Hope, with the 3-tonner and a broken-down jeep.[11]

At 09.30 the next morning, they suddenly saw a column of vehicles approaching from the wrong direction to Captain Timpson's pre-arranged position. Realising they were the enemy, Schott decided to abandon the jeep and make a break for it in the Ford 3-tonner, back to the pre-arranged RV with Stirling. This decision was so precipitate, that the first Almonds knew of it was a shout and the revving up of the 3-tonner's engines.

'Okay! We're off! Everybody aboard!' He was about 20 yards away from his blanket and rifle at the time so he had to make a choice between going to get them or diving into the back of the vehicle. Safety being the most important consideration he decided to scramble aboard and just made it as the 3-tonner was moving off.[12]

During the dash across the desert, they were chased by an Me-110 and came under fire. Fortunately, the enemy failed to do any damage because of their speed and the huge dust screen raised by the 3-tonner. They reached Stirling at 15.30, arriving just in time for tea. On meeting up again with Warr, they discovered that the mystery column they had seen approaching their RV was none other than Warr himself and party but the haze and mirages caused by this one vehicle gave the impression of at least twenty-five Italian Lancia trucks loaded with troops! Not a bit put out by the sudden disappearance of my father's party, Warr stopped at point 212 and picked up the broken down jeep, which with the help of the LRDG was eventually towed all the way back through the Depression to the Delta area for repair. Paddy Mayne later returned my father's rifle and blanket to him.

'Here,' he said with a grin. 'You might be needing these.' But it was clear that Mayne had not been impressed by the panic exit from the RV.[13]

Although the raiders had not been able to destroy aircraft on the ground at the airfields, the results of the operation were considerable. Timpson and Warr contented themselves with blowing up the water pipe between Sidi Barrani and Mersa at its lowest point, thereby draining all the water in the pipeline. The knowledge that SAS clandestine operations were forcing the enemy to observe self-imposed 'curfews' on his roads and airfields, which must have cost him dear, also gave a certain sense of satisfaction. On the basis of the information wirelessed to HQ, ten fully laden transport aircraft were confirmed destroyed by the RAF over Sidi Barrani and four on the ground at LG 05.[14] For good measure, quantities of equipment left behind by Allied troops were also destroyed, including broken-down vehicles, tanks and dumps, so preventing the enemy from using them. There were no casualties but the closing words to Schott's otherwise 'stiff upper lip' report give a hint of what they had been through.

> I should like to mention the efficiency of Capt. Timpson's LRDG patrol throughout the operation. Capt Timpson and the patrol Sgt were both extremely sick with desert sores and jaundice. Capt. Warr, Sgt. Almonds, Pct. Thompson and Sgt. Brough also showed courage and determination throughout the operation.[15]

As usual, the report was franked MOST SECRET and not released for thirty years.

From the main rendezvous, the SAS then mounted other attacks on vehicle laagers, roads and railway lines. During one of these, there was an air strike and on 12 July Robin Gurdon was killed.[16] Stirling was again devastated, for it was an open secret that he had planned to make the bold, confident Gurdon his second-in-command. But, as usual, the show had to go on. Just as when Lewes was killed, Stirling was full of enthusiastic talk about what they could do to the enemy given more resources and the right training.[17] He really was very adept at using overt emotions to mask his real feelings.

On 16 July, HQ Eighth Army issued personal instructions to Stirling. He was to discuss formation of a base at Qara Oasis with Lieut. Col Prendergast of the LRDG. His raiding priorities were spelled out: tank workshops; tanks; aircraft; water; petrol and he was given orders about cooperating with other raiding parties and engaging in 'blocking operations' to hold up traffic at a number of locations, including Sollum and Halfaya. The instructions contained an assurance that Eighth Army would, wherever possible, keep him informed of other raiding operations in the vicinity but the short notice at which this often had to be mounted meant that this could not be guaranteed.[18]

This seems to have provoked a knee-jerk reaction. On 17 July, Stirling reported on his operations against the enemy airfields. He was positive about the performance of the Bantams but at pains to point out that a lack of logistic support from the Eighth Army had meant the last minute cancellation of part of the planned raids against El Daba and Fuka. He received a sympathetic hearing.[19] After this fouling up of operational communications between Stirling and the Eighth Army and the usual tensions with MEHQ, his views were fed into some forthcoming discussions at senior level on the reorganisation of Middle East raiding forces.[20]

Then, towards the end of July, the stores at the caves began to run out. Almonds and Pleydell were among the few who remained at the rendezvous while Stirling with most of the party made a provisioning trip back to Kabrit. Being left behind does not at first sight seem as arduous or as dangerous as making that dreadful trip through the Qattara Depression. The reality was rather different. The men left behind were down to their very last supplies of food and, more importantly, water. So they lived with the knowledge that if anything happened to Stirling's party, either on the way out or the way back, they would die out there in the desert all alone. For company, they had only each other and the constant attentions of about one million flies, which pestered them mercilessly. It was difficult not to sit and think of the other men, by now back at Kabrit enjoying a beer and a swim. Nevertheless, Almonds and Pleydell got on very well together, swapping their few paperback books and stories and making geological observations on their surroundings.

In just over a week, but rather later than expected, Stirling returned. Like boys back from raiding the school tuck shop, he and Jellicoe brought as many small luxuries as they could carry, including sweets, lavender water and cigars. Stirling had been revitalised by his visit back to base and was full of plans to attack Sidi Haneish, a previously unnoticed airfield not far from Fuka and about thirty miles east south east of Mersa Matruh. It still had plenty of aircraft and was again 'just begging' to be raided. Almonds joined in the preparations for what turned out to be one of the most audacious and dangerous raids ever carried out by the SAS in the Middle East.

The plan was (dangerously) simple. They would pioneer the use of their jeeps to their full capacity as the formidable offensive weapons that they were now fitted out to be. Each had four high-speed LMGs, usually with one pair on the front right for the passenger and one pair on the back for the 'tally man'. The driver usually had a Bren gun which he kept 'handy' down beside him. This combined firepower could deliver about 1,200 rounds per minute. It was supplemented by a .50 calibre heavy machine-gun (HMG), a mortar and smoke discharges. Some jeeps were even fitted with a high power searchlight. It followed that the firepower of the raid was potentially 24,000 rounds per minute!

But the hardware alone was not enough. First they had to practise their new 'gangster-style' attack until it was perfect. The twenty jeeps were to drive in a double column formation straight down the airfield. With four vehicles across the front, they were actually an open three-sided box. They had to keep in perfect formation, with a maximum of two abreast, so that they could sweep round and back up again, shooting outwards at the aircraft but without hitting each other. Over and over again that night, out there in the desert in the enemy's own territory, they rehearsed driving in formation, then wheeling round and back again, all the time keeping their

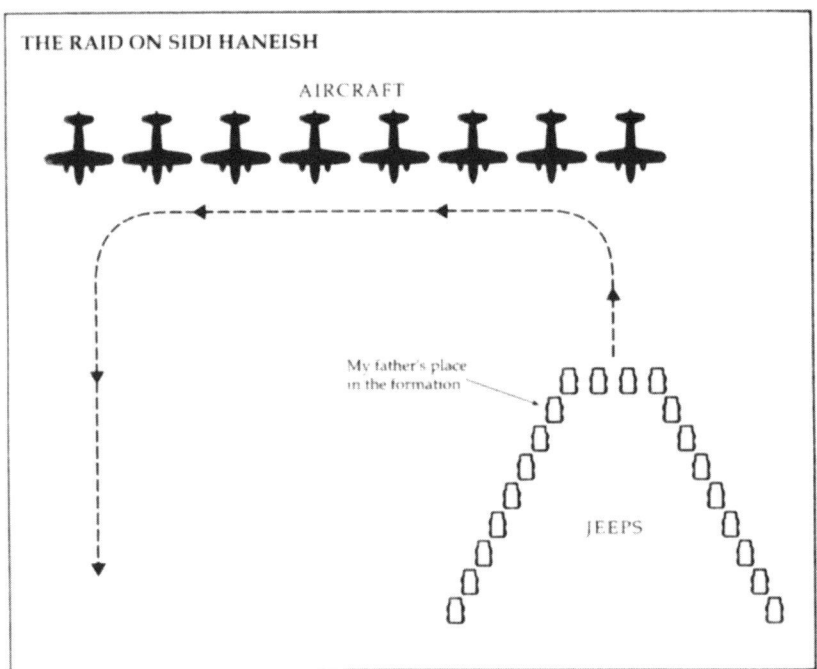

'dressing' in line with each other. The Guards parade ground disciplines were proving useful after all.

The moon happened to be full but Stirling decided to lose no time and mount the raid straight away on 26 July. Bang went another SAS norm; from then on, they would raid whatever the quarter of the moon. Next, they had to get there. Such a large convoy of vehicles travelling together meant that expert navigation to the target, and then a quick get away, were vital. The column consisted of four jeeps and T1 Patrol of the LRDG under Captain Wilder. The whole force was to move by the main Qatara-Garawla track to Bir Khal da. From there, T1 Patrol with one Bren carrier was to take up a position north-west of the airfield to create a diversion while the main body approached from the east.[21]

Getting them to the airfield was Mike Sadler's 'finest hour'. As Stirling's navigator, he rode in his jeep. After travelling for some time through the night, they stopped about twenty miles short of the target so that Sadler could make some observations. Then they drove in slowly on a bearing. Stirling gradually became increasingly agitated. Eventually he snarled, 'Where's this bloody airfield then?'

'About two miles ahead,' Sadler replied and *exactly* as he said it, all the aerodrome landing lights came on and lit up the runways! But their concealment had not been blown. It was simply that an aircraft was about to land and a couple of moments later a heavy German bomber lumbered down onto the landing strip. Without more ado, the raiders got into formation and went in, Stirling leading in the front, with the two columns of jeeps following led by Jellicoe and Mayne.[22]

Almonds was driving the second jeep in the left-hand column. He knew that he would have to focus all his concentration on keeping his position, to avoid being hit by the inside gunners of the formation. But as they got onto the airfield itself, his jeep suddenly struck a hidden defensive anti-tank trap ditch at the side of the runway and went right down into it. He and his gunners were thrown out but fortunately managed to land well and unhurt. The ditch was very deep and there was no way that they were going to be able to get the jeep out of it so Almonds set off to report the fact to Stirling. He meanwhile had called a pause and was taking stock as cool as a cucumber. 'Bad luck,' said Stirling, as if the occupants of the second jeep had just had a goal scored against them in a football match. 'You'd better join Sadler.' Mike Sadler, who was waiting at the south-east corner of the airfield as planned, picked them up and they settled down to observe the proceedings.

After sorting themselves out, the attackers drove on. As soon as they got within sight and sound of the enemy, they accelerated hard and drove in with guns blazing. The enemy immediately switched off the landing lights but there was no difficulty in seeing anything. Brilliant flashes of exploding and blazing aircraft, murderous and continuous gunfire from the jeeps and the stabbing red lines of the tracer bullets lit up the whole show. This was accompanied by the deafening roar of thousands of rounds of ammunition being loosed off simultaneously, punctuated by intermittent explosions as fuel dumps around the edge of the airfield were also hit. As if to complete the visual effects, the scene was bathed in eerie green light from Stirling's Very pistol which had signalled the open fire.

Down the airfield they charged, with a row of parked aircraft, all Ju-52s, neatly parked right across the scene in front of them. Because of their column formation, the attackers could safely blast away straight ahead of them. The combined firepower reached a crescendo, while exploding petrol dumps and bomb bursts magnified the effect. Stirling then wheeled round to the left and round they all wheeled behind him, still desperately fighting to keep in position. This meant that they could then have another go at the same aircraft as they swept alongside them before turning away and back up the way they had come. The effect was rather like the shooting gallery at a fair, except that the targets kept still and they raced past them. Finally, when Stirling was sure that there was nothing left that they could usefully destroy, they disappeared off the airfield to be swallowed up in the desert night.

For a couple of hours, Almonds and Sadler lay low but still quite near to the airfield. In no time at all, Teutonic efficiency swung into action and there were men all over the place, towing away the burning aircraft and clearing the runways for landing. In fact, the airfield was already in use again by the time the hidden raiders silently withdrew.[23] The two men stayed in position until daylight, still on the lookout for any more stragglers. When morning broke, it was fortunately very misty. The SAS raiders, with the Germans in hot pursuit were long gone. Cautiously, Almonds and Sadler moved off. After making good progress, they suddenly came upon the German convoy who had departed to chase the SAS! Unknowingly, Almonds and Sadler had approached the Germans from the rear while they were taking a break. Men had stopped by their trucks, while some were still sitting at the wheel. They looked up to see who the latecomer was. Peering through the gradually clearing mist, Almonds could see German soldiers doing the same back to him. What if they should suddenly be stopped and approached by the enemy? In spite of the danger, he could see the funny side of the situation. He and Sadler resolved that whatever happened they would avoid stopping.

They drove steadily on past the parked convoy and took the first expedient turning off. After finding a suitable spot to take cover, they quickly camouflaged the vehicles. Sadler watched as Almonds got out and went for a scout round. Carefully, he approached the crest of a low ridge. Suddenly, without turning round from what he was looking at, he gave a one armed, palm down, signal for Sadler and the others to 'get down!' A German vehicle recovery team was nearby. The SAS men's hearts sank as a group of Stukas screamed into view but, after coming in as low as they could over the recovery team, the planes flew off. The pilots must have thought that the recovery team and the escaping SAS were all one and the same unit.[24]

Not far away from them, Merlyn Craw and his patrol had been at the airfield since 01.00 hours. They had been there to deal with the defences, particularly the anti-aircraft guns, but because of the anti-tank ditches they had not been able to get close enough to do a proper job. The following morning, they too had been leaving the scene of the crime when they heard the sound of more engines overhead. A German Fieseler *Storch* reconnaissance aircraft was coming in slowly, circling low, dipping and angling to get a good look at the ground. Not content with that, it came lower and hovered, as if dithering over what to do next, then landed just out of sight. It had come down and was sitting between the truck belonging to the LRDG officer, Nick Wilder, and the one containing Merlyn Craw.[25]

The aircraft was on some flat ground between two small wadis. Suddenly, a nearby German infantry half-track carrier, on its way to Qattara Springs to stop the SAS from crossing the Depression, opened up on them with three 0.47 mm guns. Merlyn Craw recognised the outfit as one that he had passed on his way to the aerodrome the night before. Nick Wilder immediately leapt from his truck and set off in the direction of the 'plane. Meanwhile, two Germans got out of it and started to walk towards the SAS and LRDG men, apparently without realising that they were the enemy. Seeing all this, Craw decided to take no chances. He set off at once to pick up his officer, giving the empty Fieseler a 'squirt' in a matter of fact sort of way as he passed it. The two Germans immediately shot up their hands and started shouting that one of them, the passenger, was a doctor. The two LRDG men from Wilder's truck went over and took them prisoner before throwing a cup of petrol over the aircraft and setting it ablaze. Looking back before Craw reached him, Wilder saw the smoke and thought it was his two trucks that had gone up. After also being picked up by Merlyn's truck, the two prisoners were then handed over to Almonds.[26]

Without any more incidents, they all made it back to the rendezvous where Almonds discovered that the raid had destroyed twenty-five aircraft and probably seriously damaged about another fifteen. Unfortunately, one SAS man had been killed.[27] At that moment, he was glad that he had never had to send anyone into action, or go in himself, where he knew the situation was militarily hopeless. For all its daring, the raid on Sidi Haneish was far from that. On the contrary, everything about it had felt right. They had planned it themselves, rehearsed it well, and they knew they could rely on each other.

The German doctor turned out to be the Baron von Luterotti. He spoke good English so he and the pilot settled in very quickly. Given that they were now POWs, the two Germans ended up enjoying extraordinarily good hospitality. The doctor naturally struck up a sort of a semi-professional acquaintance with Pleydell and joined the quasi-scientific discussions with him and Almonds. One evening, a few days after the raid, the three of them were sitting together one evening having a cigarette. Always fascinated by the night sky and remembering his boyhood desire to escape to sea and navigate by the stars, Almonds started pointing out the constellations overhead. There was Orion with his belt of stars, clearly visible even that far south. Pleydell and the German doctor joined in, both equally of course authorities on the stars.[28] Only, with hindsight, did Almonds remember that the doctor seemed to be taking it a little more seriously, verifying that this was the Milky Way and over there was the pole star, which always pointed north.

An hour later, when Almonds had just turned in, he was called by a very disturbed sentry.

'Sergeant Almonds! It's the prisoners; they've gone!' The soldier appeared very distressed at the idea that he had let the two Germans get away. Pulling on his shorts and reaching for his pistol, Almonds asked what had happened. The sentry did not know. He had seen the pilot go round to the back of the truck to get his blanket, as he usually did. But he didn't come back. The soldier went to see where he was, but he was nowhere to be seen. Then, when he went back to where he had been before, he discovered that the doctor had gone as well. It was obviously a planned job.

Since the prisoners could not have gone far, a full-scale search was launched. But they could find no trace of the missing Germans. The doctor had clearly made the most of his observations of the sky at night.

Meanwhile, back in Cairo, Special Services in the Middle East were being reorganised. On 26 July, the same day as the raid on Sidi Haneish, the DDO had sent a minute to DCGS, DDSO:

> As a result of the conference on 24 July, a draft minute from CGS (Lt Gen McReery) to C in C attached. Any comments?'[29]

On 4 August, a submission, closely resembling the draft, was put forward to the C in C recommending that a new HQ raiding forces should be formed from HQ 'L' Detachment and that it should be entirely separate from the SOE operation called 'G R'. 'L' Detachment itself was to expand and have an administration section at Kabrit, amalgamating 'L' Detachment, the SBS and 1 SAS Regiment. There would be a separate parachute brigade but a Lieutenant Colonel Cator (late Scots Greys who had been in Eritrea with the Commandos and with 'GR' at Haifa) was to be CO Raiding Forces, working directly to a new GSO1 at GHQ and supported by a dedicated IO (Intelligence Officer).[30]

By 9 September, this proposal had been modified so that it came out with Stirling in place of Cator. The background papers and the brief from the CGS explained that Stirling was to occupy this key role. One can only surmise what had happened in between these two dates. The CO of 1 SAS Regiment, Colonel Graham, had suggested the same idea on 8 August. Stirling had been at it again with his social contacts. After some well-timed lobbying in the right quarters, and attendance at a dinner with the Prime Minister, who was visiting Saults and Alexander in Cairo, he managed a little 'bending of his ear'. The next day he received a PM Private Secretary note dated 9 August.

> Please can I have the short note on what you would advise should be done to concentrate and coordinate the work you are doing.[31]

The note was signed 'ThR'.

Stirling's ready response 'to Prime Minister' of the same day proposed a reorganisation of all combined operations forces, from single agents up to whole Commando battalions, and amounted to a 'take-over bid' by 'L' Detachment. These ideas were brought to a meeting on 25 August where

Colonel Prendergast, the CO of the LRDG, argued for no change.[32] Although the SAS and LRDG got on well together, there were some 'creative' tensions between them. Once the SAS started blowing things up, the LRDG's discreet, but very valuable, observations became much more difficult to carry out. It was surprising that Prendergast's view did not carry more weight because he was known to be an excellent organiser and administrator and certainly a better one than David Stirling.[33] Divided roles were eventually agreed for the LRDG and raiding forces. But a 'note to file' reveals something of the dynamics and the frustrations of the various interested parties.

> Stirling outlined certain larger proposals for capturing aerodromes in the Gebel [sic] which were dependent on the success of the Benghazi operation. It was pointed out that this was a matter for GHQ to decide...[34]

Essentially, Churchill had bought Stirling's version of the idea. On 9 September, the CGS, Lieutenant General McReery, wrote to Lieutenant General Holmes (Ninth Army) explaining the reorganisation of raiding forces. 'L' Detachment, SBS and 1 SAS Regiment were to be amalgamated, with Stirling as CO of the Raiding Forces. Unfortunately, the old strings remained; he was to work to a new GSO1 at GHQ.[35]

The irritant of having to report to a staff Lieutenant Colonel did not hold Stirling back. He was still fascinated by the lure of Benghazi and he agreed with MEHQ, at a price, to plan another raid on the port. It would be 'third time lucky'. The 'price' he paid for this was staff officer interference in SAS planning. But even so, when Stirling discovered that 'L' Detachment was to be used in a 'set piece' attack as part of a larger overall operation to liberate Benghazi, Tobruk and Jalo, he was furious. He went along with it, however, saying later that he had been beguiled and even 'bribed' by the promise of a free hand afterwards.[36]

He never could resist a gamble.

Chapter Ten

Attack on Benghazi

The SAS returned to Kabrit and began preparations for the Benghazi raid. Then they set off in a three-part convoy via Cairo and followed the river Nile upstream in the direction of Aswan. After passing through Asyut, they turned off south westwards between Girga and Nag Hammadi onto the Kharga Oasis track. Although the route had long been used by trade caravans, its surface was uneven and rocky so that their progress could only be as fast as the vehicles could stand without breaking down. The Oasis lay about a third of the way along the distance they had to cover to reach the Gilf el Kebir, a sharp ridge of mountains climbing to over 3,200 feet above them. From there, they were to make for the next Oasis at Kufra, then bypass Jalo Oasis, which was now again in Italian hands, before coming finally to Benghazi. This circuitous journey, which took nearly 2,000 miles and six weeks, described a huge U shape southward around most of North Africa.[1]

'*Shades of Hannibal*', Almonds thought, since they even had two lumbering Honey tanks to replicate the elephants. Already the interference of the staff officers was beginning to tell. This was not at all the SAS style. The tanks had aeroplane engines and made a terrible noise so everyone realised that the element of surprise would be impossible. In addition, the going was so slow, with the overburdened vehicles constantly becoming bogged down in sand so that some days their breakfast camp was still in view when they stopped in the evening. Eventually the heavy loads and tanks had to be got rid of, much to everyone's relief.

The parties separated and Stirling and Mayne proceeded independently. Almonds was with a third group led by Captain 'Sandy' Scratchley. One of the other officers in their party, the Hon. Douglas Berneville-Clay, was evidently the result of one of Stirling's not-so-good selections. It was apparent that in some cases Stirling did not seem to be able to see through people of his own class who pretended to be 'one of us', while actually holding quite different beliefs and values.[2]

Berneville-Clay talked constantly about the title he would one day inherit and was promptly nicknamed 'Lord Chuff' by the men, 'chuff' being one of the soldiers' more polite terms for the rear end. He was a deeply unpopular officer. Almonds instinctively took care to avoid him. Years later, he read that Berneville-Clay had turned out to be the only ever SAS traitor. The SAS misfit had apparently afterwards joined the 'BFC', the so-called 'British Free Corps', made up of Allied POWs in Germany who did not relish being sent to Siberia and were persuaded to support the Nazis.[3] So much for Lord Chuff.

The Kharga Oasis was a welcome sight. The sight and sound of running pure clear water was a balm after dry days of dunes and dust. As they approached, Almonds saw with a sudden stab of homesickness that there were even some swathes of bright green grass where a little Arab girl of about twelve years old was herding cows. As usual, he was very interested in the mechanics of oases and their perennial supply of fresh water. Underground water sources accounted for most of them, with their springs and wells, some of them artesian, supplied by sandstone aquifers whose intake areas could be more than 500 miles away, such as Dakhla Oasis which lay ahead of them slightly to the north. As with all the Sahara oases, the date palm was the principal tree and the main source of food, while in its shade grew citrus fruits and figs, peaches and apricots and even vegetables and cereals such as wheat, barley and millet.

But after only one day, they had to leave the delights of Kharga and strike out for the Gilf el Kebir. They had about 700 miles to cover to reach it over a vast waste of uninhabited desert so they had to get the navigation right. Moreover, Stirling wanted them all in Kufra in just over a week's time on 3 September. Almonds's party had been designated one of the 'fast' parties sent ahead to find the trail while the others came behind them with the 3-tonners and stores. They were not without their own problems however. At one point when a vehicle hit a rock and broke its sump, he spent some time removing its back axle and fitting it to another which had a good sump but a broken axle. He also stripped the broken vehicle of any other small and useful parts that they could take with them before abandoning it. This seemed to him just a sensible thing to do, although in the process he attracted a ring of 'doubting Thomas' spectators. Finally, they set off again leaving behind not two abandoned vehicles but only one.

The track took them to the long ridge of the Gilf running north-west to down to the Jebel in the south-east, which became a great wall of black basalt rock, barring their way. The leaders of the party included Jim Chambers, an honest-faced man in who there was a complete absence of cynicism and who was greatly liked by the men. Bill Cumper, their new Sapper explosives expert, and Pleydell the MO, made up their complement of officers. But in spite of their combined skills and attributes they were not well endowed with navigational ability and they began to include Almonds in their regular 'O' Group meetings. The party had been told to look out for a perfect cone of black rock as the landmark that was supposed to mark the only pass through the ridge at a pass called 'Eight Bells'.

As they skirted along the edge of the Gilf, at the first sight of black cones, the leaders of the party and Pleydell thought they should turn right into one of the many apparent entrances. But none of them could be sure.

'What do you think S'arnt Almonds?' they said. He doubted that this was in fact the pass, because a quick recce revealed that it petered out a little way ahead. The leaders then, with some relief he detected, delegated the responsibility for navigation to him! Before long he was sitting in the leading jeep with its fluttering pennant. At 'mushroom rock', another landmark which stuck up out of the bare ground, shaped exactly like a growing mushroom, the basalt turned into limestone and he found the way through. It was another old camel trade route. He could imagine with what joy countless camel trains over the centuries had found it before them.

Near the turning-off point there was supposed to be a dump of POL, food and water hidden in the desert for them. Once again, Almonds was put on the spot.

'You're good at this sort of thing,' said Scratchley. 'Can you find it for us?' Slowly, Almonds searched the blistering horizon in a steady three hundred and sixty degree scan. Suddenly, he brought his eyes back sharply over a section of distant sand dunes. What was it that had made him do that? Then he saw it: an unnaturally straight line in an ocean of billowing desert. It was a well-camouflaged cache. He and Reg Seekings set off to explore it and were overjoyed to find food, water and fuel. They filled up the vehicles with high-octane aviation spirit mixed with half a pint of engine oil per tank, as Almonds said, 'to steady it down a bit'.[4]

At Kufra they met up again with Stirling and Mayne, where they spent some time studying maps and a street model of Benghazi and working out details of the impending raid. The objectives were selected so as to cause the maximum amount of permanent damage as quickly as possible while they still had, in theory at least, the element of surprise. Almonds was given the role of driving a truck, packed with ammunition and explosives, into the harbour. There, he would board a ship and after overpowering the crew, pack the vessel with explosives and scuttle her across the mouth of the harbour. This would deprive Rommel of the use of the port for some time.

He spent some time studying the model of Benghazi and trying to memorise the route from the edge of the town to the harbour. This was not easy because there was a maze of tiny streets and no particularly memorable landmarks. It was then that he learned that the Benghazi raid was timed for the early hours of the morning on 13 September and that Mayne's job was to rob the main Benghazi bank! The raid was to coincide with an attack on Tobruk, supported by two other attacks: one on Barce airfield, to be carried out by the LRDG, and one on Jalo Oasis. It seemed to Almonds at the time that this was all very ambitious and that they would be doing well even to get their cumbersome wagon train with its 200 or so men, 40 jeeps and as many 3-tonners carrying all their supplies anywhere near Benghazi.

They got ready to move off again, this time on the 'home run' to the north-west. Benghazi was now within their reach. The three-part convoy pressed on. But first they had to cut across a narrow isthmus between two huge areas of the Great Sand Sea at a place called Zeighen. The Great Sand Sea itself is some 800 miles long and 250 miles wide. Passing through this area of the desert was an awesome experience. It was rightly named a 'sea', for there were no features by which to navigate other than the sun by day and the stars by night. As far as the eye could see, hills of sand shimmered and danced in the heat. They were up to 400 feet high from valley to crest and as the convoy crawled through they were like tiny ant specks in a sand dune.[5]

In this strange, vast, sand oven, instead of the usual shells and the odd artefact, they found huge lumps of glass, smooth but murky, tinged green or blue and weighing anything up to 7 kilos (about 15 pounds). Just like particles of water in the waves of the sea, the sand itself was in perpetual motion, shifted slowly but inexorably by the winds. The windward side of each giant 'wave' was fairly firm, while the leeward side was much softer. Some parts of the Sand Sea were completely impassable because the dunes were so high and the soft side so long and so treacherous that the vehicles risked sticking and sinking, never to be recovered. Such a terrain meant constant checking ahead and sometimes detours through the deep shade of the 'valleys' that lay between the giant dunes. And all the time, there was the danger of enemy aircraft, from whom there would be no cover at all in such a merciless environment.[6]

The Sand Sea was unforgiving to those who did not show proper respect for its unique environment. One young officer (who was not an SAS original) drove his vehicle straight to the top of one of the sand dune ridges and instead of turning sideways at the crest of the sand ridge to see what the terrain was like on the downhill side, he drove straight on over the top. The jeep fell 90 feet, landed upright but then rolled over, breaking the back of the passenger and killing him, a heavy price to pay for such a lack of caution. Many years later Almonds met the officer concerned in London and the pain of that death of long ago was still evident.[7]

Thankful that they had only a relatively small part of the Sand Sea to cross, the convoy soon emerged on the western side of it and at last turned north towards Benghazi. For about two-thirds of the remaining distance, they were to travel parallel with the western edge of the Sand Sea. This put another premium on navigational skills, since if they drifted off course to the north-east by only a degree or two they would wander back into it. They were now also approaching the more occupied part of the enemy's territory and as they grew closer to the northern coastal strip they needed to pay even more attention to camouflage and the risk of being spotted by enemy aircraft. Before reaching the northern tip of the Sand Sea, they passed Jalo, leaving it well to their left since it was again in enemy hands. Soon they came into country that was familiar to Almonds from his raiding days with Jock Lewes at Agheila and Mersa Brega. The brooding presence of the Jebel el Akhdar lay sprawling the horizon east to west in front of them.

At the point where the Trig el Abd, an old east to west camel route, crosses the Jebel the three parts of the convoy finally came together. This was dangerous territory because the enemy had sown it with German thermos bombs. These were scattered from the air and then armed themselves after they had landed so that they were sensitive to even the smallest vibration. One jeep in the convoy set one off and was completely destroyed with one man seriously injured.

They went over their operational plans once again. Everyone had his individual job to do. Almonds was working out the details of his jeep packed with explosives and limpet mines. He would find a tug waiting at the inner harbour mole, which he could use to tow a big ship across the harbour entrance, sink it and block the entrance. If Almonds had wanted a *Boy's Own Paper* adventure, this was it. Any language problems were to be overcome by the use of local guides and Captain Bob Melot, a Belgian who had been in the Middle East for many years. He had joined Stirling and Mayne as a fluent Arabic speaker with good knowledge of Benghazi and some potentially useful contacts. But here came the first discordant note. According to his local Arab intelligence, the enemy knew of their approach and the element of surprise was already lost. As planned, Alan Nutt and Merlyn Craw were to take part in the simultaneous raids on the neighbouring airfields in the area.[8]

History, in the form of the Public Record Office (PRO) files, can now make its statement on events. On arrival at the first RV, Paddy Mayne sent forward a party consisting of Bob Melot, Fitzroy Maclean, and a private of the LAF. The sortie was for 'the purpose of establishing contact with the Representative of the ISLD [Inter Services Liaison Department – a 'euphemism' for MI6]…with a view to obtaining the latest information'.[9] Stirling reported that the ISLD was not found, so the LAF private was sent off 'in order that he might visit his relatives and obtain … information'. The agent left at night on 10 September, returning on 12 September, having spent four hours in Benghazi. He reported to the effect that the enemy 'appeared to be expecting an attack. It was said that there were 5,000 Italians in El Abair; a German Battalion to the 'north-east of the town; that 70 truckloads of Italian Infantry had arrived the day before; and that shipping had left the port 48 hours previously[10]. This did indeed seem to suggest that the visitors were expected!

Stirling communicated all this by signal to GHQ ME. Again, the official record shows that 'on receipt of their reply, which showed that *no great importance was attributed to this information*, [my italics] the party moved off…'[11] Before leaving the Jebel, Stirling did meet the ISLD representative, who confirmed that the enemy had anticipated an attack on the date in question. Reinforcements of 200 German machine-gunners had been moved in and civilians had been evacuated. Still Stirling's orders to attack Benghazi were not rescinded.

On the way in towards Benghazi, a small group under Bob Melot attacked the Italian fort guarding the pass through the Jebel el Akhdar to Benghazi. They managed to destroy most of the barracks and silence the radio. But they did not know what messages the defenders had been able to send before this was accomplished. It was a short, sharp fight, in which Bob Melot was wounded and only two prisoners were taken. At the very least, the security cover of the Benghazi raid now appeared to be in doubt, if not completely blown. Everyone in the convoy realised that the scheme now left far too much to chance.[12] The raid ought to have been called off so why did it still go ahead? Perhaps Stirling was under so much pressure from above that it *had* to go ahead. If so, we do not know *why* this pressure was being applied but MI6 have always been known for assiduously protecting their sources. If the raid *had* been called off, the Axis would have known that someone inside Benghazi was an informer.

At last, on 13 September 1942, the day for which they had waited six weeks finally arrived. They would raid Benghazi before dawn. They were supposed to go in while it was still dark when a planned air attack was finishing. But they were so late that as the air attack was winding down they were still up on the Jebel. After being led astray on their way down from the hills, either wilfully or through incompetence by their so-called guide, and having retraced their steps, they at last found the right road. They still had to cross the open plain towards the coast. The winding line of trucks bounced over the bumpy track, towards the town, the leading jeep's headlights flicking up and down over the bleak desert terrain. During the drive, Mike Sadler heard Stirling say,

'We'll never make it unless everyone puts their headlights on. Give the order.'[13]

Almonds was inwardly full of misgivings. If ever an SAS raid was ill-conceived it was this one. If ever an example is needed of what can go badly wrong when SAS raids are not planned by the SAS, this is it.

By the time they reached the outskirts of the town it was almost daybreak. The air raid that had been intended to provide diversionary cover had long since finished. The long low outline of the town with its huddles of whitewashed, still sleeping houses lay ahead of them. Not for the first time, Almonds wondered how on earth he had got himself into his present situation. At that moment he had had enough 'adventure' to last a lifetime. But it was not to be the last time either. As he drove on letting the wheel slip lightly through his fingers to compensate for the dips and ruts in the road, he realised that the churning feeling in his stomach was not fear but hunger. In their haste to reach the target, they had not had time for a proper meal for the last 24 hours.

As the rosy glow behind them on the eastern horizon was spreading up into the desert sky, the leading jeep up ahead came to an abrupt halt. Leaning out, Almonds saw that the convoy had reached a pole roadblock. Stirling and Cumper had got out of the vehicle and appeared to be conferring. They looked at the lump of concrete in which the pole was mounted at one end; then they peered down the track and they looked out from both sides of the road into the still gloomy scrub ahead. It was faintly farcical that the whole of an SAS attack consisting of 200 men and 40 vehicles was being held up by one puny piece of wood, while Stirling and Cumper chatted as if they were considering how to play the next hole on a golf course. Then Stirling straightened up and looked back along the column of vehicles. Mike Sadler saw him call and beckon to Almonds to come out of the line of vehicles and drive up to the head of the column.[14] Stirling probably wanted him to go first because he had the furthest to go to the inner harbour mole to carry out his task of blocking the harbour entrance.

Almonds was now in the leading jeep. In fact there were supposed to be two leading jeeps together but the track was so narrow that they could not drive two abreast and so he went first. His front and rear gunners were Magi McGinn, a small wiry Scot, and a heavyset Irish Guardsman called Fletcher, whom he had never met before. Sitting beside him in the front was an Arab guide, who was supposed to show them the way to the harbour. The man kept his face well hidden and whether or not he understood English made no reply to any communications apart from a nod and a grunt. The road ahead was double lined on both sides with barbed wire. It looked like a classic ambush: there was no turning off point and no turning back either; the track was too narrow to turn round in. Beyond the pole across the road, was another roadblock about 150 yards further on.

Standing beside the barrier, Stirling looked totally lost and suddenly Almonds *knew* that in this situation and through no fault of his own Stirling *was* lost. After a few moments, the native guide decided that this sudden elevation to a leading role was not to his liking. He was only in it for the money and since his night's work now looked decidedly dangerous he suddenly whipped over the side of the vehicle and vanished back the way they had come. Almonds looked at Stirling standing beside him.

'Hello?' he said in surprise. 'What's happened to my guide?'

'Oh,' Stirling said, looking round after the vanishing scout, 'er, he's gone.'

As if pondering this development, they all remained motionless, Stirling standing beside the jeep, Cumper on the other side of the road at the pole barrier, and Almonds at the wheel of his vehicle with his two gunners waiting for the order to go forward. It seemed that Stirling did not know what to do. The enemy had not fired a shot at them so what reason did they have for just turning round and beating a rather ignoble retreat? On the other hand, the two roadblocks and the barbed wire did not look very inviting and they possibly risked losing a considerable number of men and vehicles if they went forward. Nor did they have the option of taking the jeeps in by a different route. They were on the only road into the town; the country was too rough; and the area around the track was almost certainly mined. To abandon the vehicles and go in on foot would mean that they would never get their weapons and explosives to the targets. It was a conundrum.

Perhaps it was the fleeing guide that triggered the next action. Stirling did not know what decision to make so Almonds decided to make it for him. 'Well,' he said, 'I don't know Benghazi, or where I'm going, but I'll give it a go.'

'Good show, well *done*,' said Stirling with genuine warmth. He waved his hand to Bill Cumper standing on the other side of the road, who then raised the pole like a starting gate at the races and with what has since been called his 'Stanley Holloway voice' he made his now famous pronouncement, 'Let battle commence!'

What the enemy thought of this crazy British pantomime is anyone's guess. Immediately, Almonds revved up the jeep and drove very fast through the first roadblock.[15] In a few moments, lurching and bouncing over the dry stony track, they were half way to the second roadblock. But it was not until he *got near to it* that he saw a very thick and heavy chain across the road, stretched between two massive blocks of concrete. It was to deal with such eventualities that they had originally had the two tanks that had been abandoned so many desert miles ago. He realised that he could not drive through the roadblock, which risked a fearful accident, but at the same time to stop, get out and try to open it was certain death. He was never to know which of these two dreadful options he would have chosen. Just before he reached the roadblock, the track was suddenly bathed in light and all hell broke loose. A crescendo of fire came from all along both sides of the track in front of them. Fortunately, the enemy's aim was not very good. Possibly, out of caution, they were some way away from their target. From the front, McGinn immediately gave them hell back with the twin Vickers, sweeping an arc of bullets at twelve hundred rounds per minute across the track in front of him and on either side towards the areas behind the barbed wire. But their jeep was packed with explosives. It was only a matter of time before it blew up. They had to get out and fast.

'Magi!' Almonds shouted, 'Go on back! We're not going anywhere, so go on back!'

McGinn immediately baled out over the rear of the jeep, back towards the already retreating SAS. Almonds was gratified to catch one fleeting glimpse of the nimble Scot ducking and weaving up the lane. Fletcher had already launched himself off the truck to the left and was ripping his way through under the murderous double barbed wire at the side of the road. Almonds then jumped clear and went off under the barbed wire after him. Further back up the lane, Fitzroy Maclean watched with horror as the jeep was hit in the petrol tank and burst into flames[16]. Almonds had got clear just minutes before it went up. In the face of such destruction, it is not surprising that the SAS remainder later thought that Almonds had either been killed or was seriously wounded.[17] Back behind them, Paddy Mayne gave the order to withdraw. But, too late, the first jeep had already passed the point of no return.

Had Stirling been ordered by MEHQ and ISLD to make a full attack, or merely a feint for one? If he was supposed to have pulled his punch at the last minute, then he had no need to send anyone through the first roadblock. On the other hand, if he did not intend to go any further, why did he call Almonds up to the front? Was it because he wanted someone who, when the chips were down, would do what he was asked? The ISLD may not of course have allowed Stirling to have the whole story. Considerable 'off-the-cuffery' prevailed in SAS desert operations and cock-up theory may be more appropriate than conspiracy.[18] Stirling's official report on the raid simply states

> ... it remained impossible to locate the exact position of the enemy posts, and the two leading Bantams [jeeps] were soon put out of action, not however before Sergeant Almonds, who was in the left hand leading Bantam [before they had reached the road block], had penetrated well into the enemy position. He was last seen vigorously returning enemy fire.[19]

On seeing his CO's real or perceived dilemma, Almonds had felt compelled to act on his own initiative. If Stirling was supposed to pull back at the last minute, Almonds may unwittingly, have provided a better feint than MI6 could ever have hoped for. What is certain is that for the rest of his life the Benghazi raid bothered David Stirling. Whenever he and Almonds met up at SAS reunions or on visits to France, before too long he (Stirling) would turn the talk to that momentous night and end up by apologising. This only goes to show his basic decency. The Army too concluded that there were lessons to be learned from the failure of Benghazi.[20]

As battle was joined and his jeep was blowing up, Almonds rolled over in the bottom of the ditch on the other side of the barbed wire and came to a stop. He looked up and saw that Fletcher was trying to hide in a small patch of shade afforded by some young saplings, for by now the sun was just up and shining weakly. Behind them, the jeep was providing the bonfire display to end all bonfire displays and for the moment the enemy were temporarily distracted by it. For a while the two men lay low to avoid being caught in the crossfire between the Italians and the retreating SAS vehicles that they could see were still turning round. Gradually, the shooting subsided. They found themselves in an open area about the size of a football pitch with an Italian barracks behind them and no cover at all except for the few trees. Advancing towards them was an Italian officer and about twenty men in extended order (a widely spaced row of men three ranks deep). As they came forward they prodded the ground with fixed bayonets, searching for any survivors. It was only a matter of time before the SAS men were seen and the manhunt would begin in earnest.

The two fugitives kept moving and hiding from the line of advancing men. Finally they lay in a dark patch under a tree. All the time it was getting lighter as the sun rose higher and the shadows shortened. Almonds realised that in the end they would be bayoneted or shot. The idea of being captured though went very much against the grain. He had a pistol but given the odds he reasoned that they were better off alive, with the chance to fight another day, than dead.

'Fletcher', he hissed, as the Italians grew nearer, swishing the sparse brush with their bayonets. 'I don't think we've got much of a chance here. I think our best chance is to stand up and give ourselves up. What do you think?'

'Yeah, OK,' came the whispered reply. Almonds waited until the Italians were almost upon them. Then he stood up to show himself.

'OK. Here we are,' he said simply, keeping very still with both hands high above his head. Immediately, the soldiers closed in on him, with every rifle pointing at his chest. As Fletcher also slowly stood up, the rifles swung wildly as the soldiers looked in all directions in case more prisoners should emerge. It was clear that their hunters' blood was up and they closed in again around the two Allied soldiers with whoops of triumph. Immediately, the Italian officer ran forward and stepping quickly between them and the two SAS, he pushing their rifles up with his arm. Their first few moments of captivity were utter confusion as the Italian gave his men a tongue-lashing, waving his arms and shaking his fist at them. Still yelling, he motioned both prisoners and soldiers towards the barracks.[21]

It was broad daylight. The fleeing SAS were so close to the aerodrome that they could see the 'planes taking off to come and attack them, CR42s that in the slight haze could have been mistaken for Gloucester Gladiator biplanes.[22] They had to make their way back across the plain and get up onto the Jebel before they could hope to take cover from the air attack. Their base was hidden in a valley that ran back up into the Jebel. But before they reached it, the Italians had found the encampment and the heavy vehicles. They shot everything up, set the vehicles ablaze and before long the base camp too was on fire.

The enemy also scored some hits on the retreating jeeps. Soon, there were so few vehicles that they had to travel about six men to each jeep. And the enemy was not their only problem. The stress and the danger began to reveal the lack of experience and training among one or two of the young officers. One man who was seriously injured was an ex-Commando Almonds had greatly admired, Corporal Drongin. He was a loyal friend and a very good soldier. Bob Bennett later reported that while Drongin lay in the back of a vehicle, one of the young officers who wanted him moved said to Bennett in a rather high-handed way, 'Right now, come along there. Get that man off the truck!' At which the wounded man, raised himself on one elbow and with a supreme effort said, 'Corporal Drongin to you sir,' before falling back exhausted. Not long afterwards, he was dead.[23]

The two SAS prisoners of war were taken to the barracks in Benghazi There they were kept confined with both hands shackled down to one ankle. After a while, just being kept in this position became agonising. Almonds could neither sit nor lie properly and the pain in his back muscles became excruciating. From time to time, he and Fletcher were separated, still shackled, for interrogation. In Almonds's case, there was a good deal of threatening, with fists being shaken in his face and weapons brandished. He retreated into himself, remembering all the escape and evasion exercises he had carried out while in training, glad of the purpose they had served. Even the occasion when he had been run around the old moat as a defaulter at the Tower of London, for some minor uniform infringement, now seemed to stand him in good stead. He had always been able to say to himself that he would be able to keep going long after the drill sergeant had given up. The Italians had quite a bit of fun at his expense but apart from jabbing him in the ribs with their bayonets without quite breaking the skin they did not physically ill-treat him. However, they were furious when he wouldn't talk.

They tried other methods. The next day, he was taken out, put in the back of an open truck and made to kneel down, still with both hands shackled to one ankle. At first, he thought he was being taken out to be executed. But instead he was joined by three Italian Carabinieri who kept their loaded rifles pointing at his head. Still kneeling in the back of the truck, he was towed slowly around the town, while the local populace jeered and spat and threw rubbish at him. He was the star exhibit in a 'tableau', the purpose of which was to show the local population how they could rely on Axis protection against the Allied attackers. And all the time, he did not know if at the end of this circus there would be a bullet in the back of the head.

Of course, this treatment was entirely contrary to the Geneva Conventions, which included amongst their provisions that belligerents in war must treat prisoners of war humanely and forbade outrages upon personal dignity and torture of any kind, whether physical or mental.[24] Almonds never spoke of this experience at the hands of the Italian military until many years after the war. One day in Ghana in the late fifties, there was some discussion about Benghazi and the Italian soldiers during the war and Lockie heard him say: 'Oh yes. Nice people; they put you in a cart and tow you round the town as a sideshow.' That was the first she knew of it, nearly twenty years after the event.

After being taken back to the barracks, he was put into a tiny shed inside another compound, still shackled, with other POWs. He was filthy and exhausted but mightily relieved at being with the other prisoners. While he was imprisoned separately there was always the risk of being taken out and summarily executed.

The other POWs were mostly Navy, RAF and marines. The main topic of conversation was that they were all likely to be taken to Italy. Almonds was by now extremely hungry since it was some 48 hours since he had had anything to eat. An Italian officer interrogating him noticed his condition and suggested that he might like some food and a bath. Almonds readily agreed that that would indeed be very pleasant and his captors duly gave him a meal and allowed him to have a bath. They were then absolutely incensed when he still refused to say anything. According to their rules of the game, he should have spilled the beans. The separate interrogations continued while the questioning tactics varied. He was not physically ill-treated but the mental and emotional stress he was to suffer began to tell the longer he stayed in captivity. Fletcher had not had to suffer being towed round the town, but then he had not had the meal or the bath either.

After a few days, he had to contend with rather different interrogation tricks of the enemy. A new 'prisoner' joined them. The man had a Scottish accent and claimed to be in the Cameron Highlanders. He was extremely friendly, readily volunteering information about himself, and seemed to expect his new-found friend to do the same. But Almonds instinctively did not trust the man. He was very dark, with a very olive skin and could have been a Scottish Italian who for whatever reason may have been persuaded to change sides. The SAS sergeant remained silent.

It was some weeks before Lockie received a very small brown envelope, as her father said, 'A bit like an electricity bill really.' It contained a formal notification from War Office that Almonds was missing in action and that she would receive any further news of him as it became available.

'*Any* further news?' she said to her mother, 'Does that mean I may *never ever* hear anything more of him?' Many of her friends who had lost husbands had received a letter that said, with an understatement that only War Office 'officialese' could manage, 'missing, *presumed* killed'. She tried to comfort herself that since those words had not been added, there must be some chance that he was alive.

For the sake of my brother, who was just coming up to two years old, she tried to be cheerful during the days that followed. Nevertheless, she was devastated. She could not eat or sleep properly. She could not stop herself from imagining what had happened to him, where he was, whether he was wounded, being ill-treated, sick, starving and a thousand other fates that could have befallen him. One night she would dream that he had lost a leg, or an arm. Another night she would imagine that he had come back blinded. She tried to imagine how they would cope if he came back to her maimed or 'shell shocked', a malady about which there was much talk and which seemed to cover a multitude of disabling and depersonalising horrors.

She kept an early morning vigil for the post woman. Sometimes, when there was no letter, she wanted to rush out as the girl went down the path and throttle the life out of her until she told her where her husband was. Again, the war had made her powerless. She could not remember what it had been like to be happy and life normal. With her parents, she kept a stiff upper lip because she did not want them to see her agony. But they knew and for the rest of their lives she never forgot and never stopped saying what a support they had been to her during those terrible dark days.

About a week after his capture, Almonds was again separated from the others. By now he was fairly sure that the Italians knew that he was SAS. He was put into the forepeak of a ship, where he found that one of his 'shipmates' was Merlin Craw. He had been captured in the raid on Barce aerodrome on the night of 13/14 September but only after successfully planting twelve bombs on his target 'planes. Travelling in the last truck, Craw had been detailed to place short-delay bombs on any aircraft that had not been burnt by small arms fire. He had been equipped with thirteen bombs but one fuse was defective so he put his last two bombs on one plane with a shared fuse. To quote the citation for his immediate Military Medal:

> He carried out this task at great personal risk, as aircraft were on fire and blowing up all around him, and destroyed eight enemy aircraft single-handed. As an NCO, he has always done extremely good work and in action is cool and confident.[25]

Unlike the Benghazi effort, the Barce raid had been very effective and had succeeded in blowing up thirty-five 'planes.

Merlyn was about twenty-eight years old and a real 'go ahead' optimist. A big fair-haired chap, with an open friendly face, his talk was of his farming life back in New Zealand, a life he clearly had every intention of getting back to. Sharing their confinement was Tom 'Aussie' Wilkinson, an Australian from New South Wales who had been taken prisoner at Tobruk. He was a carpenter by trade who had joined the Royal Marine Commandos and was serving on one of the destroyers.[26] A big, heavy and very tough character in his late twenties, he had determination stamped all over him. Unlike Almonds and Craw, Wilkinson was not married. But he had left his mother running the family fruit-canning business and talked as often of her as the others did about their wives. These men were known as the 'bad boy' prisoners and the enemy had wisely decided to keep these likely troublemakers in close confinement.

Once again, Almonds was to go to sea – destination unknown.

Chapter Eleven

Living with the Enemy

The prospect of being deported by the enemy did nothing to dampen Almonds's usual curiosity about his environment. The forepeak in which he was imprisoned was well below decks and in fact not far above the bilges. The ship had clearly been bombed at some stage and the holes nearest the water line had been plugged by makeshift wooden bungs. By removing one of these and enlarging the jagged bomb splinter hole in the bulwark of the ship, he soon made himself a little peephole from which he had at least a partial view of the world.[1]

But before the ship left harbour, the POWs underwent their last 'softening up' interrogation. While not exactly questioning as such, it was very unpleasant and was definitely designed to put the captives in a co-operative frame of mind. There were no latrines other than a row of holes in a wooden frame arranged high up over the ship's side facing toward the docks. So, if the prisoners were not to foul their living area, they were forced to use these (very public) conveniences to the ridicule of all people in the harbour. At the time Almonds was not counting, but this was the third breach of the Geneva Conventions.[2]

A couple of days later, very early in the morning, he awoke from a fitful sleep to the sound of a general hubbub. Engines were throbbing, instructions were being shouted and there was the sound of scurrying feet on the decks above. Through his peephole, he watched with one eye as the forward lines were cast off. Slowly, the ship turned and headed out into the Mediterranean, first in a north-westerly direction until she was well out from the coast and then swinging round she set a course due north-east. They were on the way to Italy. At that period of the war, the Mediterranean was being heavily bombed as the Axis forces struggled to prevent the island of Malta from being used as a supply point for the Allies. Almonds therefore reckoned that the ship would hug the North African coast and comparative safety. He hoped too that they would not be at risk of being bombed by the Allies, for it would not do for them be sunk by their own side and drowned like rats in a barrel. He thought of Ernie Bond and Mike Sadler and how many times both had told him,

'Don't worry about the enemy; it's the RAF we need to watch out for!'

From his limited vantage point on one side of the bows, Almonds could not tell how far they were from land but after a few days he saw lush green shores with hills and mountains rising in the background. The land was so close and the slope of the hills so steep that he thought the ship must be passing through some sort of straits. By the time of day and the angle of the sun, he judged that they were travelling north-east. The sea was an idyllic blue and before long he could see small islands – the Greek islands. Towards evening, the boat rounded a promontory to starboard and turned sharply north-west. They were in the Gulf of Saronikos and approaching the entrance to the Corinth Canal. By this circuitous route, the Italians had avoided enemy attack and would only have to make the short crossing from Greece across the Ionian Sea to Italy.[3]

The next morning, they were one of a series of ships queuing to pass through the tidal waterway at the isthmus between Corinth and the rest of the Greek mainland. When it was their turn to begin slipping through the canal, Almonds was glued to his peephole. The steep sides of the canal, which appeared to have been cut out of the solid rock, towered high overhead, at times blocking out the sunlight. Although he had heard of the Corinth Canal, he had had no idea that it was so narrow. From the distance he could see from his peephole to his side of the canal, he thought it must be about 80 feet wide in all. The ship was going forward very slowly but from the estimated speed and time it took to pass through he thought the waterway must be about 3½ to 4 miles long (or just over six kilometres). For a while, the war was forgotten as he admired the canal. It truly was a work of art and engineering. Late that afternoon, they emerged from the canal into the Gulf of Corinth and sailed on, now westward to Patras. Without further delay, they sailed again on the late evening tide and docked the next morning at Taranto, Italy. All was very beautiful and peaceful as they sailed through the narrow walls of a brick-walled channel at the harbour entrance where several warships were moored.

On the jetty, they all had their hair shorn and were completely unrecognisable to each other. Looking like a bunch of 'boot camp' recruits, the new arrivals were then loaded into open trucks without seats and taken to a POW transit camp in Altamura in the province of Bari. This was *Campo* No. 51. A winding ribbon of road connected it to another camp, Altamura Camp No. 65 at Gravina. *Campo* No. 51 was fairly newly built of long low wooden huts and laid out rather like a village. From what could be seen of it, the surrounding country looked rather like rough moorland. Altogether, it was a depressing sight for the new arrivals, who had no idea how long they would be forced to live in this forbidding place.[4]

First impressions were totally borne out by experience. Surviving in the camp was a terrible ordeal. By now, it was late September and even at that latitude the nights were beginning to get cold. In their undernourished state they felt it more. The POWs were forced to live out of doors and to add to their discomforts, the ground was so rocky and hard that it was impossible to 'dig in' or level out the bumps underneath them. The Italians gave them groundsheets, which they buttoned together and stretched over low wooden frames to rig up low-slung bivouacs, but these offered little protection against the elements. The weather was also unusually harsh for that time of year. It rained steadily for days on end and it was impossible to prevent the water from pouring into their palliasses.

In the camp, Almonds, Merlin Craw and 'Aussie' Wilkinson, met Jan Folscher, a former South-West African mounted policeman in the BSAP – the British South African Police. Folscher was a big raw-boned man of German extraction. In his late twenties, with flaming red hair, he was naturally nick-named 'Ginger'. He had been captured when Tobruk, which was then being held by the South Africans, had fallen to Rommel in June. He and the South African POWs had arrived by all accounts with everything except their rifles. Folscher had been left behind in the transit camp when the previous occupants had been moved on, some to Germany and some to work in the copper mines in southern Italy. His job was to welcome in the new 'intake'. Apart from taking an instinctive liking to Folscher, Almonds cultivated the acquaintance because Folscher knew the ropes, could speak Italian and German and was moderately trusted by their captors.

Life in the camp was appalling. Rations were very low. The prisoners' diet was also very deficient in salt because there was a shortage in Italy at that time. Mussolini had taxed it and had forbidden the extraction of salt from the sea. Their daily menu consisted of nothing for breakfast and for lunch a bread roll small enough to disappear into the palm of the hand, together with a tiny cube of cheese. In the evening, there was a small bowl of watery soup made from boiled mangolds with some penne pasta. This menu was the same every day except for Saturdays and Sundays when the soup was supposed to be made from meat. It was so rare even to see a speck of meat that a great cheer went up whenever anyone found a bit in their bowl. However, their guards were not much better off. They appeared to have only a piece of bread to nibble at midday and they too had no breakfast so they were more or less the same as the prisoners – except that the prisoners had the Red Cross parcels. In fact, these Red Cross parcels literally saved lives.[5] Years later when I was a little girl, I can remember that whenever a Red Cross collecting box came around my father always gave most generously. He knew the value of their work.

All the Red Cross parcels had to be opened to prevent hoarding or the laying-in of stores in preparation for escape, but most prisoners teamed up and developed a paired arrangement for sharing a perishable item from one parcel for a perishable item from another. One of the most treasured items was the delectable tinned condensed milk. Although the men trusted each other at one level, this condensed milk was an incredible temptation. Once a man started tasting it, it was so difficult to resist that by mutual agreement if one of the two had to go away to work etc. they would leave a little dipstick in the milk so that they could see whether any had been taken or not. In spite of their deprivations, the thinking prisoners used some of their precious condensed milk, chocolate, coffee or soap for 'chumming up' the guards. But it was usually preceded by quite an inward struggle as to whether or not to sacrifice it in this way.[6]

The enforced lack of hygiene also took its toll. There were outside cold water taps but no soap – soap from the parcels was very scarce and highly sought after. Their heads were kept shorn but body lice were a terrible and constant scourge. These were not just a nuisance but a real health hazard. Just to keep the numbers of lice under control, it was necessary to spend a considerable part of one's day systematically going down all the seams of each garment where the parasites used to hide when their 'host' was not asleep. When caught, they then had to be killed by cracking them between the thumbnails otherwise they would just jump aboard again. One man eventually became so distressed about not being able to keep the upper hand over his lice and then so depressed that he took to his bed and just gave up the struggle. He would not do anything for himself and in the end he died.

The battle for cleanliness, like the battle for survival itself, came down to a personal decision about attitude. The Sikhs in the camp were marvellous at keeping up their morale, fitness and even their hygiene. They would be up in the morning while it was still dark, washing under the cold outside taps and meticulously going through their clothing to remove all lice. They also had a first class Regimental Sergeant Major who really stood up to the Italians. He insisted that he had an extra blanket for each of his men and even when the Italians refused he kept on making his demands. They threatened him with punishments and even with being shot but he kept on until in the end he got his blankets. He also insisted that they must have fresh meat that they killed themselves and that it had to be goat. After a few months, he even got that for them too. So each man had to keep up his fitness of body and mind in his own way.[7] As winter arrived, conditions worsened. Snow fell and when it melted it ran down between their makeshift tents. The low rations became a starvation diet. Malnutrition, TB and other illness stalked the camp. There were no POW officers with them except for some RAMC Medical Officers. However, all the time Almonds was there he was not seen by any doctor, nor was there any system for carrying out the most basic medical inspections of all the men, not even a preliminary check on admittance. One other SAS man who had been captured earlier developed what seemed to be severe bronchitis and one night he just died there where he lay in the damp and cold. No doubt he did not realise how very ill he was and nor did those around him. Alan Nutt began to suffer from severe dysentery until Merlyn persuaded the guards to allow him to have some plain boiled rice, which seemed to help his stomach to settle down. However, diet and illness could be very confusing. One young nineteen-year-old seemed to be getting fatter and fatter so Merlyn thought he must have a secret supply of food but actually he had beriberi and before long he died as well.[8]

These deaths really affected Almonds. When he saw how easily these very fit men had become ill and just slipped quietly away, he was determined to stay physically and mentally fit. He thought constantly of escape and resolved to get away at the first opportunity. Round and round the perimeter fence he paced. He never went too close to it for fear of alerting the attention of the guards. But all the time he was estimating the distance to it, the height of it, how far up it he would have to run before he could get his hands on to the top and how long he would have before they started shooting at him. He came to the conclusion that he could do it *if* he could be sure that his feet would not slip on the fencing. He thought of all the times he had achieved such a feat running up the school yard fence in his boyhood, but then he had not had someone waiting to shoot him if he failed.

When he was not thinking about escape, he tried other ways to keep his mind occupied. He longed for something to read. Pleydell had leant him

H. G. Wells's *The Short History of the World*, which he was in the middle of reading before the Benghazi raid, and he missed it very much. It occurred to him that if the opportunity arose he would get hold of a Bible because they sometimes had maps in them. Jan Folscher used to talk endlessly about the wealth of the cocoa veldt. In South Africa, the barbed wired diamond reserves had to be policed to keep people *out* because the diamonds could even be found lying on the surface. He was always busy 'recruiting' fellow POWs into a scheme to get back into diamond mining as a living. Innovation also abounded. Occasionally, Almonds would come across a scruffy bearded group discussing how to make a cake with the contents of their Red Cross parcels. And by taking the top off a Red Cross Klim milk tin and rigging up a handle with the pocket out of a pair of trousers, it was possible to use the resulting 'billy' to make tea. There were a great many pairs of trousers in that camp with no pockets, but then the prisoners had precious little to put in them anyway.[9]

It was in mid-October, just after her twentieth birthday, that Lockie received a second small brown envelope notifying her that her husband was a POW. Having seen a 'Movie Tone' News film about life in the POW camps, which of course was about German POW camps, she was relieved to learn that he would apparently now be enjoying a good life and singsongs. She thought that all the danger was over and he would stay safely put until the end of the war. She should have known him better.

The Joint Council of the Order of St John issued a map of all known POW camps in Europe free to the next of kin. From this, my mother could see that the camp where my father was, not far from Taranto, was PG 51 (Altamura). His first POW letter gave details of what he could be sent and said that the Red Cross arranged parcels.[10] He could not say very much in the letter because he was now subject to an Italian censor, but she was used to that. However, she spent some time puzzling over the wording, which evidently had to be read 'between the lines'. He asked for a warm sweater. 'I need a good thick one,' she read. 'It's freezing cold here. And as for colour, well make it so that I'll know when washday comes around.' He was thinking of a white one for camouflage against the snow-covered Italian mountains. But the rules that the British Red Cross had sent her stated very clearly that any clothing she sent had to be khaki. She only had disposable income of £2.10s a week and so could not afford to send him very much. But then, oh joy! She won £5 – a considerable sum in 1942 – in a magazine fashion competition (she had excellent taste in clothes and always looked beautiful). She was able to buy warm vests and underclothes to send, along with one long-sleeved polo-necked pullover, in the regulation khaki. It was an incredible relief that at last there was something she could *do* for him.[11]

Life in the camp was very grim. It was constantly stated that there had never been a successful escape and this did not do much for morale. Nevertheless, Almonds's group continued to speculate about how they could get out. But they had to be very careful about these discussions. There was another suspected 'watcher' who seemed odd and kept asking a lot of questions. He was probably in the employ of the enemy. Then there was also the 'Italian Scotsman' POW, who had accompanied them from Benghazi. He continued to press his unwanted attentions and Almonds later reported him to the authorities. To this day, there is a file at the National Archives which was to have remained closed until 2020 but was released in 1972. The only piece of paper in the file is a one page Appendix to a letter dated 7 September 1943 from a Lieutenant Colonel GS, A.C. Simmonds, to a Captain F. P. Falvey. Under a heading, 'Personalities', it reads

> Watch out for [still censored], of the Cameron Highlanders, probably a stool pigeon.

The censored name is asterisked to a footnote 'deletion retained under section 5(i) of 'the Act'.[12] If this person is still living, he is now in his nineties.

Alan Nutt became so ill that he had to be moved to a hospital. He had also been captured after the raid on Barce aerodrome. The day before the raid, an Allied spotter 'plane had flown over and sighted numerous 'planes on the airfield, mostly Italian, and some German. Nutt's patrol had been sent in to destroy them but it was sighted on the outskirts of Barce. As Nutt put it:

> We had to get in somewhere handy to raid the airport. It ended up that we attacked at about 11 o'clock at night and we had to fight our way in. Each person was responsible for each of his bombs. We went on to the Barce airport and it was like fairyland. We had to do it with the ten minute bombs as we were getting sniper fire from round about but to cut the whole thing short we were credited with the destruction of thirty-two planes on the ground that night, 13/14 September 1942.[13]

Being in hospital was no picnic either. By now, Nutt knew that he had tuberculosis as well as dysentery. He was quite literally carted off to hospital behind an old dray. However, the change of scenery did not mean that he got any treatment. He had no medication and nothing to relieve his pain. The hospital was run by black-habited nuns. 'What's your religion pal?' said the man in the bed next to him. Nutt could see that the other chap was a POW. Before he could answer, some ministering nuns arrived and the man hurriedly whispered, 'Whatever you are, you'd better be an RC (Roman Catholic) in here and start crossing yourself, otherwise you'll get nothing.'

Whenever a prisoner died, the nuns would bring a tiny piece of cake on a saucer to the bedside. The prisoners used to say that the fittest was the first out of bed to get the cake! The 'nurses' would even take things from the sick and dying men, especially soap and chocolates. Nutt's verdict on them was that 'They were a right pack of bastards.'[14]

Almonds was fortunate in still having men like Merlyn Craw, Aussie Wilkinson and Johann Folscher around him. These three thought that their British colleague had had more training and experience from his Guards Commando and SAS escapades than the rest of them, so he was duly 'elected' leader of their small escape committee. It began by engineering themselves into a suitable position on the inside. Soon, Almonds and Folscher managed to get onto the working party that received and unpacked the Red Cross parcels. Gradually, as 'vacancies' occurred, they arranged for Craw and Wilkinson to be co-opted onto it as well.[15]

It did not take Almonds long to work out a plan of escape but then they had to prepare. It was going to be very difficult to save food. Every item of rations that arrived in the Red Cross parcels had to be publicly opened. He and Folscher would stand behind the big bench where the parcels were unpacked, solemnly raise their metal spikes on high and puncture every article, even the tins of milk and cheese. This was done precisely to prevent hoarding for the purposes of escape. However, Almonds began to save the little pieces of string from the parcels. It was time to deploy his old rope-making skills again. Slowly and very patiently he started to splice the little bits of string into bigger pieces of twine, then into cords and then into a rope that might come in handy for tying up their guards. He made one end of the rope into a lasso, which he intended to use to pinion the arms of the overpowered sentry. Merlyn Craw, using his LRDG techniques, carefully 'blew up' a small map that Almonds had torn out of a Bible. A visiting priest had left one unattended for just thirty seconds too long. Craw then 'extended' it onto an opened out piece of canvas which was a traditional square of material wrapped around the foot and used as socks by the Italian soldiers. These preparations helped to give purpose to their dreary prison life.[16]

Chapter Twelve

'Empire' Effort

In England, a short entry appeared in the *Supplement to the London Gazette* of Tuesday 24 November 1942:

> War Office, 26th November 1942
> The Military Medal
> The King has been graciously pleased to approve the following award in recognition of gallant and distinguished services in the field:-
>
> No. 2655648 Sergeant John Edward Almonds, Coldstream Guards.

For once, David Stirling had got round to doing some admin.

Towards Christmas, the POWs started to work outside the camp. Whenever the Red Cross parcel deliveries arrived, a working party had to go out to collect them. Almonds now had a smattering of Italian and with Jan Folscher's fluency and good relations with the guards they managed to get their group allocated to the task. For the first time, in addition to their plans and improvised map, they began to have opportunities, albeit fleeting and under surveillance, for a real escape. They decided to work on several prepared 'scenarios' of delaying tactics, all with the purpose of prolonging their return to camp until after dark. But they needed to engineer both lateness, so as to be able to escape under cover of night, *and* some ruse to separate their captors so that they could deal with them one by one.[1]

Whenever they were alone, they discussed and planned their escape. It was a microcosm of an SAS-style operation based on a group of four, each with their different skills and strengths. Almonds had the military training, intelligence and operational ability to plan an escape and put it into effect. Jan Folscher had excellent language skills, including mother tongue German as well as Italian and English. He also had 'local' knowledge of the Italians and their systems. Merlyn Craw was an LRDG-trained navigator who was tough, energetic and a total pragmatist when it came to doing the necessary. Aussie Wilkinson was a carpenter in the Navy. He therefore knew about ships, and putting to sea if they needed to, and he had a wealth of practical skills.

In charge of their daily work detail was an Italian officer, Lieutenant Tinenti Mikeli of the Bersciglieri Regiment. This was one of the 'crack' Alpine Regiments and he wore a splendid headgear richly adorned with feathers. Working for him was a C*aparalli* and a private soldier, '*Dragonetti*'. Somehow, these three would have to be dealt with effectively but humanely and, above all *quietly* because directly above the shed where they worked was the Italian Officers' Mess. This was a splendid mansion just outside the camp that had been commandeered by the military.

The four would-be escapees knew that the time for breakout had come when they heard, through their guards' careless talk, news of a Allied landing in Sicily. When the first opportunity and the right conditions presented themselves, they would make a break for it. But the weeks dragged slowly by, made worse by having to suffer very bad winter weather.[2]

Their patience was rewarded and on 4 February 1943 the moment came. In a sort of 'Empire' effort, Almonds, Jan Folscher, Tom Wilkinson and Merlin Craw broke out of the camp. They had gone out to work as usual and spent the day outside the compound opening the parcels. As usual, Mikeli was in charge, accompanied by the Caparalli and the Dragonetti. By now, a great many parcels were being received and it was necessary to organize the stacking and repackaging of the empty boxes so that they could be returned to the Red Cross in Switzerland. The unpacking of parcels had now also been got down to a fine art so that similar items were unpacked and collected together for easier distribution.

As the normal time to return to camp approached, Merlyn and Aussie began to 'play for time' by rolling around big bales filled with the contents of parcels, such as clothing, under the pretence that all these unpacked items needed to be properly organized, otherwise they would not be able to distribute them to the rightful owners when the time came. Just before it began to get dark, Almonds looked across the bench at Folscher and gave a barely perceptible nod. Folscher looked at Mikeli.

'You want coffee?' he said winningly. Mikeli started and then stiffened slightly. He looked around. Almonds was deliberately lifting up his large spike, stabbing it down into the parcels and passing the ripped open boxes along to Aussie Wilkinson. The Australian was busying himself taking out the contents. The Italian thought for a moment. Real coffee was only available from the parcels; the Italians did not have any. 'Eh…Grazzia', he said rather stiffly. It was always difficult for the captors to maintain proper 'face' and dignity while at the same time demeaning themselves to accept small luxuries from the hands of their prisoners. On this occasion, Mikeli could not resist the thought of some freshly made coffee. Then he looked outside. 'But,....' He looked at Folscher and tapped his watch meaningfully. 'Si, si,' said Folscher cheerily, 'Is OK; is OK. Uno momento'. But then, oh dear, there was no water. So Dragonetti was sent off to get some. Then Jan Folscher said that there really were an enormous number of empty boxes that needed to be shipped back to Geneva and he took Mikeli outside to show him. That left the Caparalli standing in the doorway surveying the scene with his back to them … Almonds stepped quickly and noiselessly up behind the Italian, put one arm around his neck and mouth and with the other twisted and pinioned his enemy's arms behind his back. Conscious of the Officers' Mess above, he suggested in low urgent tones that if the Caparalli wanted to stay in one piece he should keep very, very quiet. After gagging his captive, he put the noose made from parcel string around his shoulders and fastened his arms behind him before stowing him away in the corner. With what turned out to be perfect timing, Dragonnetti then reappeared, all unsuspecting, with the water. The look of happy anticipation on his face (he was hoping to get some of the coffee) froze. Slowly, it changed to a look of terror. His eyes darted from Almonds, to Craw, to Wilkinson and back again. He did not seem to notice his corporal tied up like a parcel on the floor. In a split second, he too was quickly overpowered, gagged and tied up. He put up barely a token resistance.

No sooner had this been done than, just like a well-rehearsed West End play, Folscher walked in with Mikeli. Everyone immediately flew at him and he got the same unceremonious treatment. But by now it was getting quite dark. Inside, in the gloom of the unlit hut, the four escapees could not really see what they were doing. The struggling continued for several minutes while the only sound in that small place was of desperate scuffling, heavy breathing and Mikeli's muffled attempted shouts. In their endeavours to ensure that not a sound was made, the gropings in the gathering gloom became farcical. A huge hand was clapped over Almonds's mouth. 'That's me you fool!' he whispered hoarsely as soon as he could free a hand to prise it away. The four dealing with the Italian had ended up trying to muzzle and gag each other! Finally, Almonds managed to reach Mikeli's officer's pistol. He carefully removed it and put it away up on a high shelf.

'*Right*', he thought, *'that's got that up out of the way where it can't do any harm.'*

Having got Mikeli under control, they took off his shoes and used his own linen foot cloths as extra gags, an unforgivable dent to his *amour-propre*. The desperadoes then quickly helped themselves to the pick of the Red Cross parcels. Shoving everything they could lay their hands on into a sack, they put their escape plan into action. Above them, rooms with windows overlooked their main avenue of escape so they had to get out to the side of the building. Having got safely out, they dodged through some ornamental shrubs to the perimeter wall a few yards away. In a matter of minutes, they had helped each other up and over. Once away, they knew that they had to cover 18 miles overnight to reach the nearest cover. The only danger then was being discovered before nightfall. They were the first ever to succeed in breaking out of the camp.[3]

At daybreak, they came to an area of sparse bushes with cows grazing the short grass in between. The fugitives split up and hid, inserting themselves each into a separate thorn bush. An inquisitive terrier dog came periodically and stared, amazed, at Almonds in the middle of his bush. He stared back at it without moving a muscle. Puzzled, the dog kept returning. Its owners were nearby but it did not bark. At dusk, without having had any sleep, they moved on. The next evening, they chose a prominent spreading bush to sit in. In the gathering dark it was safe to light a fire but they had no water. By this time, they were very thirsty. Almonds crept out of the bush and, with many glances back behind him so that he would be able to find the bush again, he eventually came to a muddy cart track. He found some puddles and spent some time carefully scooping up the water. It was then very dark and he could not see his way back to the bush. He decided to stay put and woke up with his battle dress frozen stiff. In the early dawn he spotted the prominent bush and headed towards it. They brewed up and had some tea. As their fire was dying down, a man came by and shouted, 'Eh, Boscali! Boscali!'[4] But they made no reply and he did not probe any further.

The four were aiming for the Gulf of Taranto, and followed the coast southwards. They were assuming that the Allies would work their way up Italy, which in fact they did not. The weather was appalling and they were soaked through in the icy rain and sleet. They had to keep to the mountains so as to avoid detection but it also at least doubled the distance they had to cover. The hills were made of clay and this made the going even harder. The first 'casualty' was the bag of rations with all the unperishable goods that they had take from the Red Cross parcels. The bag was quite heavy so they took turns to carry it. But as the going was steeply uphill, the bag was pushed forward first and then half leant on so that it got used to climb with. Gradually, the contents were mashed together. They had even taken soap with them from the parcels and soon it was studded with raisins and tea leaves. In the end, after eating biscuits that made them froth at the mouth, they had to abandon the inedible sludge that was left.[5]

They continued to trudge through snow and wade rivers in the freezing cold as they made their way to the coast. Toiling up the next hill usually warmed them up again. Once, close to shore, they saw a sentry box, just too late. The lone occupant shouted at them, 'Qui va là?'

They quickly escaped by crossing another stream. Later they discovered that this sentry and various other people had reported their whereabouts to the Italian authorities. Hunger became impossible to ignore and they resorted to living off the land. They tried eating raw nettles and at night they dug up some planted broad beans. Almonds found that once he had his finger in the soil at the right angle, he could whip it along the row like a plough turning back a furrow and up would come the beans. He thoughtfully swept the earth loosely back over the small trench and wondered what the farmer would make of it when in due course no beans came up. At a hut in the hills they found some very old hard broad beans in a tin and tried to eat them uncooked.

They were down to their last cigarette. In the teeth of a howling gale, it proved impossible to light it until they found an old hollow tree. Through a hole in the side of the trunk, they took turns to insert their head and arms and smoke the cigarette.

The next day, without any warning, they bumped into a group of charcoal makers. With admirable quick thinking, Ginger Folscher spoke volubly to them in Italian, explaining that they were looking for escaped POWs and offering them a reward if they could give any clues as to their whereabouts. The Italians were unable to help and the escapees went on their way. By now, they had been out of the camp for two weeks. It had rained, snowed or sleeted for thirteen out of the fourteen nights they had been out. Almonds was going well but before long it became clear that Aussie had very bad bronchitis, if not pneumonia.[6]

While deliberating over what to do, the decision was inadvertently taken out of their hands. They lit a fire and spread out their sodden clothes and footwear to dry. Craw, Folscher and Wilkinson were wearing cheap Italian cardboard-soled boots and before long they had burned the bottoms out of them. There was no more walking for them. In any case, Aussie was by now very ill. The others decided that they had to get help for him or he would die. They gave themselves up at a farmhouse. The friendly peasant family called the Carabinieri while also taking them in and looking after them extremely well. One old lady broke down and cried when she saw the state that they were in. She immediately started cutting up a large loaf of bread for them, wiping away her tears as she did so. The Carabinieri took them to Rocoimperialia, where the people were also very kind and appeared equally upset at their condition. The next day they were taken to the railway station.[7]

On the return journey to Altamura, their guards had to move a group of officers so that prisoners and guards could all travel together. Down the side of the seat where the officers had been sitting, Merlyn Craw unexpectedly found a pistol. But he knew they would be thoroughly searched again so he left it there. He still had a British prismatic compass. He had managed to get this through the body search by tying it to his penis. Slowly, they chugged through the wintry Italian countryside. There were still a couple of enemy soldiers in their compartment, but these were Germans and since there was little else to do, they began to make conversation with the POWs.

One blond Arian who looked as if he had jumped straight out of a Hitler Youth propaganda poster mistook them for Allied pilots. Smiling, he offered round cigarettes and asked if their aircraft had been destroyed.

'No, no, mate'. You've got it all wrong', the captives explained, 'We're *escaped* prisoners of war, right?' The Germans were fascinated and clearly quite delighted. On learning that their enemies were not downed pilots but had managed to get out of Altamura and then stay out for two weeks, they thought it was a huge joke.

'Bloody good show, Tommy', they said, not understanding the Commonwealth dimension. 'Ja, ja, ganz bestimmt,' said the Hitler Youth, grinning and nodding approvingly, much to the annoyance of their Italian escort who immediately separated them. By this stage of the war, there was clearly not much love lost between the Germans and Italians.[8]

On arrival, back at Altamura station, Mikeli was waiting for them on the platform. He was so furious that he was literally hopping from one foot to the other, the peacock feathers in his 'crack' Alpine Regimental hat quivering with rage. At the sight of Almonds and Folscher, with whom he seemed particularly angry for betraying what he thought was a trust, he began shouting loudly and waving his arms about. The escape, and the ignominious assault he had suffered at their hands, had clearly been an enormous blow in terms of wounded pride and loss of standing in the Regiment. On the other hand, Almonds did not think that he could have been a very highly regarded officer to have been given the job of looking after the POW parcels detail in the first place. It was with some relief that the delinquents were placed under close arrest and driven off to the camp.

Numbers in the camp had greatly reduced during their absence. Their escape had in fact been timely because it had prevented them from being transported to Germany. The reprehended men were lined up and paraded, heavily guarded, in front of the Royalist Colonel Commandant of the camp. He was an elderly gentleman who had spent summers in Scotland with the Earl of Arran, the CO of 8 Commando. The Commandant was clearly very put out. He said that it was a very bad thing that they had done and, having some understanding of the English, attempted to make them feel guilty about having tried to escape. They were now the special '*quatro prisonieri*' and likely to receive harsh treatment and living conditions because they could not be trusted. But in spite of all this blustering, Almonds felt that the Commandant was really on their side and hardly likely to be very pro the Fascist Government.[9]

Under the Geneva Conventions, the Commandant could only punish them to a maximum of thirty days on bread and water, not that on past experience the prisoners had any expectation that those rules would be respected. To punish them more severely, the Commandant had to take more formal steps and he gave them to understand that he would. He pointed out that striking an Italian officer was a capital offence and they would be tried accordingly. Having delivered this decision, the Commandant handed the four men over to others who did not share his gentlemanly background. The '*quatro prisonieri*' had a few bad days during which they believed (and the guards did nothing to disabuse them) that they were going to be taken out and executed. Instead, they were told that they were to be formally tried by a Court Martial and that a summary of evidence would be taken.[10]

While awaiting trial, Almonds was separated from the other three and sent to a bigger brick-built camp, No. PG 65, at Gravina which was visible from Altamura, where he was placed in solitary confinement. The other three men remained in PG 51 in the same appalling living conditions as before. They passed their time playing bridge with a pack of cards that had come from a Red Cross parcel. Just before Easter, an envoy came, apparently from the Pope, to help prepare their trial defence. He began by blessing their tent but quickly got round to trying to barter half a bread loaf for their warm singlets. Eventually, Tom Wilkinson could stand it no longer. 'Get out of it you black bastard!' he shouted. The Italian darted back out of the way. The word 'bastardo' is recognisably similar in Italian. As if to make up for this very un-Christian behaviour, the Franciscan monks were always very good and smuggled in cakes and other small treats for the prisoners whenever they could.[11]

This time, the enemy were taking no chances. Almonds's cell was tiny. He had no windows, no exercise, nothing to do and no one to talk to. For a man used to roaming outdoors and leading an energetic life, it was a particular cruelty. He paced up and down and at first passed the time by counting the bricks. He soon realised that this was not sufficiently intellectually demanding. He developed other mental exercises. He started with a scheme for an electrolyte car but then turned to designing and memorizing the plans for an ocean going boat. He found that he could keep the plan going. Each day, he added more details. At night, he memorised the day's building progress. Rather like the Kim's tray (a test of memory achieved by showing a trainee a tray of objects, removing them and requiring the objects to be recalled) which he had practised in SAS training, he took a series of mental pictures and did not go to sleep until he could recall them. Each morning, he began again. The craft was a 32 foot ketch, with maximum beam of 9 feet 6 inches, 7 foot draught with centreboard down and a dead weight of 8½ tons. It was not until many years later in 1960 that he eventually completed the design, built the boat by hand in Ghana and sailed it back to the UK.[12]

Plans for his court-martial progressed. The Italians charged the *'quatro prisonieri'* and began preparations for a trial and a summary of evidence. The charges included assaulting an officer and attempted murder. The noose made of parcel string was produced as evidence. Almonds pointed out that he had not attempted to kill anyone. He had, after all, left behind Mikeli's pistol. He was told that he would be taken out and shot anyway for striking an Italian officer. When interviewing him for this book, I asked him if at this stage he had not sometimes wondered whether he would ever see England and my mother again. Quick as a flash came his surprisingly vehement retort.

'No! Not once. I know where I'm going and I knew it then. Once you start wondering and doubting, then you don't know where you're going or which way is up.' After a few more weeks he was taken out of solitary confinement but still kept in a small compound within the main prison and not allowed to mix freely with other prisoners. Altogether, he had seven months of confinement that breached the Geneva Conventions.

Towards Easter, he too was visited by an emissary of the Pope. After splashing holy water all around his cell, the Roman Catholic priest settled himself down to talk to the prisoner. The dialogue was conducted in a mixture of broken English and Italian and was therefore somewhat restricted. The man had with him a book of prayers and hymns in English. But any spiritual content of his mission was completely nullified by his attempts to barter with his interlocutor. Throughout their conversation, the visitor kept furtively displaying the tip of a little bread loaf peeping out of the pocket of his black robe, while at the same time pointing to the prisoner's woollen Red Cross vest. It was still very cold and damp in the unheated cell and Almonds was deeply shocked at this attempt to barter with him for his clothes. It confirmed for him that captors, captives and the Italian population all had to share the miseries of the war. While the man left the cell for a few moments, leaving his book behind him, Almonds leafed quickly through it looking for maps and blank pages to write on. There were no maps but he tore out two suitable pages, one of which was empty. On the reverse were a calendar for April 1943 and a prayer for speedy and universal peace. Easter was very late that year.[13]

More dreary months passed. On 3 July 1943, it became clear that the Italians had more to worry about than holding a court martial. Almonds was reunited with his fellow escapees when they joined him in Camp 65. The Fascist Government was in the final stages of its existence and Mussolini's days were numbered.[14] In addition, the Allies landed in the south of the country on 10 July.[15] Two days later, all the POWs were put onto a train and sent 300 miles north to Ancona to a POW camp with other British prisoners. This was Campo 70 at Monturano, a working camp that was a disused jam factory. But the four 'bad boys' were still kept apart from the other prisoners and locked up each day earlier than the rest in a sort of camp within a camp. There they stayed, with no freedom of association and no exercise, well into the summer.[16] On 24 July, Mussolini was deposed by the Fascist Grand Council and two days later the Badoglio Government took over.[17] But after having to establish martial law the new regime was rumoured to be already on the brink of collapse.

In September, Almonds's talent for getting selected for things came to the fore again. The Italian Commandant of the camp came to see him; it seemed strange that he did not simply send for his captive. The

Commandant had accompanied the prisoners northwards from Altamura and so he knew all about Almonds's escape and evasion skills. The old man explained that on 8 September an Armistice had been announced and Italy was now on the side of the Allies. He asked Almonds if he would go and carry out some reconnaissance around the little harbour of Porto San Giórgio to find out the disposition of the German troops in the area.[18]

Almonds agreed with some alacrity. Any chance outside was better than remaining a prisoner. His very dark brown hair and brown eyes meant that he could easily pass as a local. The Italians fitted him out with civilian clothes, a black jacket and some khaki trousers. The clothes were slightly too short for him and whenever he knew that he was being observed he had to slouch as he walked to try and make them look as though they fitted him. Early in the morning of 12 September he slipped quietly out of the camp. After making his way to the coast and scouting around the area, he was able to assess the local German troop strengths and movements. He also discovered that the Americans had captured Palermo on 22 July. A few days later, while he was still 'at large', he heard that the Germans had taken over the camp at Monturano.

Having carried out his assigned task, Almonds reported by telephone to the CO. There were no Germans in the immediate vicinity. Equipped with this information, Almonds had already decided to make good his escape. 'Good. Thank you', said the old man in his strangely courteous way. 'And now you return'.

'I'm so sorry', Almonds said equally politely, 'but I'm afraid I'm about to take my leave of you. I'm going home.' There then followed a stream of protestations from the other end of the line, to which the only answer was the gentle click of the receiver being replaced. Even as an escaped POW, it went against the grain to hang up on an officer and a gentleman.

Without having been able to make any preparations at all, Almonds set off again on the even longer trek south.

Chapter Thirteen

The Italian Picnic

Almonds made a month-long journey south. It took place in a strange vacuum in which the Italians were officially neither friend nor foe. After Montgomery's Eighth Army had crossed the Straits of Messina on 3 September 1943 – the fourth anniversary of the conflict – the conduct of the war in Italy was fairly chaotic. The advance was very slow because only two good roads ran up the coasts of the 'toe' promontory of the 'boot' of Italy. Secret Allied terms for Italy's capitulation had been agreed the same day. Patton had earlier demanded an unconditional surrender but this only served to delay things for six weeks after Mussolini's removal. The deal was that Italy would be treated as leniently as it would deserve by the part it would play in the war against Germany. The capitulation was actually announced on 8 September.[1]

A largely US force, the Fifth Army under General Mark Clark, made equally slow progress. After landing at Salerno on the 'shin' of the boot on 9 September, it was not to reach Naples until 1 October. A last-minute strike on the 'heel' of Italy, by a single British Division, the 1st Airborne, took the Germans by surprise and captured Taranto and Brindisi. But the invaders lacked the resources to advance swiftly and consolidate a hold on the ground as far as Foggia.

The Italian government, acting on an agreement between Eisenhower and Badoglio, the General and statesman who had extricated Italy from the war by arranging the armistice, did not declare war on Germany until 13 October. This was the day before Almonds finally reached the Americans. The Germans' Gustav Line ran for a hundred miles from the mouth of the River Garigliano on the west coast, through Cassino and over the Apennines to the mouth of the Sangro on the Adriatic coast. The enemy also managed to hold onto other lines across Italy. The most southerly of these was the Viktor Line, which ran from the mouth of the River Volturno on the west coast, north of Benevento to just south of Termoli in the east. All the time Almonds was north of this line, he was in enemy territory and forced to play another, more protracted game of hide and seek.[2]

Unknown to Almonds at the time, the Allies were making some attempts to put in place systems to help men in his situation. In London, there had been considerable preoccupation with the problem of what to do about the Allied POWs in Italy. At the time of the armistice, there were roughly 75,000 of them. The Germans made known that they were taking about 50,000 of these to Germany. Of the remaining 25,000, a few thousand were heading for Switzerland via the area north of Rimini-Leghorn. Several hundred were reported as being with partisan bands all over Italy, presumably thinking that they could serve their country best by carrying out sabotage work behind the lines. The rest, more than 20,000 of them, simply vanished into thin air.[3]

Options as to what could be done about this situation were limited but that did not prevent some of the most unlikely from being considered. A draft cable to Dudley Clarke, master of British counter-intelligence, shows that the British were even considering exploring an escape post in the Vatican, arranged via MI6 under diplomatic cover.[4] In the end, pragmatism prevailed. In southern Italy on 30 August, HQ 15 Army Group's Tac HQ 'A' Force had issued an operation instruction to a young British captain, A.C. Soames, the future Minister of War and son-in-law of Winston Churchill.[5] Almonds had known 'Soapy' Soames when he was 'bouncing around' as a young Coldstream Guards officer at Pirbright but they were not to meet in Italy.[6]

Soames's Operational order detailed him to command No. 2 Field Escape Section. His mission was to take responsibility for the conduct of all rescue work in the forward areas during the course of military operations. He was to be based on the leading Corps in any future operations conducted by the Eighth Army and maintain close liaison with operation and intelligence staffs, without compromising the security of pending military operations. He was to use all known means to produce a network of helpers behind enemy lines and make local plans for the early rescue of ground troops and air crews at large in enemy territory. To help him, Captain Soames had a supply of 'aids and devices' and the money required for the payment of local helpers. Nevertheless, it was a tall order.[7]

Back at Monturano, Merlyn Craw realised that Almonds was not coming back. The SAS man had not said anything before leaving because he had not known himself that he would not be returning. Grasping what had happened, Craw had the presence of mind to write at once to Almonds's Lincolnshire address, but to his sister Beatrice in her married name. His aim was to ensure that the censor would let the postcard through. In deliberately scrawled handwriting, Craw buried the essential phrase

'Haven't seen Jim for some time,' in amongst the most boring inconsequential verbiage he could think of. It worked. The card got through and Lockie was duly alerted.[8] Then there was a sudden turn of events.

Later in the afternoon of the day when Almonds left the camp, the prison gates were opened and all of the prisoners were let out. The camp had about 8,000 prisoners in it and there were two other POW camps in the area, each with about 8,000 prisoners. This was a lot of men to have roaming the countryside. Merlyn and Tom Wilkinson were among those who immediately went off out through the gates but later that night, having nothing to eat and the local environs being unable to support so many men, they returned to the camp. Then they heard a message being broadcast over the camp broadcast system by a British major in the RAMC.

Through the crackle of the tannoy, this major (whom they had never met in any official medical capacity) announced to all POWs that he had information that the British would land on one side of Italy and the Americans on the other. They were therefore all to stay put until further notice. Normally, in camps of Allied POWs the senior RSM was IC POWs and known as the 'Camp Leader' but this one had apparently let the RAMC major take over. This might have been intended to add verisimilitude to such an unusual broadcast and make the order not to escape appear more authoritative.[9]

That night, Merlyn whispered to Aussie Wilkinson from the bunk above.

'Aussie.'

'Yup.'

'I don't reckon I like the sound of this so-called message. You know, about staying put. I think I'm going to make a break for it. What do you think?'

Wilkinson said that he was still trying to piece together the meaning of the gates being opened, then the announcement not to escape. He suggested that they see what happened the next day.

The next morning, they realised that fifty Grenadier Guardsmen were also watching the POWs along with the usual Italian camp guard. The prisoners were actually being guarded by their own side! Then all of the inmates were given half a Red Cross parcel each. The reason was not clear because the gates remained closed. The mood in the camp was anxious. Merlyn did not think that the tannoy announcement sounded quite right. But it was real enough.[10] This behaviour of the Guards fitted with Merlyn's impression that British soldiers obeyed their officers without question. It was all part of the culture of deference. At that time, the average British soldier (apart from the special forces) relied on his corporal or sergeant to tell him what to do and was not encouraged to think for himself. This was a problem when the occasion called for him to use his initiative, for example when in a POW camp or on the run. The Guards were different again: they would obey to the death. By contrast, in Merlyn's view the colonial soldiers only did so if the orders seemed reasonable.[11]

That day did indeed turn out to be 'make your mind up time'. They were presented with an opportunity to escape. Before the arrival of the '*quatro prisonieri*', four POWs had escaped from Campo 70 by getting the others to bury them almost completely in the outer compound, which had only a wire perimeter fence, and later making off under cover of darkness. Although they had been recaptured, the breakout had cost the prisoners the use of the compound. The prospect of escape arose through a game of football. One of the Welsh prisoners had received a football in a Red Cross parcel but had never been able to make use of it because the Italians would not allow them a makeshift football field in the compound. The Welsh were still dying for a game of football and when they heard the news of Mussolini's fall they saw their chance to get a game. Italy was now no longer an enemy of the Allies so, they argued to the guards, there was no reason for the prisoners to escape or the guards to keep them inside the camp. Eventually, it was agreed that they could play but as Craw said, 'It's all stones in Italy,' so he and Aussie managed to persuade the guards that they needed to go out and clear the rocky surface for a makeshift pitch.

Craw and Wilkinson were still on 'restriction of privileges' as a punishment for their earlier escape. As Almonds had been allowed in the later stages of his confinement, they could only spend one hour a day outside their cell. That day, the day of the longed for football match, was also 13 September, the anniversary of Merlyn's capture. This added a certain incentive to his desire for freedom.

'Are you coming then?' he whispered to Aussie Wilkinson, as side by side on their knees they cleared the gravelly ground. 'Nah.' Wilkinson looked uncomfortable. 'Reckon there must be a reason for those orders to stay put. I'll just hang on here and wait my moment.' Merlyn had meanwhile enlisted a young parachutist called Sam Schoeles who was definitely on for the escape. The rest were more interested in the game of football. As the game started and the players rushed forward at the kick-off, Merlyn and Sam went under the wire. The Welshmen were most upset when the breakout again ruined their chance of any more games of football.[12]

Travelling alone, Almonds moved at his own speed, which was fast. This time it was summer and the going was much easier. To escape detection, he again had to go by way of the mountains, the Apennines, which run down the length of Italy. But first he turned his back to the sea and travelled by night until he came to Ascoli Piceno, about 60 miles from Ancona as the crow flies. Beyond the town, he quickly followed a river valley up into the safety of the hills. Then he turned southwards and started to run. Crossing at right angles all of the little valleys and gulches that run up into the mountains, meant that he ran downhill some of the time and uphill the rest of the time, doubling at least the distance he had to cover. In spite of his imprisonment, he was still fit. Like an uncaged bird that has regained its liberty, he exulted in the physical exercise. Sometimes he ran all day, covering 20 miles or more, and that is the enduring picture that I have of him, running through those mountains.

A massive crest began to appear ahead of him. As he got closer, he realised that it must be the 'Gran Sasso d'Italia' (the Rock of Italy). War or no war, he was so fascinated by its towering beauty that he took time off to visit the Gran Sasso and marvel at the views from as far up as he got towards the summit. Italy lay spread out below him, warm, burnt sienna coloured and deceptively peaceful in the late summer sunshine. To the east, the mountains slipped away to the strip of green that ran along the coast and beyond it he could see the faint blue haze of the Adriatic. High up, he spied an impregnable looking fortress and gave it a wide berth. Unknown to him at the time, it was the stronghold where Mussolini had been held and rescued by a German parachute raid only a few days previously on 12 September.

After exploring the Rock of Italy, he rejoined the war and followed the track across Abruzzi leading south to Campobasso. Occasionally, he met friendly Italians foraging in the hills. 'Where do you sleep at night?' they asked. 'Here,' he said, with a generous sweep of his hand southwards along the mountain ridge. They reacted with horror. In a mixture of broken English and Italian they told him that it was not safe. There were bears in the mountains. Almonds laughed and waved goodbye. It was only after the war that he read that the European brown bear still survived in parts of the Apennines.

One evening, he looked down into a small corrie and saw a man lighting a charcoal fire. Seeing that he was alone and unarmed, Almonds went down and chatted to him. The man was at first very nervous; this was not surprising since he was half the size of his uninvited guest. He was cooking a small lamb and motioned to the Englishman to sit down and eat some. They passed a tolerable couple of hours together until it was dark. Then the escapee withdrew again up into the lonely higher reaches of the mountains.

He reached the village of Civitella Casa Nova. Walking towards it, he was not particularly worried about the Italians. But, as he sauntered into the village street, he saw a parked lorry with Germans loading up stores. A soldier looked enquiringly at him. Almonds carried on casually but adopted his slouching posture, so that his trousers did not appear too short. This probably helped his disguise, since the bearing of a Coldstream Guardsman might have been something of a give-away.

He turned into the first open door that he saw. Pushing through a dingy passage, he heard the sound of chatter and the clinking of cutlery and glasses. In a small cluttered room, bright with sunshine and painted pottery and warm with the smell of pasta, an Italian family was having a meal. They stopped and stared. There was a gasped intake of breath. A large Italian mama put her knuckles up to her mouth as if trying to stop herself from screaming. 'Sh!', my father said, putting a finger to his lips, 'Inglezi'. The ring of faces looked back. They sat motionless. Without saying anything more, the intruder quickly crossed the room and climbed out through a low open window. Outside was a lush and fortunately well screened garden. He made his way to the far end of it where he found a deep, narrow stream. A large dead trout was floating downstream, belly upwards, another unclaimed casualty of the war. Several more drifted past, completely unmarked but lifeless. He wondered what could have happened upstream to cause such annihilation. Following the stream uphill, he was able to make his way out of the village. He came to an orchard full of peaches and walnuts and bit into the soft and bitter fruits that were growing all around. Before moving on, he loaded his pockets with a few more meals.[13]

He came to crossroads where the road from Pescara to Rome runs in a valley that crosses another valley running north-west to Aquila. Eventually, somewhere, he had to cross a secondary road in continuous use by Germans coming to and from the direction of Campobasso. He lay face down in a ditch at the side of the road, waiting for the right moment. In the end, he shot across it into a field and came face to face with an elderly Italian hoeing up between some rows of potatoes. Almonds threw himself down between the ridges a few rows away but he knew that he had been seen. The man looked at him, as if about to open a conversation. The fugitive really did look like an Italian. Again the finger raised to the lips.

On the road about 20 feet away, some German trucks rumbled to a halt. Soldiers shouted to each other as they spilled out of the vehicles to relieve themselves and take a break. The Italian, somewhat wild-eyed, kept on hoeing feverishly with short mechanical movements, all the time keeping one eye on Almonds but trying to appear as if he had not seen him. Ten minutes went by. The soldiers threw away their cigarettes and heaved themselves back up into their cabs. They started up their engines and revved up noisily. It seemed an age while the SAS man lay with his face down, smelling the freshness of the earth, listening to the crashing of gears and nearby the quick regular scraping of the hoe. Then came the long drawn out rising note of the vehicles pulling away and changing up, until their sound finally died away into the distance. The two men in the field looked at each other. 'Grazzia', Almonds said, and as if by way of explanation, 'Inglezi'. The man shrugged his shoulders. 'Prego', he said, relief written all over his tired face.[14]

Shortly afterwards, Almonds met some more Italians on the bank of a river. They were a family: a rather well dressed man, his wife and some children. They spoke a little English. The man had been fishing and had caught a trout, about a one pounder Almonds judged. He noticed that the man was fly-fishing, with refined skill. 'You come. Stay; eat', said the Italian and smiled at him. His family nodded welcomingly.

'Thank you,' their visitor replied as courteously as he could. 'But I'm an Englishman; and I'm going home. Anyway,' he added so as not to appear unfriendly, 'you should eat your catch,' and he gestured towards the beautiful fresh trout. 'Is a no problem,' said the man, smiling widely. Carefully, he selected a fly and cast again. They chatted amiably while they waited for the fish to bite. He was an excellent fisherman and before long had caught two more trout, cleaned them and had them over hot charcoal. Almonds thought of the fish he used to cook for Pat Riley; it seemed a lifetime ago. They shared the food together. He had forgotten what it was to do these simple family things. While they were eating, the sun began to go down. They said their goodbyes. It was time for the escapee to make himself scarce again. Never had he felt more appreciative of such genuine hospitality. He always found that the ordinary Italian people were decent and kind.[15]

Soames's first problem was the situation he inherited on the ground. The broadcasts to POW camps had not helped him in his task of recovering the missing men. The instructions to camps telling the men to stay put had originally been passed in late June and were in the nature of 'standing instructions', meant to deal with conditions likely to arise at the end of the war. Moreover, they were not specific to the invasion of Italy but applied to POW camps everywhere. In the case of the Italian camps, there had been no time to take account of the peculiar and totally unforeseen circumstances which arose when Italy capitulated but Germany fought on.[16]

Merlyn Craw was right. Those in charge of the camp at Monturano had simply slavishly followed the standing instructions without applying them intelligently to their own situation. As a result, 20,000 of the Allied POWs missing in Italy (but not including Almonds who had already gone) had been given the clear message 'Do not escape'. At the same time, so Tac HQ 'A' Force informed Soames just before the armistice was announced, steps were to be taken by the Italian authorities to release all Allied POWs immediately.[17] The Italian authorities would try to supply ten days' rations and instruct the POWs to move south, using the east coast road. This then was the reason for the opening of the gates on the first day after the armistice and the issue of half a Red Cross parcel. Two conflicting sets of instructions were operating at once.

Soames's second problem was that after the armistice, not all elements of 15 Army Group Tac HQ were working to the same policy. The young captain lost no time at all in pointing this out to his superiors. Three 'A' Force letters referring to 'FORKS' (code for personnel sent forward to find and help recover escaped prisoners) made no mention of getting the escapees to move south. Rather 'A' Force's view of the task of the FORK was to organise helpers to *shelter* the fugitives ('ELKS') for as long as possible.[18]

All this Soames explained painstakingly in a memo to a Squadron Leader Dennis:

My FORKS, on the other hand, have all been sent with the same orders – completely contradictory to those mentioned above – [in the three letters], namely to ORDER, ASK, or BESEECH the ELKS to come south, no matter what the ELKS themselves may say about it. On arrival at an area about 10 kms beyond the front line, they are met by guides who bring them through ... It does seem pointless that TAC's FORKS should be ordering the ELKS to do one thing and mine ordering them to do completely the reverse. I am convinced that the ELKS must be told to help themselves and to get moving – otherwise no one can help them. All reports got to show,[19] it is NOT dangerous for them to come south as long as they keep moving and do not spend more than one night in the same place until they reach an area stretching back about 10 kms from the front line, when it is dangerous, mighty dangerous ......[20]

Meanwhile, Craw was making a clean getaway. On 14 September, the day after their escape from Monturano, he and Sam Schoeles met an Englishwoman married to an Italian. She told them that there was no need for them to skulk around at night. According to her, they could travel quite openly by day. They were sceptical about this because at the entrance to each village underneath its place name there was a sign giving details of the reward offered for information leading to the recapture of escaped POWs. This was usually between 20 to 25 pounds in gold. For good measure, the penalties for harbouring or assisting escapees, which included the death penalty, were also listed. They were unarmed except for a pistol that had been given to Craw in the mountains by a young man whose father had had it in the First World War. In the face of this conflicting evidence and in the generally confused situation, the two escapees decided to play it safe. They kept moving south east by night and lay up during the day.

Back in the camp, seizing his moment, Aussie Wilkinson also made a second breakout. It was in the nick of time. Four days later, the remaining 8,000 POWs woke up to find German sentries in the goon towers! Within a week, they were on their way to Germany.

About ten days after escaping, Craw and Schoeles heard of five men who were trying to pick up escaped prisoners. From the descriptions of these men, they sounded like the SAS, but obviously SAS who were prepared not to remain under cover. They finally met the SAS men on about 23 September at Porcia, about 25 miles from the east coast. The SAS were wearing overalls and Craw was convinced that they were the real thing. They said that they had orders to pick up thousands of escaped men and could organise boats for up to 20,000. But after three weeks of looking for escapees they said they had found only twenty! The main problem was apparently Italian government policy. Escapees could not count on a positive civilian reception, for fear of the Italian authorities. If bribed, civilians would assist, but not usually hide POWs. Consequently, many escaped POWs preferred to lie up in the hills waiting for the Allies to come to them. Some managed to get taken in by Italian families, where a life of eating pasta and drinking Chianti was infinitely more attractive than risking death, injury or semi-starvation on the run. But staying put was in fact just as hazardous since it often led to discovery and recapture.[21]

Of the five SAS men, two or three had parachuted in; the others had come in by boat. One was an RSM but he quickly went down with a bad attack of gonorrhoea and the others spent some time trying to get medicines for him. In the end, a farmhouse agreed to take him in and look after him, since going to hospital would have led to a fate worse than death. Finding that the SAS men could not really help them, Craw and Schoeles looked elsewhere. They met a friendly Alpini officer who gave them cigarettes and blankets. He also arranged with a trawler, run by a rather piratical bunch, to take them off. But the Germans had taken the fuel injectors out of the engines. Then a boy came and told them that the injectors had been replaced. So the two men went down to the nearby port of San Geórgio. But the boat was heavily guarded and they needed to get across the open road to the sea front. When the air raid warning was sounding and everyone else dived for the shelters, they dashed across the road and grabbed the trawler.[22] For the rest of the war, Merlyn Craw was a free man.

Almonds still ran all day. It was so good to be free that he felt as though he had wings. He came to the village of San Juliano. Germans were in the vicinity in ever-increasing numbers so he knew that that he could no longer hope to dodge them as he continued on his journey. They seemed to be moving northwards so he started to look for somewhere to hide until they had moved through. He carefully avoided a group of Germans from an 88mm gun battery. They seemed to have been having some success. Some distance away, he saw an American single-engined Thunderbolt fighter plane with smoke billowing from one of its star-tipped wings. He watched and then with relief saw a parachutist bale out.

On the edge of San Juliano, he came to the home of Liberato Coapaulo on the outskirts of the village. Coapaulo was about forty years old and had a wife and a daughter of about nine years old. His house was built into a hillside and on the north, uphill side was a doorway from the hillside directly into a hayloft.

'Prego,' said the Italian, gesturing towards the hayloft. Then in broken English and pointing again to the little door, 'You go in where I put food for animals.'[23]

That evening, Coapaulo invited the escaped POW inside for a family feast of a *pegara*, a roasted sheep. Without much ceremony, the Italian cut its throat over a large bowl. Almonds had nothing with which to pay the man and yet he was not only helped, but also hidden. Apart from the danger of German reprisals if discovered, this hospitality was at some additional cost to the little Italian family. They had precious little to eat themselves.

It quickly became apparent that the danger was all too real. Before they had finished their meal, the Germans came to 'requisition' provisions. Almonds was quickly smuggled back up into the loft. Hiding in the hay, he looked down through the cracks between the floorboards. It was a strange vantage point since he could not see the Germans' faces, only the tops of their helmets as they moved about accepting 'hospitality' from Coapaulo and his wife. Before leaving, the Germans cut off the heads of the chickens they had 'bought' with their worthless requisition slips.

The next day, Coapaulo reported that an American downed pilot was in the vicinity. Almonds took the opportunity to use one of his most precious resources – paper to write on – and made a belated diary entry on the blank page that he had torn from the priest's book:

MEMORANDUM 10 October 1943

In a hayloft of a little farm at St Juliano, province of Campobasso, Italy, while in hiding from the Germans. It is a month today since I left the camp at Termo [sic], Ancona to rejoin my own people. An American pilot [Capt. M. Nielson] is also in hiding somewhere in the neighbourhood. I saw his plane shot down and watched him make a successful parachute landing. Since leaving the camp, I have walked about 300 kilometres. Shall I make our own lines this time? Yes, I think so. Lockie darling, I shall be with you for Christmas.[24]

The ever-helpful Coapaulo went off and came back with a note from the American pilot. He had also been looked after well by the local people. Almonds replied but, wary of any trap, suggested a meeting before daybreak. The American turned out to very pleased to make contact with an ally. He wanted them to stay together and Almonds agreed, on the one condition that they kept moving. Nielsen accepted and they took to the road together.[25]

The night was moonless and inky black as they headed southwards. After covering a few miles, Almonds suddenly heard a noise to his left like the 'chink' of a mess tin hitting something. In the darkness, all they could see was a long dark mass outlined against the sky. Something about it was decidedly eerie, as if people were all around them but maintaining silence. The two men froze and after a long interval, very slowly, they inched away. As dawn was approaching in that short summer night, they saw that their way ran down a hill, a stony, loose dirt track. Something about it made Almonds stop. Involuntarily, he put out an arm out to stop Nielsen too. Suddenly, he was back in the days of his night recces with Jock Lewes. *'This is exactly the sort of place to lay mines'*, he thought. He looked again and saw here and there the telltale signs where the partially metalled road surface had been turned over to lay the devices. Dropping to his knees, he explored as he had done in the desert and confirmed the awful truth. If he had never had the experience of minefields with Lewes, he and Nielsen would probably both have been blown to bits as they trudged down the track. Although it was getting light, Almonds set about surveying the extent and density of the minefield. The Germans were retreating and he knew that sooner or later the Allies would be coming this way. He memorised every available natural feature and landmark, making a detailed mental map which he then committed to memory. Then the two moved on together, travelling by night down the Apennines.[26]

Living off the land, ducking and hiding and lying low whenever they had to, at last they reached the German front line at Benevento. In thirty-two days, Almonds had covered 230 miles from Ancona, as the crow flies. But his way was across valleys and mountainous terrain, so it was probably more than twice that distance, giving him an average rate of progress of about 15 miles a day. Since he had spent some time lying up, on some days he must have done considerably more than that.

By the time they got to Benevento, the two fugitives had become rather careless. In spite of having seen some bivouacs, they arranged to be put up by a man they met in a village. Perhaps thinking to make something out of it, he went and fetched the owners of the bivouacs who turned out to be US Forces, a lost and rather disgruntled troop of about half a dozen US Rangers. They were about to eat, so without more ado, my father and Nielsen simply joined the food 'line'. The Americans were also heading back south to meet up with their main force and having been satisfied by Nielsen that my father was 'a limey' and 'okay', the two went along with them. The Americans grumbled a lot and seemed to be finding it all rather heavy going so Almonds carried their automatic weapon, a light Bren gun, for them.[27]

A few days later, they reached the American Main HQ. For a few hours, Almonds suffered the indignity of being a prisoner of the Americans. He sat in a tent with a US intelligence officer wagging a loaded pistol at him. The man seemed unable to make a distinction between an Italian appearance and an English accent. Eventually, this problem was sorted out and Almonds's identity confirmed. He said goodbye to Nielsen before being handed over to a British Liaison Officer. The American pilot was fairly emotional and asked Almonds what he could do for him when he got back to civilisation. Almonds said that he would really appreciate it if he could send a small present to John since it was impossible to buy toys in England.[28]

Feeling strangely as if he were again in captivity, the repatriated ex-POW was taken by car to Castellammare in the Bay of Naples. There he was checked at the Medical Centre before being interrogated and debriefed at some length. Intelligence were delighted with the information about the enemy minefield and immediately got him to produce for them a hand-drawn map. The information probably saved many lives and vehicles, since the main Allied force had yet to make its way northwards.[29] He also provided details of the POW camps in which he had been held and the insider 'stool pigeons'. Then he was kept hanging around for two months waiting for information and orders.

This was a very difficult time for Almonds. After a year as a POW, there was no joyful reunion, no home-coming nor even at that stage any recognition by his own side of his achievement in escaping twice, surviving a perilous journey through occupied territory and surveying an enemy mine field on the way. On the contrary, he felt as if his own side somehow regarded him as 'contaminated' by his year of imprisonment, seven months of which had been in very close confinement. The end of his dash for freedom was an unexpected anti-climax.

Meanwhile, Captain Soames was putting on record his views of the performance of the ELKS. One particular, rather senior ELK, a Brigadier Cooper, provoked Soames into an explosion of indignation. On 7 November, he wrote to the long-suffering Squadron Leader Dennis:

SILVESTRI arrived here yesterday... I am simply horror-struck.

The sole object of my wretched FORKS, sent a month ago to the very area where this note was written, was to get ELKS moving southwards. How <u>can</u> one expect ORs [other ranks] to comply with this, which I am convinced is their main hope of salvation, if this is the attitude taken by Senior Officers? "We are eagerly awaiting the arrival of the Allies." It is more than pathetic.

It is not as if my wretched FORKS were lying up like dog-ferrets and doing nothing ... I sent the guide back to Brig. COOPER stressing that:

a) He should order others to come down, and that
b) He should do so himself.[30]

Later in the month Soames wrote to Dennis again on the general subject of the missing 25,000 thousand POWs:

Dear Squad,
During the past two months, only about two thousand of those have reached our lines – half of which are very largely thanks to the activities of 'A' Force. In other words, out of twenty-five thousand Officers and ORs, only one thousand have had the foresight; intelligence and gumption to take any active measure to carry out what is surely their duty – i.e. to reach our lines... Daily, reports come in of both officers and other ranks sitting tight with no intention of moving. They believe implicitly the intensely exaggerated reports from local Italians of the impassability of rivers and the numbers of Germans about, the 'impenetrable barrages' put down in the fighting area, and the general insuperable difficulties and dangers incurred in walking south. Reliable reports say that the vast majority of ELKS never think of going to look for themselves. No, they find a farmhouse with an Italian family. They ensconce themselves there.... The ELK has not proved himself the man he ought to be. He has let himself down badly. If they get recaptured, it is entirely their own fault.[31]

Dennis's reassuring reply on 25 November reveals something of the prevailing attitudes to repatriated POWs:

Don't be too hard on the lads inside until we get the full picture and this won't be until the war is over – if we get it then......

> Altogether I don't think the picture looks too black, for we must allow for the 'PW/complex' which must affect people in different ways; and after two or more years in a P/W Camp it would be unfair to judge by normal standards.[32]

Gradually, Almonds began to fill in the gaps in his missing thirteen months. He learned that Stirling had been captured in the previous spring and was a POW in Colditz. The SAS had since become two Regiments. Paddy Mayne had taken over part of the original Regiment as CO of the SAS Special Raiding Squadron, which was by then in action at Termoli on the other side of Italy. They had landed by sea and after bitter fighting and many painful losses were holding a position there. It was rumoured that the SRS would become 1 SAS Regiment again, with Mayne in charge.

He had no news of Lockie and did not know if she knew whether he was dead or alive. Nor did he know any of the men he was with and he longed to get back to the SAS. To keep his spirits up, he fell back once again on his practical creative skills. He found a big metal file in a bombed out factory and started shaping it into the SAS winged sword. Before long it was stolen from his bedroll. The mystery of who took his piece of handicraft was never solved. It may have been discovered during an accommodation check and mistaken for an intended weapon. The 'P/W complex' no doubt.

Paddy Mayne heard that Almonds had made a comeback and started making plans to come and get him by car. At about this time, Mayne wrote to the Medical Officer, Malcolm James Pleydell, who was still in the Western Desert:

> I have heard that Sgt Almonds – you remember he was captured in the Benghazi raid – has got through to our side. I am trying to meet him....[33]

But the SAS were pulling out of Italy so Almonds drove to the ship which was to carry them and him at last back to the UK. They boarded and set sail for North Africa and Sfax. Time had been passing. After reaching Algiers, they set sail again for England on Christmas Day. Unlike the excitement and eager anticipation of the trip out to the Middle East three years before, Almonds felt nothing and the details of that journey home refused to imprint themselves on his memory.

On arrival in the UK, he was taken to a place somewhere near Croydon, probably Latimer House, for several days' more debriefing and rehabilitation. Again, he felt as if he were being treated as if he had gone native. The process of checking his sanity and stability ended with a question.

'And what job would you like to do next?'

'I would like to rejoin my Regiment', he said very firmly. But they obviously thought that he was in a pretty bad way, emotionally and mentally if not physically. It was to be many months before he could stop pacing up and down. In January, after he had been away for three whole years, he was finally free to go on two weeks' leave. He reached Bristol early in the evening and made his way to 15 York Street. That day, my grandfather had come home and noticed what looked like one of the very small cards that used to come as wireless licence reminders. But on looking at it more closely, he realised that it was from his son-in-law. It was so cryptic that each sentence had to be completed by the recipient, for example 'I am being sent …' meant 'I am being sent home!' 'Emily,' he said to my grandmother, 'Jim's coming home and May's gone out!'[34]

Coming up the road in the darkness, Almonds was mesmerised to see a large banner stretched across York Street. It was strung from the cross bar of the lamp post outside number 15, where he had first seen Lockie, to the upstairs window of the house opposite. 'Welcome home Jim!' it said. Colourful bunches of balloons bobbed and tugged at each end of the banner, hastily organised by my grandfather and the neighbours. After the three months that had passed since Almonds had rejoined the Allies, he could not believe that it was really for him. He walked into what my grandparents called 'the living room'. In front of the fire, a small boy was playing with a few toys. He was in his pyjamas ready for bed, his face shiny clean, his hair smoothly brushed, still damp, across to one side. They stared at each other for a moment. Then the boy's eyes swivelled immediately to the photograph of his father on the mantelpiece and back to his father. A small frown clouded his brow.

'Hello Daddy', he said rather severely. 'You've been a long time.'[35]

In the Eastville Hippodrome cinema, the Wells Fargo stagecoach was being chased by bandits. Lockie had gone to the 'pictures' without having seen the card informing her of her husband's return. The outlaws pounded across the screen. Superimposed among the dust of the horses' hooves, there appeared a curled up scrap of paper with a message in scrawled handwriting. Her friend dug her in the ribs. 'May, May.' The whisper was so loud that everyone around them set up a chorus of 'Shhhhh!!'

'May, that's for you.' Startled, Lockie realised that the message on the screen had indeed been flashed up for her. 'Mrs Almonds should go immediately to the foyer,' it read.

She made her way outside, anxious in case anything had happened to her parents or John. There she met an elderly police Sergeant, Williamson, who had been a friend of Almonds from his Bristol police days. Seeing Lockie's anxiety, he said 'It's all right my dear. Nothing's wrong. He's home.'

'Who?' she replied. She had not heard from her husband for many months. Having learned from her sister-in-law that he had probably escaped again, she knew that he was unable to write. It was a moment before she could take it in and then another before she dared to believe that her husband was not only free but already waiting for her at home!

She said nothing to poor old Sergeant Williamson but without even waiting for her usual bus, she just ran off, all the way back to York Street. She had no thought for what state he would be in or what she would find. She only knew that she could not stay separated from him for one second longer than necessary. When she reached home, Almonds hugged her, swung her off her feet and then held her tightly to his chest. It was a long time before they could let each other go. My grandmother was crying while John looked gravely from one to the other, taking it all in.

But readjustment took time. Three years' separation is an age in a young married couple's life. During his short leave, Almonds was sometimes quite strange. He could not sit still, but had to keep getting up and walking around the room. The photographs of him that appeared in the Bristol papers showed a thinner, temporarily more haggard face than my mother remembered.[36] On occasions his behaviour was very odd. Once when he was out with Lockie and John shopping in the town, he suddenly stopped and said, 'What do you two want? What the hell are you following me for?' Fortunately, Lockie was able to understand and tried to make allowances, although it hurt. Putting on a brave face for the sake of their son, she just said, 'Oh, all right. Come on John; we'll just make our own way home.' In addition, her husband would not talk at all about any of the things that had happened to him, or even what he had been doing, so that Lockie had three blank years to cope with.[37]

In spite of his expressed wish to rejoin his unit, Almonds was posted to the Prime Minister's country residence at Chequers. There he was put in charge of security. He complained bitterly and as soon as he could, he went up to London to see Ian Collins. By then his old Troop Commander was a Lieutenant Colonel. They met at Collins's office in Whitehall, where he was doing a staff job at the War Office. Collins had lost none of his boyish charm and greeted Almonds like a long-lost friend. During the previous three years, Collins had often remembered Lockie and had sent some beautiful children's books, courtesy of Collins publishers, for John.[38]

After thanking him for this kindness, Almonds explained that he hated his sedentary job and wanted to get back to the SAS. Collins said he would get in touch with Paddy Mayne to see what could be done. But Almonds was not the only one complaining. Lockie was bitterly disappointed that after three years' separation, they still could not live together. Leaving John with her parents, she went to see her husband at Chequers. They stayed in a little thatched house called Rose Cottage with a huge brown teapot as big as a pumpkin.[39]

Within two weeks, Mayne was on the case. He contacted Almonds to say that he was arranging for him to be 'extricated' from Chequers to rejoin the SAS in Scotland. The Regiment was reforming and already in training for the invasion of mainland Europe. Lockie was devastated. This time, her husband had not even consulted her. In the inner struggle between his two sets of obligations, she was even more in second place than she had been when he had set sail to the Middle East in January 1941. Probably because she knew it, in a moment of high passion, she even said that she wished he were still a POW. 'At least then I'd know where you are! I'd know that you weren't in any immediate danger.' Of course, she later regretted it. But the damage was done and they were estranged for some days.[40]

Ironically, it was at that time that a solitary entry appeared in Almonds's name in the *London Gazette* under 'War Office, 27th April 1944, Bar to the Military Medal'.[41] This was for his services when escaping from the POW camp and mapping the minefield at some personal danger to himself. A Military Medal and Bar is rare. This is because quite often the recipient of a first Medal was commissioned and if he was decorated again for similar gallantry received a Military Cross, the equivalent decoration for officers. In Almonds's case, he had been taken prisoner after being recommended for his first MM and soon after breaking out of POW camp got another one.

Mayne acted fast. In mid February, Almonds was posted to Scotland, accompanied, as a 'consolation prize', by his wife and son. On the long train journey north, their carriage was packed and they had to stand for most of the way. Three-year-old John rose to the occasion and spent his time entertaining the troops with his antics. Much later, it was the usual non-drama, with the couple walking the streets of Edinburgh at midnight looking for somewhere to stay, this time carrying a sleeping child between them. Eventually, they found a hotel and the next day caught a bus to Darvel in Ayrshire.

While the little family was united for the first time, preparations began for parachuting behind enemy lines in France.

Part III

1 SAS in Scotland, behind enemy lines in France and leading the advance into Germany
January 1944 – May 1945

Chapter Fourteen

The French Picnic

After his timely 'escape' from Chequers, Almonds was very pleased to be back with the Regiment again. Paddy Mayne was by now the CO of 1 SAS. David Stirling's earlier views of his Second in Command's fitness to command the Regiment had not prevented that. Mayne seemed equally pleased to see the sergeant who had vanished through the road block in the Benghazi raid. He appeared to study Almonds intently. Did he see any after-effects of the previous eighteen months of imprisonment, escape and evasion? After a lowering look Mayne, ever economical with words, said, 'Well, pleased to see you back. How did it go in Italy?' Almonds said that he had been superbly fit just before he was taken prisoner and felt that this had been crucial to his survival. In addition, the Commando and SAS training had proved the prerequisite for survival when the chips were really down.[1]

'It's some time since you parachuted, isn't it,' Mayne said. 'You'd better do some jumps.'

Without any refresher training, Almonds went straight up and did his first jump for nearly three years. He was met on the ground by Mayne, Lockie and John. "Fine,' Mayne said. 'You haven't lost the knack.' Even at three and a half, John was conscious of Mayne as a huge powerful man. It was the first time that he realised there could be a man bigger than his own father. Holding tightly to Lockie's hand, every time he looked round, he met Mayne's cold disapproving stare. This was not because Paddy disliked children: on the contrary, he was very fond of them. But he actively discouraged the presence of wives and children in Darvel. However, he had not reckoned with Lockie who was equally determined after being separated for three years to see something of her husband.[2]

The whole of 1 SAS was regrouping and gearing up for action. By the middle of May 1944, SAS Brigade HQ was advancing its plans for 1 SAS involvement in Operation *Overlord*. According to Brigade Operation Instruction No. 6, dated 17 May, classification Top Secret, these plans relied on building up bases in the areas north east of Château Chinon (codenamed Operation HOUNDSWORTH) and west of Châteauroux (code-named Operation BULBASKET) from D-Day onwards. The aim was to carry out clandestine strategic operations against the enemy lines of communication to prevent them from moving supplies or troops up to the battle area. The Germans would then be forced to retreat by the advancing Allies without the reinforcements they needed. To achieve this meant that the 1 SAS men had to be dropped in by parachute at night to a waiting reception party of the French Resistance. The SAS would then carry out a recce of the area to assess the strength and organisation of Resistance groups, the danger of enemy interference and the availability of supply dropping zones and storage possibilities. 2 SAS would be operating to their east.[3] On 19 May, SAS Brigade Operation Instruction No. 12, also classified Top Secret, stated that 'Operations of 1 SAS against the railways in SW France will be known as GAIN".[4]

These plans were being drawn up in response to SHAEF (Supreme Headquarters Allied Expeditionary Force) intelligence about German formations and their likely troop movements on D-Day and thereafter, up to D + 28 days. The cutting of road and railway communications south of the Loire should therefore delay the arrival of 276, 277 and 272 Infantry Divisions and hinder the movements of 273 Panzer Division and 271 Infantry Division. The railway lines most likely to be used for movements included the one from Toulouse to Orléans via Brive and Vierzon. 1 SAS were to be ready to begin operations against these lines from D + 4 onwards. Airfields in the area were to be considered separately but attacks would still need SAS assistance locally. Although operations could be mounted from the UK, information sent back by radio was invaluable in deciding which airfields were worth attacking and how to target the bombing.[5]

The reforming of the SAS at Darvel marked a turning point for the Regiment and for Almonds too. He had been a sergeant since 1940. In the intervening time, he had been mostly on active service in the desert, or a POW, or escaping from the Italians, 'the Italian picnic' as he called it. On rejoining the SAS at Darvel he was promoted to staff-sergeant. 1 SAS then formed a new Squadron – 'D' Squadron – commanded by a young Major called Ian Fenwick. He was the only SAS Squadron Commander appointed by Paddy Mayne who had not experienced active service with the SAS in the Western Desert or Italy. This was evidence of how highly Mayne regarded him. Almonds was then promoted again, to Warrant Officer Class II, and made Squadron Sergeant-Major of 'D' Squadron. From the start, he and Ian Fenwick got on. Both were good-looking, superbly fit and confident leaders of men. In addition, they shared the same dry sense of humour. Fenwick was a brilliant cartoonist who had been working for a national daily newspaper before the war. He had a perceptive eye and merciless wit, which he deployed mostly to debunk the mores and attitudes of the society of his day, including Army officers. His work is still often seen today.[6]

Many of the new recruits to the SAS were destined for 'D' Squadron and Almonds's job was to give them specialist training and inculcate the ideals and culture of the Regiment. Hardly any of them had seen action before. Some were not really of the best calibre for the SAS and would not have been selected by Stirling in the early days. But by 1944, human resources were no longer plentiful and it was a question of working with what was available. As always, they were all volunteers and knew that joining the SAS would mean dangerous operations behind enemy lines, most probably in occupied France. Like Almonds, the new men had originally been attracted by the excitement and the idea of something new.[7]

ONE OF IAN FENWICK'S CARTOONS

Training was typical – walk them till they drop and then bivouac them out in the countryside. This was fairly arduous because they began in the depths of winter with an exercise carried out in February, dropping onto Carradale, half way up the Mull of Kintyre. In addition to having to endure the harsh weather conditions, the lack of sleep and the need to live off the land while at the same time avoiding capture made for a harrowing experience. But it later proved invaluable in equipping the men with skills that were not just essential for survival but for carrying out effective operations in occupied France.[8]

From his own experience of Italy, Almonds was convincing proof that no amount of head knowledge can replace actual practice in the field. He was able to add a flavour of reality to the training and to share with the new men something of the loneliness and constant danger of operating alone in a foreign and hostile country. In his view, final survival in such an alien environment depended on expertise that had become so ingrained as to be second nature. It was also about adaptation; a matter of dropping in and either fitting into the countryside or not. Men from the cities had more difficulty with blending into the landscape, even in their own country. But many of them made up for it in courage, intelligence and fitness. In addition, the new volunteers underwent training in resourcefulness and intelligence work. Just prior to departure, after they had been 'caged' – placed within a compound within another compound to prevent them from disclosing any information about the raid, even unwittingly, before departure – they were briefed and given French money and a code, which took the form of a silk word square. There was very little language training: there was no time to make the sort of investment that would have been necessary.[9] Sometimes, the men needed more than training. Most welcomed some support and a chat. Some inwardly felt guilty about feelings that they did not dare to express, fear of going into action, or even fear of parachuting. Almonds's approach was not to deny that fear existed, but to accept it as a reality. He told them, 'Fear is a constant companion. One never really gets over the natural fear of jumping, very unnaturally, out of an aeroplane. It is a question of not thinking too much about it but just getting on quickly with what has to be done. Parachuting is only a means of transport.' But some men remained desperately afraid. At a dance the night before they all left for the drop into France, Lockie noticed that some of the men were tense and silent, standing white-faced around the edge of the dance floor. She remembered that they were among those who did not come back.[10]

An additional stress factor was caused by false alarm departures. The SAS moved down to the south of England near Swindon ready for despatch to France. When they were placed on stand-by, the men would be given a final briefing and then caged. They were then taken out to the Stirling or Halifax aircraft that would take them to the DZ. Only then did they learn their destination. Sometimes, they would get as far as boarding the planes and then, for some reason, the drop would be cancelled. Parties that were all 'psyched up' to go were often stood down at the last minute because of a technical problem or bad weather in France. Almonds was used to sitting in aircraft waiting to jump but some of the younger men were very tense. They would deplane, knowing that they would have to repeat the whole process again.[11]

Launching an SAS operation into France, even a fairly small one, was no easy matter. Unlike the raids in the Western Desert, four-man parties could not simply get into vehicles and drive pretty well all the way to the target. The *SAS Troops War Diary* for June 21 1944 shows that active concurrence with a plan was required by a whole range of interested authorities:

SHAEF at Kingston
Main HQ 21 Army Group at Portsmouth
(Sometimes) HQ AEAF at Stanmore
SFHQ and EMFFI in central London
HQ Airborne Troops at Moor Park, West London
Tac HQ SAS Troops at Moor Park, with Bde Signals WT terminals
(Sometimes) Main HQ SAS Troops at SORN, Ayrshire
Unit HQs at Fairford transit camp, Gloucestershire
(Sometimes) unit rear HQs in Ayrshire
Bde dump and packing station near Fairford
HQ 38 Group RAF at Netheravon
Up to six 38 Group airfields in Oxford, Gloucester and Dorset shires
(Sometimes) RAF station Tempsford
Deployed SAS parties in the interior of France[12]

The dominating factors in arranging operations at short notice were, therefore, the telephone and teleprinter facilities in the UK, which were efficient, and the WT (wireless telegraphy) contacts with the field, which were, at best, tenuous. The main impression which those who worked at Bde HQ in this period would retain was of the constant ringing of telephone bells, to the sound of orderlies' boots arriving with more wireless and teleprinter messages.[13]

But in spite of these difficulties, it was seen as crucial to the success of *Overlord* to drop the SAS into France. The destruction of railway communications across the Rivers Seine and Loire, and the damage to the 'ceinture' system around Paris, had canalised all German rail communications to the battle area. This made the gap between Paris and Orléans particularly important to the enemy and therefore to the Allies' 21 Army Group. The only good double-track railway still available was Troyes – Orléans – Tours – Le Mans – Argentan, but a number of lower-capacity switch lines also remained in the area. On 12 June, SAS Brigade issued its Operation Instruction No. 22 – Operation GAIN, again classified Top Secret. The object of the operation was to cut the German lateral railway communications in the bottleneck area Rambouillet – Provins – Gien – Orléans – Chartres and to continue to interfere with German rail 'comms' in the area between Paris and Orléans for a period of about three weeks, beginning as soon as possible. Six parties were to be dropped, code-named SABU 70 to 75. The *War Diary* for 11 June summed up the plan as follows:

> Bombing of Seine-et-Loire has made gap between Paris and Orléans of special importance. 21 Army Group attach great importance to it; SAS Tps directed to put in a few parties to attack rd and rly comms.
> Op Instr 22 (Appx III/22 issued to 1 SAS Regt)[14]

The stated aim of the Operation GAIN Instruction was to drop on the night of 13/14 June (D+8). It was mounted at only a couple of hours' notice when the order came on the evening of 14 June that 'this was it'. That night, Almonds, Ian Fenwick and their parties were to parachute into France. They had been living mostly in the transit camp at Fairford. Although Lockie was not far away, living with her parents in Bristol, there was no time for Almonds to say goodbye. Shortly after he left, she was officially notified that he was once again on active service and guessed that it was France. A sudden fear gripped her. While she had never really worried about him in the desert, she was anxious for every moment of the time that he spent on the other side of the Channel.[15] By now, the war was a desperate and evil business.

After the usual planning and preparations for a drop, the SAS men went through the familiar procedure of packing, caging and briefing at

RAF Fairford. They got into the big four-engined Stirling bomber. They knew only that the DZ was on the edge of the forest of Orléans. Each man had a kitbag strapped to his right leg with a drawstring release. After jumping, the kitbag was allowed to dangle at the end of 25 feet of line, so that as it hit the ground it would warn the man above to be ready for the ensuing impact. The heavy dangling weight also acted as a counterbalance to limit drifting if there was a stiff wind blowing. The Stirling revved up its engines and lumbered noisily off the ground. Before long they crossed the Channel and were soon over Caen, whereupon the German gun batteries promptly opened up at them. Below them they knew that Allied troops were still on the beaches. They eased themselves into position near the gaping hole in the floor of the Stirling, dragging their leg bags with them. The minutes seemed like hours as they sat there waiting to jump into black nothingness to an unknown fate. Suddenly, the jump light came on and out they went, Fenwick first, followed by Almonds and then the rest.[16]

They hurtled out into the dark rainy night. It was very windy. After dropping through the blackness for a while, he felt the leg bag rope slacken and braced himself for the shock of landing. With a huge jolt, he landed with one leg on the edge of a ditch while the other went down into it, dislocating the knee he had 'left behind' so that he could not walk on it. As he pulled his canopy round to ensure that the wind did not fill it and drag him along, he saw through the gloom an approaching figure. Quickly, he pulled out his pistol, a US issue Colt automatic. To his immense relief, the dark shape turned out to be M. Poulard of the French Resistance. As planned, they had been met by special forces reception at a DZ 2 kilometres (1¼ miles) west of Pithiviers.

Almonds and M. Poulard exchanged passwords and a few phrases in English. The rest of the party then came together. All except one, who had injured his back very badly, had landed safely. The Resistance reception party were very efficient and extremely helpful. They buried the 'chutes and helped to gather up their kit and the containers of supplies. M. Poulard then offered to fix up the dislocated knee. He got my father to his farmhouse and sent for the local bonesetter to put the knee back into place. While they were waiting for him to arrive on his bicycle, Almonds was offered some *eau de vie* as a painkiller. This is a clear, fiery liquid, that tastes rather like schnapps, distilled from fruit wine. A licence to distil this remarkable beverage is still required in France today and is often passed down in the family. The bonesetter arrived and the knee was manipulated back into position and strapped up. Whether due to the effects of the *eau de vie* or the skill of the bonesetter, the operation itself proved not to be too painful. The injury could not have been serious, since Almonds quickly recovered. Unfortunately, reports of his accident were, in this instance, greatly exaggerated and someone radioed back to England that he was wounded. This news was passed on to Lockie and caused her a good deal of needless anxiety.[17]

The next arrival on the scene was M. Blanchard, the local baker, who was driving his *camion*, or baker's van, and one or two 'D' Squadron personnel who were already in the vicinity. Of the six SABU parties scheduled to drop on the night of 14/15 June, bad weather and aircraft unserviceability meant that only two had done so. But another drop had been made on night of 13/14 June, consisting of Lieutenant Watson and party and Lieutenant Jock Riding, along with Sergeant Dunkley, Corporal Langston, Lance Corporal Sadler (who was no relation to Mike Sadler, LRDG), Lance Corporal Alibert and Trooper Ion. When all the arrangements had finally been agreed, Almonds was crammed into the van, along with Troopers Ion and Packman and Sergeants Dunkley, Duffy and others, and driven away deeper into the forest of Orléans. Even at that urgent hour, there was about it all an air of the faintly comical; as Almonds said later, 'Not a million miles away from the TV series *'Allo 'Allo!*'

Almonds and his party began their life in the forest at a place not far from one of the forest warden's huts. The warden was an acquiescent Frenchman who was prepared to turn a blind eye to the presence and subsequent activities of the new arrivals. Nearby was a triple road junction with a road branching to the left. The Germans later set up a machine gun post on it but that was a bit of a stable door job because by then the British visitors had already done a fair amount of damage to the surrounding road and railway communications. On arrival, Almonds did a quick recce to secure their position and then they bivouacked down for the rest of the night. Although they had dropped with three containers of food, ammunition and explosives, they were dependent on a follow up supply drop due two days later.

For communications, they had one MCR 1 'midget' radio receiver and a Jedburgh set, which was a wind-up hand-generated affair and very hard work to use. The arrangement was that messages from Brigade HQ were to be broadcast and repeated through special forces channels to the appropriate Resistance groups. GAIN radio operators would liaise with the local Resistance group and call in for messages at stated intervals. Two-way communications with the field were established by the Jedburgh set outstations working to two 12 HP sets in the UK. All radio traffic was passed by WT using one-time-pad encryption. This meant that the coded letters for each word were used only once and only the sender and receiver had the same pads. The code was therefore very difficult for the enemy to break, unless of course he captured a one-time-pad.[18]

Owing to the limited number of trained operators and base stations in the UK, only five outstations were ever manned at any one time. Time schedules allowed about two hours a day to each outstation. A third 12 HP set stood by on an emergency radio frequency, on which any outstation could call at any time if it were not already engaged. This meant that the field could contact base at any time but the base could not contact the field, except at scheduled times.

The wireless skills of the men in the field made a huge difference to successful communications. Limited time and facilities in the UK meant that comms with the field were restricted to the laying on of air operations and the passing of immediate intelligence reports and brief operation orders. The passage of long situation reports, location statements and operation instructions was out of the question. Once a party was committed to the field, little was known of its movements and little control could, or needed to be, exercised over it. The need for a very high standard of telegraphese and faultless ciphering was apparent. Most messages arrived either mutilated or much too long or, as the *War Diary* observes, in the case of 4 French Battalion, both. Operation GAIN was a conspicuous exception and sent short, clear reports.[19]

For one-way communications, the Op GAIN personnel were occasionally able to benefit from BBC radio broadcasts sending speech on two frequencies. This was a useful channel of unclassified news bulletins but could only be used for the vaguest operational traffic and only then to stations that were not co-located with a Jedburgh set. It could never be known for sure whether that particular station's one-time-pads had fallen into enemy hands since the party was last heard of. Still, it was sometimes useful for urgent, unclassified communications, including those of a personal nature. While Almonds was in France, one of his friends from 'L' Detachment days, Johnny Rose, wrote to Lockie and said she could relay any emergency message. Messages could also be got back, although this took some time. How Lockie would have wished for such a system in 1941 when John was feared dying and Almonds so far away in Kabrit. Fortunately for all three of them, in 1944 it was not necessary.[20]

The day after they landed, Ian Fenwick and Almonds decided that he and three others from his party should blow the railway line between Orléans and Montargis. They lay low for the rest of the day, hid their equipment containers and then, as soon as it was dark, they set off. It seemed to Almonds as they trudged the 12 miles or so to the target that only the venue had changed since the days in the desert when they had first used guncotton and learned to pick the most vulnerable spot at which to sabotage the rails. But that night, they could not find any railway points, or parts of the track that would have to be remade by hand, or any curves. Such stretches of line were tightly guarded. So they had to content themselves with planting their charges at a couple of places where two straight pieces of line joined. This meant that at least two lots of rails would have to be removed and repaired or replaced. Having fitted a pressure switch and time delay and feeling satisfied that at least they had started their work in France, they made their getaway and set a brisk pace back through the few remaining hours of darkness to their base. A little while later, the dull distant sound of the explosion confirmed that Operation GAIN had opened for business.[21]

A few days later, on the night of 16/17 June another GAIN drop took place a little further to the south, not far from Nibelle and Vitry-aux-Loges, where two officers and their parties landed together. Seven containers were also dropped for the SF reception party.

One of the new arrivals was Lieutenant Leslie Bateman, whom my father had known slightly at Darvel, and who was one of 'D' Squadron's officers.[22] He and my father did not meet up again in France until towards the end of their time there.

Bateman was a fair-haired young man, with an intelligence and air of purpose that inspired trust. He had the added advantage, rare among Englishmen in those days, of speaking very good French. Fortunately it was not *too* good and on one occasion this probably saved his life. Fenwick asked him to go and recce a French roadside café, *l'Aubèrge de la Cour Dieu*. This was located on the Pithiviers to Orléans road and was used by the Germans to entertain their '*amours*' and consequently usually had a good selection of transport parked outside. Fenwick indeed had his eye on these vehicles and wanted more detailed information so that a raid could be planned. Bateman was chosen because of his good French and he took with him Corporal Bert Baynham who although he spoke no French was otherwise an excellent 'accomplice'. They both got into some borrowed French civilian clothes and with Colt .45 automatics hidden under their clothes they wandered nonchalantly into the *Auberge*. Having abandoned their uniforms they ran the risk of being shot as spies if discovered, but Hitler's illegal decree against the SAS meant that they ran that risk anyway.[23]

Bateman and Baynham approached the inn on foot and sat down at some tables and chairs outside. A middle-aged Frenchwoman who was wiping cups behind the bar came out and Bateman ordered two beers. When the woman reappeared with the drinks, Bateman engaged her in conversation. While he chatted, he offered her a cigarette. It happened to be a 'Favorit', a German brand that he had acquired from one of the recent night-time train 'hold-ups'. During their conversation, the woman never commented on Bateman's good French and, in spite of his fair hair and blue eyes, he thought he was genuinely being taken for a local Frenchman. He idly asked some questions about how much the inn was used at weekends but the woman's answers were not very revealing.

While they were sitting there, both men took stock of the layout, then after a while they drained their glasses and left. This turned out to be in the nick of time. As they were walking out, a German vehicle came up behind them, pulled in and stopped at the inn. The two SAS forced themselves to stroll on while every nerve in their bodies urged them to take flight. Once under cover of the trees, they gave into their instincts and took to their heels. Whatever the woman may have said to the Germans, they did not give chase. It seems that the woman had decided that Bateman, with his blond looks, fluent but obviously non-native French and flashing 'Favorit' cigarettes, was part of Hitler's Gestapo or the SS. The terrified Germans probably did the obvious thing and went in the opposite direction. London, however, did not allow a raid on the *Auberge* to take place. The attack could have resulted in vicious German reprisals but in any case, the GAIN contingent was told, the necessary jeeps were on their way, by parachute.[24]

Because it was safer for the parties to be separated, Fenwick and his group had set up their base at HQ about a quarter of a mile away from Almonds' group to the north-west. Fenwick had the cooks and radio operators, including Sergeant Bunfield and Troopers Ion and Packman, with him. Two nights later, on 19 June, the longed-for supply drop took place. Almonds's section was waiting for jeeps, more weapons and explosives, and POL. The parachuting into France of such requirements were nothing short of a miracle. When the Americans later arrived on the scene, they found it hard to believe that he and his men had been gaily driving around on French roads in a jeep that they *hadn't* stolen from Uncle Sam.

The delivery of a jeep required some prior partial dismantling and reassembly *in situ*. With the drop came the familiar Vickers-K machine-guns to be mounted in pairs on the front and rear, together with ammunition. Each jeep, minus its steering wheel, was sitting in the middle of a giant tray. Lines were attached to each corner of the tray and to a junction box some feet above the jeep, which was connected to a central parachute above. Four more parachutes were deployed from each of the corners. Jeeps had to be dropped from a Halifax and once the five parachutes had been deployed, there was nothing to be done but wait for it to hit the deck.

Almonds and his party went to the DZ and waited. Eventually, they heard the faint sound of a Halifax bomber. As it got louder and roared overhead, they saw a dark shape against the sky. They watched as their jeep floated down, beautiful in the moonlight. But at this point, the problems began. The tray landed fair and square in the top of a broad oak tree, right next to a road used by the Germans. It had to be got down and hidden before daylight; otherwise their cover in the area would be blown. The only way was to try and saw off the right branches so that the jeep would land upright. After some hours, the last key branch was sawn through and the jeep thundered to earth with an almighty crash. Although it did land the right way up, the four engine mountings were broken off. Nevertheless, they managed to drag the jeep away from the road and have it hidden before daybreak.[25]

It was at this point that Almonds met Antoine Kroutchelnitsky, the local *M. le garagiste* in nearby Nancray-sur-Rimarde. Like most of the Resistance, he had a trade that he plied by day while working with the underground the rest of the time. Such people ran the most frightful risks because even if they were individually careful and very professional so that they did not get caught, the Germans were known to commit atrocities collectively if they were subject to local attack or harassment. The village of Nancray-sur-Rimarde put itself completely at the disposal of their British visitors and the occupants literally worked day and night for them at great personal risk. People like the Abbé Thomas, who was later murdered by the Germans, Roger Vallée, Bernard Bertrand and Léandre Beauvy offered invaluable help and support.

The SAS did not need anyone to lead them around or help them to carry out operations but the value of local and up-to-date information, together with practical help cannot be overestimated. So it was that under dark the next evening, Almonds got the wounded jeep to Kroutchelnitsky's garage where he set about repairing it through the night by candlelight. Eventually, they had three vehicles, which meant that they could nip out and around the surrounding environs, wreaking havoc but, like lightening, never appearing to strike in the same place twice.

On the night of 17/18 June in the forest of Orléans area, another eight men and seven containers were dropped, according to the *War Diary* to a fifty-strong reception party. On 19 June, having established their base, attempts to put more troops into Operation GAIN were frustrated by three nights of bad weather. On the night of 27/28 June, three men, one jeep and twenty-four containers were dropped in the Pithiviers area but the guns and petrol were smashed on landing because of a faulty container parachute, probably due to a delay action device. According to the *War Diary*, 31 'D' Squadron personnel were dropped into France in June.[26] They were reinforced in early July by another 16, but this included an ill-fated party of twelve led by the Squadron 2IC, Captain Pat Garstin.

Life in the forest was not as bad as it might have been, provided that one took account of the danger and planned around it. The Germans never came deep into the woods, probably because they knew that it was occupied by unwanted visitors and they didn't want to run into them. Almonds and his men 'cammed up' the jeeps in the same way as the Germans by removing the lamp masks and putting sprigs of foliage all round. Although the enemy made good use of camouflage, they did not bother with routine roadblocks and the checking of identity cards on main roads until about the beginning of August, when the Allies advancing from the north-west were getting too close for comfort. This was something of a charter for the SAS whose whole philosophy was still predicated upon the element of surprise and the fact that the enemy was not expecting to find them so far behind the front line. Throughout June and July, they were able to roam more or less at will using the jeep headlights at night as the Germans did, but turning them off if they found 'the Boche' doing the same.

The Germans in the area seemed mainly preoccupied by the possibility of aircraft attack from above. They tended to keep to minor roads in the area and drove around with one man hanging out on each side of their vehicle, one on the radiator and one on the roof, all heavily armed and continually watching the skies.[27] The enemy's methods and fighting value received a mixed assessment from the SAS. They were poor at restricting behind-the-line activity and carried out no identity checks. German sentries were not inquisitive and were not seen using torches. If in pairs, they usually stood together. Railway lines were ineffectively guarded by Frenchmen. On the other hand, their fighting quality was regarded as good. Germans were never seen to surrender, and in retreat weapons were usually carried to the last. German prisoners openly stated their mistrust of Hitler and blamed everything on the Nazis, SS and propaganda.[28]

Unfortunately, one of the danger factors to be taken into account turned out to be the local Maquis. Unlike the Resistance, they did not have occupations during the day and many of them were motivated mainly by a wish to avoid conscription into forced labour in Germany. Worryingly, some of them were also rather shady characters. Their main aim appeared to be to get hold of as many weapons as possible and hold the local farmers, or anyone else against whom they had a grudge, to ransom. To make matters worse, they were persistent in wanting to camp near the SAS which increased their risk of detection by the enemy and caused them to break camp more than once.[29]

The quality and effectiveness of the Maquis varied throughout France. In some places, they did very good work. Sometimes, they were badly organised and had too many chiefs. They would begin to operate too soon, before even the most basic training had been undertaken and some sort of discipline had been established, and were often active too near their own camp. Consequently, they were detected and dispersed by the Germans just as their best moment to strike a real blow for France was arriving. Since they were badly organised, they also tended to go to pieces when attacked.[30]

In the forest of Orléans the local Maquis (called the Maquis de Loris) were under the command of Colonel O'Neil (pronounced with a French accent, whose family had left Ireland some 300 years before). He was ably supported by two French Army captains, *Capitaine* Giry and *Capitaine* Albert. There existed a sort of *modus operandi* between the Maquis de Loris and the GAIN teams against their common foe.[31] Jock Riding and his men sometimes acted as escort on Maquis missions, one of which at Bellegarde benefited them to the extent of 17,000 Boche cigarettes – including the 'Favorit' that Batemen offered at the *Auberge de la Cour Dieu* – and huge quantities of sugar. On another occasion, they obtained enough butter and cheese to keep them going for the rest of the war. In all cases, these missions were rather like a circus with lights blazing, and the Maquis making as much noise as they possibly could.[32]

Just as in the old days at Tobruk, Almonds started from the basis that any fool could be uncomfortable, whereas if they established a proper base they would be much more effective in striking at the enemy. The first thing they did, under his supervision, was to build a log cabin that would take him and three others: Vic Long,[33] Sergeant Lambert and one other. Using 'borrowed' timber that had already been felled and sawn, they soon erected a passable abode. Almonds notched the wood in strategic places so that the timbers would lock together when assembled. The whole thing was then lashed tightly together with parachute cord and had not a single nail in it. They covered their new home with two parachutes, first a white canopy suspended above it from the trees and, higher up, a green parachute, so that seen from the air they blended into the forest. Like latter-day Robin Hoods, they had a safe retreat from which to sally forth and right wrongs in the surrounding countryside. Apart from comfort, which enabled them to rest and maintain their morale, the log cabin ensured that they could keep their weapons, ammunition and maps dry. This turned out to be a wise move because it rained quite often during the two and a half months they were there.[34]

The SAS lived partially off the fat of the land. The wood had plenty of wild pig and they rustled the odd chicken for the pot. Water was rather more of a problem because it had either to be brought in cans by the French or collected from one or two natural springs. Apart from the need to drink and cook, it was quite important that they shaved fairly regularly so that they did not attract attention when driving around in the jeeps. Probably because of his Guards background, Almonds shaved every single day while he was in France. Cooking mostly had to be done after dark and before dawn so that the smoke of their fires did not give away their position. To augment their issued tinned and other rations, the Resistance brought them milk, bread, butter, cheese and eggs. Although they were efficiently supplied by container drops, the diet of largely tinned stews and vegetables became rather monotonous. There was never enough tea, chocolate, sweets or cigarettes and the lack of these commodities was crucial to morale.[35]

One thing that was missing was help in the house – it was *very* hard to get good servants in those days in that part of France. But towards the end of their time in the forest, they acquired a semi-volunteer. The Maquis had stretched a trip wire across a road that ran near the edge of the wood and they succeeded in unseating a German motor cycle despatch rider. Rather than let him come to a sticky end (the Maquis did not normally take prisoners but killed all the Germans they captured, a practice which the Germans tended to reciprocate) Almonds and his party took the German on as a batman-cum-cook. 'Fritz', as they called him, was a clerk typist by trade but while he was on temporary detachment to 'D' Squadron, 1 SAS, his duties became rather more mundane. He peeled all the potatoes, cooked all the meals and did all the washing up. He never complained and didn't try to escape, because he knew when he was well off.[36] He was at least fairly safe where he was and no longer had to make hazardous journeys around the locality waiting to be ambushed by the Maquis, the Resistance or both.

By now, it was a commonly held view that that the Allies were going to win the war. It was only a question of how long it would take. Fritz was a cheerful soul who relaxed considerably when he realised that he was going to be well treated. He spoke a little English so it was possible to have some sort of a relationship with him. Towards the end of their time there, the moment came when it was right to let him slip away. Almonds did not want him to be accused by his own side of fraternising with the enemy, or end up being shot or captured by the Americans.

During the many daylight hours when the occupants of the log cabin were not sleeping but could not carry out any overt action against the enemy, they resorted to various pastimes to keep themselves amused. Almonds made them bows and arrows and soon had them practising the age-old skill of English archery. He also spent many hours making a plaited sennit lug-line for the boat he had designed in his mind while in solitary confinement in the Italian POW camp and still intended to build. He had learned this seventeenth-century skill as a boy from an old uncle who had been a sea captain. The line needed carefully crafted knots at accurately measured intervals. It could then be fitted with a device with fins that would measure distance as it turned through the water. First he stretched two lengths of parachute rigging line between two trees about fourteen paces apart. Then he began to plait around the two lines with nine other lengths of parachute cord to produce a very thick strong rope. This was slow, time-consuming work, but exactly what he needed to fill the hours of enforced idleness and yet give him the satisfaction of producing a useful product at the end of his labours. When he finally left the forest, he did not forget to take the finished line with him.[37]

Operation GAIN was well established and the teams quickly blended in with their surroundings. Nor were they fettered by being over-managed from home. Command and control was exercised from the UK with a very light hand. Once parties were in the field, only the broadest directives were ever sent to them. In one or two special cases, they were directed onto particular targets but, in general, their *modus operandi* were left to the discretion of party commanders. They had been well trained in the SAS Brigade's doctrine on what types of operation and organisation were feasible. It was always accepted that the local commander understood local conditions, was doing his best, and should be left to fight his own battle as briefed with as little redirection as possible.[38]

The lessons of Benghazi had been well learned.

Chapter Fifteen

No Gain without Pain

Once properly established in the Forest of Orléans, the Operation GAIN contingent got down to serious business. They would go out at night in one or two of the jeeps to carry out *ad hoc* raids, mostly on railway lines but sometimes to attack unguarded German vehicles or ammunition dumps. As the Germans in the area gradually realised that the damage was not all being carried out by the French Resistance or the Maquis, these activities became increasingly hazardous. The most vulnerable points of target installations became very heavily defended. Fenwick and Almonds decided to focus instead on a stretch of railway line that ran eastwards from Orléans towards Fontainebleau, between Bellegarde and Montargis. Here there were a couple of stretches where the line ran parallel to the road for some distance, presenting an ideal spot from which the SAS men could blast a train until it stopped without even having to get out of their own vehicle. There was a manned level crossing on this road and given its importance the Germans had gone so far as to install one of their own men as crossing keeper.[1]

It was a deep black night when they set off for the first of these attacks. Light summer breezes tossed the trees along the roadsides as they sped towards their target. They expected a train at a particular spot in the early hours of the morning. At about 01.00 hours, they forced the German crossing keeper to open the gate for them. Finding himself staring down the barrel of a gun, the German looked the other way and let them through. This was not entirely surprising since his predecessor in post had been killed when he had attempted to attack another raiding party trying to get through the crossing. Having once let them through, it was unlikely that the new crossing keeper would then blow the whistle on them. While they were waiting for the train, Fenwick and Almonds decided that there was in fact little risk that the German would call for reinforcements. There was therefore nothing to be gained by harming the man, since it would simply blow their cover, and everything to be gained by getting him to open the gate for them on their nightly sorties.

Shortly after the raiders got through the gate, sure enough, they heard the distant clackety-clack of the approaching train. Just before it got level with them, they opened up with the Vickers-K machine guns and then continued so that the hapless train was strafed all along its side as it ran past them. They carefully avoided hitting the driver's cab, because he was likely to be French. As the stricken train began to slow, they made off back the way they had come, leaving it to be stripped by the Resistance. They repeated this operation quite frequently. As they crossed back through the level crossing, the German would come out and obligingly let them through, knowing very well what they had been up to. But it never seemed to occur to the Germans to reinforce the guards on that part of the railway line or to double up the guard on the crossing. In any case, the guards were often Frenchmen pressed into service who really had no interest in doing the job properly. The Germans themselves were rather bad sentries. They were not inquisitive enough and mostly spent their time in pairs chatting to each other rather than maintaining active observations.[2]

The contents of the trains were always unknown. They were predominantly goods trains but there was always the risk that one would be a troop carrier and hundreds of Germans would come spilling out.

They really started to get into their stride. The *War Diary* for June records that three railway lines were cut in the Paris – Orléans area on the night of 21/22 June by Op. GAIN.[3] Their determined efforts are marked by another entry for the night of 23/24 June in the same area where the Paris train was partially derailed.[4] On 29 June, a locomotive was reported destroyed[5] and Almonds submitted a group of heavily guarded petrol bowsers at Montargis for bombing.

On the night of 4/5 July, the initial parties dropped into France were reinforced. Twelve men landed in one stick while another four men and three jeeps were dropped separately. A week later, on the night of 10 July, another jeep was delivered.[6] So the erstwhile Robin Hoods did not lack for transport and drove around the countryside as bold as brass. They became even more confident about driving around at night with their lights on. Although the Germans may have suspected the presence of unwelcome visitors who occupied the woods, it does not seem to have occurred to them that these interlopers would have the audacity to have vehicles delivered and then to drive around in them.[7]

One of the reinforcing parties of 4 July party was under the command of the 'D' Squadron 2IC, an Irishman called Pat Garstin. Mike Sadler was on board the aircraft with the party, acting as the Intelligence Officer observer. His job was to observe on behalf of the SAS and debrief the air crew when the show was over. As the Stirling lumbered its way to the DZ, some of the men appeared very jittery. Sadler found that this was something that varied between drops. Even the state of mind of the air crew could make quite a difference to morale. Sadler himself felt rather vulnerable, perched in the nose of the aircraft in the great glass greenhouse where the bomb aimer normally lay. The bombing equipment had been removed to make room for the observer. Suddenly, the flight became very bumpy.[8]

'There's another aircraft around,' said the pilot peering out of the cockpit. But it was too dark to see anything. Eventually, they saw the usual few lights on the ground and the pilot lined up on them before coming in over the dropping area. As the stick went out, Sadler looked down and was dismayed to see flashes of gunfire and more lights on the ground. Although the DZ and reception had been arranged through SFHQ, the parachutists appeared to have been expected by a detachment of Germans who had opened fire on them without hesitation. The aircraft banked, circled round and headed for home. But even before they had left the area, they were attacked from the front by a Messerschmitt 110. The pilot immediately began to throw the aircraft all over the place and managed to avoid taking any serious hits. But the enemy followed them for most of the way back and gave them quite a pasting. The whole encounter seemed strange to Sadler because Messerschmitt 110s did not normally attack head on.[9]

The descending men were greeted on the ground by a group of men in civilian clothes who greeted Captain Garstin with the words 'Vive la France'. Then came a burst of what sounded like Bren gun fire and they replied with their carbines.[10] One can only imagine what thoughts raced through their minds. Had someone in the French Resistance betrayed them, or had there been some other mistake? Whatever it was, it led to tragedy. Two of the men, Troopers Morrison and Norman, tried to rescue their badly injured Lieutenant, Johnny Wiehe. But he told them to go on and save themselves. The two men managed to evade capture and got clean away. Another trooper was eventually caught but escaped a few weeks later. Four were wounded and two were sent to hospital, where one died the next day.[11] In any case, hospital was only a brief reprieve for the SAS. They all knew that that unless they could escape they would be shot because of Hitler's decree to kill all captured SAS.[12]

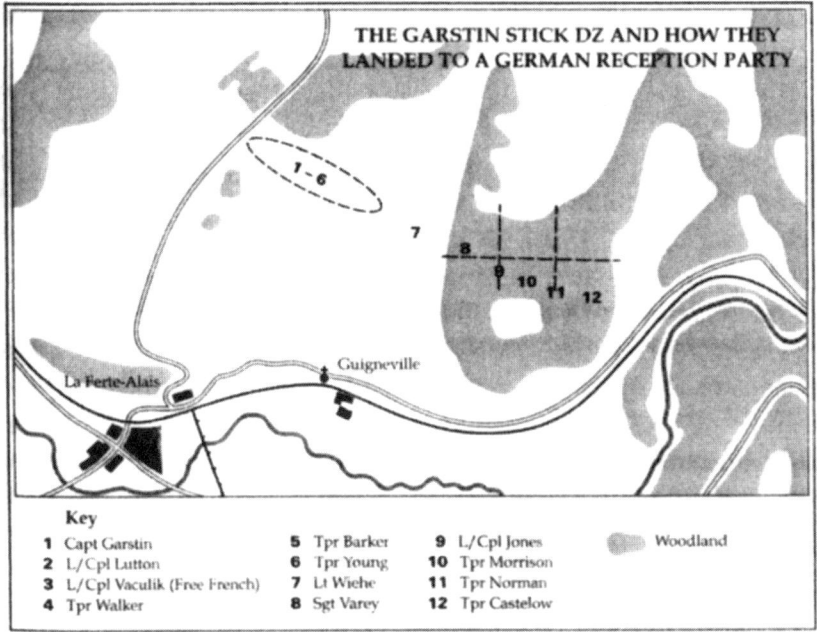

The remainder were taken into Paris, first to a converted hotel behind the Champs de Mars and then to Gestapo Headquarters in the rue de Saussaies. There, 'interrogation was carried out in a forcible manner'. Three days later they were returned to the hotel where they were rejoined by Garstin and one other who had been in hospital. Garstin was in a very weak state.[13]

After the war, Almonds heard a full account of what then happened from one of only two survivors, 'Ginger' Jones. According to Jones, while they were held in prison the Germans tried to convince them that if they changed into civilian clothes then, under the Geneva Conventions, they would be exchanged in Switzerland for German POWs and repatriated. Pat Garstin, who was wounded and could hardly walk, seems to have believed what the Germans said. They kept repeating that because this exchange was to take place under civil extra-territorial law, and the POWs would have to pass through a neutral country, they would need to change out of their uniforms. The SAS usually operated behind enemy lines in uniform which means that they were not spies. The fact that they did so successfully during the Second World War was a constant irritant to Hitler and may have provoked him into issuing his decree.[14]

Ginger Jones did not like the sound of this story. Nor did some of the others. In vain they tried to persuade Garstin that Jerry was up to no good and should not be believed on any account. But Garstin seemed convinced that they should co-operate with their captors. Perhaps he was tempted by the thought of pulling off a successful negotiation with the enemy that would at least get his men and himself safely back home. He must have been feeling very unhappy about the situation they were in, although there is no evidence at all to suggest that it was his fault. *Did he stop to ask himself the question, 'for what other reason would the Germans want them to change out of their uniforms?'* It is very difficult to change the clothes of dead men, especially if they have been shot. But in spite of the briefings he had had about Hitler's edict, Garstin appears to have believed the Germans.[15]

After some mistreatment by the Gestapo, on 8 August, the remnants of the Garstin stick were eventually made to change into civilian clothes that had been provided for them. Handcuffed and carrying their uniforms in bags, they were loaded into a lorry and driven away into the darkness. After a while, Garstin said to one of the Germans

'If we're going to Switzerland, why the hell are we going north-west?' The German told him to shut up and the driver increased his speed.

Just before dawn, the lorry stopped near Bauvais in the French Département of the Somme and they were all herded out. Ginger saw that there was a second truck in the woods with a tarpaulin over the back of it. Serge Vaculik, one of the Free French operating with them, asked if they were to be shot and received an affirmative reply. They were lined up with Ginger Jones and Vaculik standing either side of Garstin who was too injured to walk unaided. A Gestapo agent in civilian clothes stood beside two uniformed Gestapo with Sten guns while a third interpreted a sentence of death as it was read out. It ended with the words 'will be shot', at which the men all made a spring for the woods. Vaculik, pursued by firing Germans, managed to get clear. Jones tripped and the Gestapo ran past him, probably taking him for dead. When he got up four bodies were lying on the ground. They had been shot in the back wearing civilian clothes, perfect for a German version of events that these were captured spies, killed in the act of escaping.[16]

Jones and Vaculik managed to evade recapture and made their way separately safely back to England. Jones told Almonds his story at a very early post-war SAS reunion. They never met again at any of the other SAS gatherings. It was as if, having survived such a fearful appointment with death, Jones had had enough of the SAS to last for the rest of his life.[17] A few months after the war, Sadler had the sad task of finding the bodies of the men who had been shot. To cover their traces, the Germans had buried them in a different wood but the local people were very cooperative and soon revealed where they were.[18]

The men of the Garstin stick who evaded capture at the outset also had a remarkable story to tell. One of them was Trooper Castelow, a twenty-eight-year-old brick-maker from Stockton-on-Tees. He dropped with the party of twelve near the village of La-Ferté-Allais. Fortunately for Castelow, he landed a little way away from the others in some woods.[19] He realised that things had gone wrong, cut free from his parachute and hid himself. The next morning, he walked to the village of Vert-le-Petit and contacted the head of the French Resistance who gave him some civilian clothes and a French pass. He later discovered that the Resistance man who was signalling them down had been killed by the Germans and that was why they had dropped into a trap. Castelow then worked with the Resistance for six weeks, ambushing German road transport. He travelled about quite freely and even spent two weeks in Paris during this time. But by about mid-August, the Gestapo realised he was in the area and it became too dangerous to remain. Wearing a French gendarme's uniform, he set out to cycle to Etampes in an attempt to reach the Allied lines in Normandy. On the way, he got caught up in the German retreat and had his bicycle stolen about 10 miles from Etampes. Unfortunately, on discovering it he swore loudly in English and was promptly arrested by a German patrol.[20]

At first, he was going to be shot out of hand as a spy, but the German officer present decided to send him further back behind the front line for questioning. He was put in a lorry and taken to Verdun, where he was kept in a small cell and given very little food once a day. He was made to stand all the time during questioning and during one period was kicked about to encourage him to talk. He refused, however, to tell them what he had been doing, or that he was a paratrooper. After a second week in Verdun, the US advance threatened the town and Castelow was again put in a lorry and driven towards Germany. On 9 September, they crossed the Moselle between Metz and Nancy and stopped for the night about 2 miles from the river.

The prisoner was put in a cottage with one SS guard. However, he was not tied down and his report states succinctly, again using the typical military precision for 'midnight', '… at 23.59 hrs, I killed the guard and took his rifle.'²¹ The enemy had grossly underestimated the calibre of the man they had captured, confined and ill-treated for so long.

Castelow then walked out of the cottage and climbed a wall into the street. He was not challenged and was able to make his way without opposition to the river. He swam the Moselle and started walking back towards the Americans. After meeting US forward units at about 19.00 hours on 10 September, he was taken to their Divisional HQ about ten miles from Verdun and repatriated via Paris on 21 September. Given the amazing performance of this remarkable man and other SAS men like him, it was hardly surprising that Hitler had ordered all captured SAS to be shot.

Troopers Norman and Morrison had an equally eventful time. They had been in the second half of the stick and were among the last five men to jump, landing in the woods, slightly away from the DZ.²² They were in the party of six led by Lieutenant Wiehe, which also included Sergeant Varey and Trooper Castelow. Norman and Morrison made their way towards the main party. It was not difficult to decide which way to go because it was a bright moonlit night; Norman had seen the stick in the air and actually saw some of the men touch down. At the edge of the wood, they heard Lt Wiehe call out, 'Who's there?' On responding with their names, Wiehe shouted that he 'had caught a packet' and was unable even to crawl.²³ Wiehe, who was a Mauritian with relations in the Corbeille area, had in fact requested a fateful exchange of places with Leslie Bateman who had therefore gone on the earlier drop in June. Wiehe was hospitalised by the Germans and on the liberation of Paris was found in La Pitié hospital paralysed from the waist down from a bullet wound through his spine. Bateman later visited him in hospital in Ashtead, Surrey, before Wiehe was moved back to Mauritius where he died two years later, still a young man and a tragic casualty of the war.²⁴

In spite of his appalling injuries, Wiehe refused Norman's and Morrison's offers of help and ordered them to remain under cover and to make for the Allied lines. While heading off in a north-westerly direction, the two men were fired at as they left the wood but the first bursts were high and they were able to get away and crawl through a field. In the vicinity of La-Ferté-Allais, they heard troop movements on the road and lay low for an hour before continuing on to the main Paris railway. After checking for sentries, they crossed the railway but were amazed to find themselves suddenly in the main street of the town. It was a nasty moment. Did they go on, or turn back?

They resolved to go on but, according to Norman, 'the idea of walking through the streets of the town did not altogether appeal to them so they decided to get into the gardens of the houses and move from garden to garden'. The idea was fine but each garden was surrounded by a high railing with a high front entrance gate, on the top of which hung a large bell. This fact was not discovered until they tried to open one of the gates. The bell clanged, a dog barked and an occupant stuck his head out and delivered a volley of voluble French. As neither Norman or Morrison understood a word of the language, they made off without endeavouring to reply.

They then spent some time trying to get across a deep river. After toying with the idea of using their issue escape file to cut through the rather thick mooring chain of a boat, they decided against it for reasons of time and noise. They crossed a small bridge and found themselves in the back garden of another house. Moving quietly around to the front, they came up against 'another one of those confounded railings, complete with the same kind of gate and bell'. But they managed to climb the railing without disturbing anyone and made it to a nearby wood. The next morning, 6 July, Norman asked a French woman at a house not far away for some food and she willingly obliged with some milk, bread and very fat bacon. After rejoining Morrison, they 'soon had the old Tommy cooker going hard at it'. They continued on and at Corbreuse, they were helped by a Frenchman who brought food into a wood for them. He told them that a small detachment of SS troops were stationed in the village.

On the night of 10 July, they set off on a compass bearing, heading north-east, crossed the main Auneau to Dourdan road and railway, noting enemy convoys on the road and finished their march at Prunay-sous-Ablis. On the night of 11/12 July, a good deal of noise nearby turned out next morning to have been enemy troops digging slit trenches and bedding down for the night. The motor vehicle tracks and a litter of envelopes and letters suggested that these were men returning from a forward position who had just received their first mail for some time. Late on 12 July, the track they were following suddenly led them onto a road that according to the map was a third-class road but had unexpectedly been improved to second-class status. Norman looked left and Morrison looked to the right. Suddenly, Norman could not speak. On seeing the expression on his face, Morrison followed his gaze and froze when he saw a road block barricade with a solitary German sentry. Fortunately, the guard was looking in the opposite direction and without even the briefest sign of agreement between them the two SAS men nipped smartly over.

They continued across country to a first-class road carrying an almost continuous stream of enemy traffic away from the battle area towards Chartres. After negotiating this formidable obstacle, the two fugitives reached a wood between Maintenon and St Chéron where they lay up all day on 13 July. The next day they found a farm, where a friendly woman of about thirty gave them some food, and they retired to a nearby wood. When the family came home from work, they visited the two British soldiers, accompanied by four friends, making a total of ten visitors! The French were eager to help and insisted that since the Allies were expected any day, the best thing that Morrison and Norman could do was to stay where they were. The local Maquis also sent a message to say that they were unable to help their British 'camarades' because the Boche were 'sur leurs talons'. So the son of the family at the farm arranged for 'quelqu'un d'autre' to help them.

The 'someone else' turned out to be a Frenchman in glasses whose identity card said that he was the headmaster of a school. He visited them regularly and said that he had almost completed plans to have them repatriated to the UK by air, having passed various messages to London via Paris. He promised to visit them at the end of July but failed ever to reappear. A few days after the failed assignation, Norman and Morrison paid a visit to the farm. They were just coming out of the house when they walked slap into a German officer. Morrison calmly stepped to one side and walked past him down the garden path, while Norman turned to the right and 'shooed' some ducks away from a nearby pond. Both men made their way back to the wood and, fortunately, all was well.

After a further period of time with still no sign of the Frenchman, the son of the family turned up with two young women school teachers who could speak English. They told Norman and Morrison that 'their' Frenchman had made a foolish mistake, been captured by the Gestapo and finally shot. As if in some way to make up for this unhappy turn of events, the young women brought with them four books in English, which Norman thought were 'a bit old, but welcome'. On 15 August at about 19.00 hours, the two schoolteachers turned up in a jeep accompanied by an American officer. Norman and Morrison dug up their uniforms, which they had hidden in the wood, and set off in search of a ride back to Blighty. After forty-three days behind enemy lines, one of the longest evasion operations in SAS history was over.[25]

By mid July, the Operation GAIN men knew that the Allies had landed on the Normandy beaches and were advancing towards them from the north-west. The Germans had begun to retreat and were so short of petrol that most vehicles passing through in convoys were towing another vehicle. Anything that could be done to impede their progress was worth considering. Almonds learned of a factory on the outskirts of Montargis which the Germans had set up to re-tread tyres to help replenish their dwindling stock. When he told Ian Fenwick about it, his reaction was instant. 'Excellent. Let's blow it up!'.[26]

Together, with Fenwick in his jeep and Almonds in his, they set off through what was by now 'their' level crossing. They skirted around Montargis itself and came in again behind the back of the factory which was right on the edge of a small wood. Sneaking down a cart track that led to the back of the factory, they hid in the wood and settled down until daybreak so that they could then do a crawled recce of the building. As dawn came, they suddenly realised that some Germans were coming down the same track. They were in a staff car with an entourage of vehicles including outriders. The Germans stopped, got out, set up some camp tables and spread out some very large maps. 'They must be doing some sort of planning exercise,' Almonds whispered to Fenwick. 'They're probably preparing for a strike or a defensive operation.'

For some reason, the Germans' interest seemed to focus on the wood in which Almonds's and Fenwick's parties were hiding. The soft babble of German floated across on the crisp morning air and the British 'sardines' began to feel more and more uncomfortable. Were the Germans about to launch forth into their part of the wood? Every so often, a German officer would gesticulate to his assembled audience and, sweeping an arm wildly around the site, end up pointing right at the hidden raiders. Fenwick and my father exchanged glances. 'We'd better cam up the vehicles quickly', Almonds said. As usual, the Germans were driving around with bits of foliage sticking out of their trucks. The SAS needed to replenish theirs so the men started grabbing bits of brushwood and twigs and decorating the jeeps, German style.

The Boche continued to gesticulate and several times made as if they were about to come into the wood. It was the moment for decision. If the SAS stayed where there were, a shoot-out against superior numbers was inevitable. There was nothing for it but to take the initiative and move out. Bearing in mind that the SAS always operated behind enemy lines in uniform, the one concession to discretion they decided to make was to turn their berets inside out. By this time, the Regiment had adopted the red beret of the Parachute Regiment, although Paddy Mayne disdained to do so.

The two jeeps set off, with Fenwick in the lead. Almonds was driving the second jeep with three other men in it. They drove steadily, but not too fast, right past the German party. One stepped forward and began to flag them down. Almonds waved back, as if to say 'Sorry, can't stop, we're in a hurry'. Looking back in his rear view mirror, he saw the Germans piling into the staff car. The two SAS jeeps continued on down the track and came to the main road, followed by the staff car. The surprise was total; the Germans must have wondered who they were but could not have dreamed that they were the enemy, so far behind the front line.

After driving along the main road for a while, Fenwick turned off and Almonds followed him down a side road. They were hoping to lose the enemy but instead ended up losing themselves in the process. Unfortunately, the staff car still followed. They came to a clearing with a large building, the front door of which was flanked by two German sentries. Mercifully, the German staff car stopped there. So the two jeeps turned around, went back and turned onto a different main road. Almonds became aware that they were entering a built-up area. The road began to converge at an angle with a railway line. But it was impossible to turn off anywhere. This was what made operations behind enemy lines in France so much more dangerous than the Western Desert.

Suddenly, they were at a knife-rest railway crossing. Fenwick waved impatiently for the crossing keepers to open the gate. This they did and saluted as the two jeeps passed through. Fenwick and Almonds solemnly returned the salutes. Gradually, however, the traffic that they were caught up in slowed to a crawl. They were in the middle of the town of Montargis, where a large German convoy happened to be passing through. Almonds was conscious that he was sitting right in amongst the enemy, wearing a beret inside out with 'Kangol' written across the top of his head. Of all the dangerous situations he had been in, he knew at that moment that this was the most perilous of all. It only needed one of the Germans to decide to get friendly and engage him in a chat, the game would be up and they would all be shot. But he only allowed himself to entertain this thought for a split second.

He spoke quietly to the others. 'Don't make a move. Don't do anything at all. If anything needs to be done, I'll do it.' He rarely needed to give orders as such, but when he did he spoke with authority. This was a situation where one person needed to be in control and the others needed a lot of faith. The occupants of the jeep sat motionless. The convoy, half tanks and half trucks, was taking a break, blocking the road in the process. Germans crossed to and fro in front of the bonnet of the SAS truck chewing buns and swigging beer. Almonds spoke very little German. He sat, one forearm hugging the wheel, but all the time his mind was racing, working, planning what he would do if it came to a confrontation, if the engine stalled, if they were asked to pull over, and a million other possible scenarios.

They continued to crawl through the town, with the Germans smiling at them and nodding to pass the time of day. It seemed an age that they were inching slowly through the town until they finally found themselves out on a clear road again. They had to pass through two more road blocks, where German sentries saluted them and obligingly opened the gates. Fenwick and Almonds still solemnly returned the salutes and drove through, apparently unperturbed. They were never more relieved to reach 'their' German level crossing keeper as he opened the gates and let them through to safety. After the war, Almonds unexpectedly met up with all three of his men at an SAS reunion. To his embarrassment, they were 'all over him' and it was with difficulty that he stopped them from plying him with drinks and expressing their gratitude for bringing them safely through such a nightmare situation.[27]

Fenwick decided not to return to have another go at the factory. They had other fish to fry. At about the end of July, the detachment was warned by radio to prepare for 'an important drop'.[28] Their preparations for this included wider reconnaissance sorties around the area and further dispersal of their locations. After discussing the options, it was decided to leave Almonds and Sergeant Lambert *in situ*, while Jock Riding and his stick occupied Fenwick's original base. Fenwick and the parties with the young officers, Watson, Bateman and Parsons then dispersed. Riding took Lieutenants Bateman and Parsons in civilian cars that they had 'borrowed', to the Château d'Ouchamps, a Resistance base near Thimory. Leslie Bateman was to stay there for a few days and then move on to the Maquis de Lorris, who were understood to be planning a fairly large-scale attack on the German garrison at Orléans. Fortunately, this attack never took place. It would have proved an over-ambitious project, since the Germans were much better organised than the French realised. Such an attack would have brought down the wrath of the enemy, not only in the form of a devastating defeat but in reprisals against the local community.[29]

Indeed, as it happened, the Germans were already planning attacks of their own against both the SAS infiltrators and the Maquis themselves.[30]

On the Sunday morning, 7 August, the day after Almonds had turned thirty years of age, Sergeant Bunfield, the Signals sergeant, received a wireless message that Colonel Paddy Mayne would be dropping that night if a DZ was given to him. It was up to the GAIN contingent to radio London later in the day to confirm which of the various DZs in the area would be the one to use.[31] But that encouraging event was not to take place. At 15.00 hours that day, the Germans attacked Jock Riding and his party at Fenwick's old HQ. Clearly, the enemy had had enough of the nightly devastation of their installations. The GAIN position had been 'direction found' by the enemy. Two enemy radio receivers had tuned into SABU's radio transmission signals. Each had taken a bearing on the direction from which the signal it picked up was emanating. The point at which the lines of these bearings drawn on the map crossed had revealed the exact location of the transmission source and Fenwick's base.

The Germans proceeded, somewhat hesitantly at first, to the edge of Almonds's part of the wood, halted at the place where the road divided into three forest rides, and set up a machine-gun position. They detected Fenwick's camp and started to mortar it heavily. Almonds was with HQ at the time, but decided that he had to get back to his own men and left immediately.[32] It is rather a compliment to the SAS that according to Jock Riding's report, the Germans then surrounded them with some 600 troops and engaged them in a pitched battle for about seven hours. Eventually, Riding and Bunfield managed to get their jeeps through the cordon undetected, while the enemy continued to blaze away at the space they had left.[33] The remainder of their party was also successfully dispersed with instructions to RV with Watson later. Riding and Bunfield, who had the wireless gear in his vehicle, then lay under cover only 400 yards from the bombardment until midnight when it was safe to move to a new location.[34]

Meanwhile, Almonds had slipped through the forest to get back to his base. Making his way carefully through the undergrowth, he looked up suddenly and saw the machine-gun position at the triple road junction where a road branched left on his way back to the log cabin. He paused. He took stock.

'Now then. I've got to be very smart here,' he thought to himself. There were in fact several machine-guns, trained so that they covered all the forest rides. The enemy was behaving just like a cat patiently watching a mouse hole. Well this mouse was not going to oblige. He worked his way round to a part of the track that was only covered by a very narrow angle from one of the machine-guns. He squatted in the bushes at the side of the road, coiled up like a spring, ready to do a world speed record-breaking sprint start. Suddenly, he made a dash for it and got safely across. The hail of bullets never came. They had not seen him. He went along the side of another track for a while, which he had to cross to get back to his part of the forest. Near to the forest warden's hut, he let a truck go by and then fled across behind it. On reaching the log cabin, he discovered that everyone had left. What to do? He went in the most likely direction. Behind him, he could hear the thump of the mortar fire but he knew that the enemy would not venture themselves deeper into the forest.[35]

At nightfall, Almonds went to a pre-arranged rendezvous. Wild pig grunted in the undergrowth around him, as he made his way. He walked all night and reached the RV just before daybreak. Suddenly, through the bushes, he came face to face with a man. It was Jock Riding. They were mightily relieved to find each other. Having finally decided that the Germans had left, they made their way in Riding's jeep back to where Almonds's vehicle was well cam'd up. It still had not been touched, nor the log cabin itself. There they regrouped with Jimmy Watson. Sensing that the end of their stay in the forest was nigh, Almonds packed a few things in his kitbag, including his piece of sennit work and a few days' rations and said goodbye to his woodland home. For their remaining days in France, they bivouacked down near to where they were operating. This gave them flexibility, less likelihood of detection and meant that they were ready to move again at a moment's notice.[36]

The aftermath of the German attack was, however, to have fatal consequences. The following morning, Ian Fenwick returned to Nancray-sur-Rimarde. Unfortunately, he was given some intelligence by the local French Resistance which was not well founded.[37] Once again, reports of accidents concerning Almonds were greatly exaggerated. This time, Fenwick was told that Almonds and Riding were dead and all the jeeps had been lost. Fenwick was aghast. These two were his right and left hand men. To have lost them and all the vehicles as well, had it been true, would have been a terrible blow. In fact, the opposite was the case: not a man or vehicle had been harmed.[38]

Fenwick decided to go and see for himself what had happened. He set off in his jeep, in broad daylight, with Sergeant Dunkley, Corporal, later Sergeant, Duffy, an SAS original from Kabrit days, Lance Corporal Menginou, who was attached from 4th French Parachute Battalion, and a

French Sergeant from Paris who was helping to organise the French Resistance in the area. As they drove towards the scene of the previous night's battle, they saw a German convoy that was out looking for the saboteurs. Fenwick saw it first and resolved to attack. However, he reckoned without the enemy's superior resources, in particular, air power. At about mid-morning, Almonds looked up in the forest and saw a German spotter 'plane, a German Fieseler Fi-156 *Storch*. The aircraft saw Fenwick's jeep speeding towards Chambon-la-Forêt and unbeknown to him, it radioed a warning ahead of him.

Meanwhile the Germans, infuriated by the lack of anything to show for their previous night's efforts, together with the losses they had sustained, had already begun to exact vengeance on the local inhabitants. All the men and boys in the village of Chambon-la-Forêt were rounded up and put into the church. The French dignitaries at the Mairie were told that unless information about the saboteurs was disclosed, all the male inhabitants of the village would be shot.[39] Consequently, the women began to flee from the village for fear of what would happen to them afterwards. One of these women met Ian Fenwick's jeep on the way to Chambon and bravely flagged him down. She told him that the Germans were waiting for him, that they had laid an ambush for him further up the road and that it would be impossible for him to get through. She begged him to turn back. But Fenwick's shock and distress had turned to anger. He thanked her politely but said very firmly that he was going to attack them.[40]

By the time Fenwick reached Chambon, the Germans had already mounted a machine-gun at the beginning of the upstroke of the 'T' junction to ambush him. He drove through the first of the German positions in true SAS style with all guns blazing. It was an attack worthy of any of the daredevil personal feats of Paddy Mayne. But this was not the desert. And Fenwick did not have the element of surprise. The Germans were ready for him. They had set up another position, further up the road at the cross-stroke of the 'T' junction in some houses that faced back down the road towards him. As he started the run past to strafe the convoy, a hail of machine-gun fire met him. He was hit in the middle of the forehead by a 20 mm cannon shell and died instantly. Since he was at the wheel, the jeep immediately ran out of control and careered wildly into the wood at the side of the road.[41]

Fenwick was dead but his death gave life to the people of Chambon-la-Forêt. Delighted with their prize kill, the Germans released all the men and boys from the church and the women gradually reappeared from hiding. Nor was it lost on the enemy that Fenwick had continued on and attacked them, in spite of knowing that an ambush lay ahead. In the face of the sheer bravery of this British lion, the enemy's own courage must surely have failed him.

Two of the other occupants of the vehicle, Cpl Menginou and the French officer also died in the shoot-out. Corporal Duffy was hit by a bullet that went right through his jaw and knocked him out as the jeep smashed into a tree. He regained consciousness momentarily and caught sight of Sergeant Dunkley, with blood on his face either from the accident or a wound, being led away handcuffed. The next time Duffy came round, he found himself in a truck on his way to hospital in Orléans. He had been carrying a code book and the Germans therefore had an interest in keeping him alive long enough to get him to tell them how to use it. From there, as a POW, he was taken with a wounded foot, two broken fingers, a broken jaw and temporarily blinded in one eye, to a German hospital just north of Fontainbleau. From what he could see as he was taken inside, it might previously have been a school or a convent. Here he was put into a ward alongside German wounded.[42]

The German medical services were usually very good at treating injured POWs, putting them in with their own patients and treating them with exactly the same standards of medical care as their own soldiers and airmen.[43] But as far as Duffy was concerned, it was the other patients that turned out to be a problem. They were extremely aggressive towards him and after several altercations he had to be moved to another ward. He learned later that they had mistaken him for a captured Typhoon pilot. They were the sole survivors of a German gun battery who had unwisely attempted to shoot it out with some Typhoon Tank Busters and they were, not surprisingly, very hostile.

Duffy realised that his situation was desperate. He was in a ward with eight Germans and a Russian. But in spite of his injuries, his mind was very active. As an SAS original, he was made of stern stuff. He had no intention of being resuscitated, only to be tortured, then taken out and shot. On the lookout for escape possibilities, he quickly struck up an acquaintance with one of the local French girls who came in to clean the hospital. She said that she would do what she could to help him escape. On 22 August, the girl told Duffy that the Americans were at Chartres and that now was the time to escape because the hospital was being evacuated. Since Duffy had no wish to be carted off with the other POWs back to

Germany, he readily agreed. The girl appeared later and put down a covered bucket beside his bed. While her friends shielded Duffy from view by crowding round the other patients' beds, he was able to help himself to the contents of the bucket, a German Medical Officer's uniform. While the other patients slept during their habitual afternoon siesta, Duffy was able to examine the clothes he had secreted under his bedclothes. Fine. The only problem was that there were no shoes. He got out of bed, hobbled to the door and peered out. He was in luck. The corridor was empty and after a few minutes one of the girls chanced to pass by. He motioned to her and pointing to his bare feet mouthed the words 'No shoes.' The girl's eyes flashed understanding. Duffy went back to bed and waited. Later, unfortunately after the German patients were awake, the girls reappeared and the performance with the bucket was repeated to deliver Duffy some shoes. One can only marvel at the courage of those young women.

There then ensued a tedious time waiting for the other occupants of the ward to go to sleep again. As soon as they did, Duffy did 'one of the fastest, if not *the* fastest, quick-change acts in history'. When he got dressed, he discovered to his dismay that the shoes were two sizes too small. Nevertheless, in spite of having one injured foot, he crammed the shoes on and walked painfully out of the hospital and into a courtyard. It was crowded with wounded soldiers and vehicles getting ready for the evacuation. As he got to the gate, he was horrified to see a sentry standing there. But as Duffy approached him, the German drew himself up and saluted. Naturally, out of courtesy, the SAS man returned it.

Still wearing the crippling footwear, Duffy walked in the direction of Milly, along the main road from Milly to Fontainebleau. As soon as he was able, he took to the woods, glad of the first opportunity to free his poor feet from the 'confounded' shoes. Eventually, he came to a deserted log cabin, where he slept the night. At dawn, he awoke to the sound of firing. He limped in that direction, this time on his bare feet. Coming out onto a road south of Milly, he met an elderly man leading a horse that was, as Duffy put it, 'drawing' a cart. As much as his broken jaw and the language barrier would permit, and in spite of his German uniform, Duffy managed to explain that he was an escaping wounded English POW! It is to the Frenchman's great credit that he took a chance on believing this story and immediately helped Duffy up onto the horse's back.

As they carried on down the road, to Duffy's consternation, they met two 'Huns' on motor-cycles who stopped and appeared to be asking directions to somewhere. The game was nearly up. Duffy realised that by now he was too weak to engage in any more escape and evasion. However, the Germans kept pointing down the road and suddenly he realised that they were asking the way to a nearby town. He had not the faintest idea where it was but he nodded vigorously, pointed in the same direction and made encouraging noises. The wound to his face and mouth gave him at least some excuse for not being too articulate. Without seeming to suspect anything of the bareback-riding, barefoot German medic who could speak virtually no German, the two motor-cyclists thanked him, revved up their machines and sped off down the road.[44]

A little further on, the horse and rider and their attendant came to a German tank that had been knocked out. Around it stood several men who turned out to be a French Resistance group. They took Duffy to a house where a doctor bandaged up his more recently acquired wounds – twenty-one blisters on his left foot and twenty-eight on his right. After being taken to the American hospital at Milly, Sergeant Duffy was awarded the Purple Heart, which is given to all Americans wounded in action.[45]

It seemed to Almonds that it was what Duffy did *after* being wounded in action that deserved a medal.

Chapter Sixteen

Mission Accomplished

In England, Mike Sadler went to have afternoon tea with his parents. Having no transport of his own, Paddy Mayne had lent him his CO's staff car and when he arrived in style it made quite an impression on the Sadler household. Parents are always pleased to see their offspring doing well. By midnight, he was in France.

The SAS departure from England was not entirely uneventful. They crash-landed on take-off from the Transport Command airfield at Brize Norton. The undercarriage of the aircraft collapsed and did a cartwheel down a line of aeroplanes before coming to rest in a pool of petrol. Sadler and Mayne were out of there in less time than it takes to think about it! The aircraft was very heavily loaded with containers and baskets which then had to be transferred to another plane. Since they had also lost their dispatcher, who had been injured in the crash-landing, the contents of the containers had to be packed loose, along with the basket. After taking off without a dispatcher, they prepared to throw out the container contents and baskets, before jumping out themselves.[1]

Mayne and his group were met by a reception party, accompanied by Johnny Wiseman, at the Operation HOUNDSWORTH area, about 100 kilometres (62 miles) to the south-east of the Operation GAIN area. In broad daylight, Mayne and Sadler then left separately to drive up to the Forest of Orléans. On the way, Sadler spent the night in a château with a French countess. She plied him with champagne which was shared with her collection of downed British and US pilots. The next day, he ran into a German column and drove right through it without them noticing that there was a Union Jack on the front of his vehicle![2]

On Ian Fenwick's death, Jock Riding assumed command of Operation GAIN. Two days later, Mayne and Sadler met up at the forest rendezvous. Sadler's map-reading skills were every bit as good as his desert navigation had been.[3] He spent a few days with Almonds living in the small log cabin and being looked after by Fritz, the German prisoner. Sadler was struck by the need for constant checking of everyone coming in and out. There were many different groupings, and factions within groupings, of the

French Resistance and the Maquis, not to mention some political and criminal elements. It was all very stressful.[4]

After keeping a low profile for a few days, Mayne decided to send out recce parties to watch the main roads between Orléans and Pithiviers and between Orléans and Montargis. In typical LRDG style, all information was carefully recorded and passed back to England. A good deal of information about the enemy withdrawal through the Paris – Orléans gap was gathered.[5] Then the enemy struck another terrible blow. The third patrol, two signallers, Troopers Ion and Packman, did not return. Some days later, news filtered through via the Resistance that on their way back in Jock Riding's jeep they had been ambushed by elements of the German SS. They had been taken to an old château at Chilleurs-aux-Bois where they were held for a day and then shot.[6]

About a week after learning of their deaths, Almonds went to the château to try and find out more about what had happened to them. There he met a very old man, who was obviously still very distressed. He was the owner of the place but it had been commandeered some time ago by the Germans. He took Almonds to a spot where the moat surrounding the château was entered by a small feeder stream. There in that beautiful setting, beside a little wooden bridge, Ion and Packman had been shot in the back of the head. Once again, Hitler's edict had resulted in murder instead of imprisonment as POWs.

Having done the deed, the Germans had departed hastily before the Allied advance, leaving the old man to arrange for the burial of the two dead British soldiers. Their bodies had obviously been left to lie in the nearby bushes for some days. Almonds could see on the ground some skin which had sloughed off from their bound hands and arms, still bearing the imprint of rope marks and some blond curly hair recognisable as that of Trooper Ion. He waited while a French Gendarme gave Jock Riding some personal effects which he recognised, including Trooper Ion's signet ring.[7]

Leslie Bateman was at the Château d'Ouchamps when he learned of the sad news of Ian Fenwick's death. Mayne then asked Bateman to attach himself to the Maquis de Lorris as a Liaison Officer, taking half a dozen men with him. Bateman contacted 'Agrippa', the Maquis leader and arranged to move in with 500 or so maquisards. While he was in the Maquis camp, an injured American pilot called Edward Simpson was brought in. He had crash-landed a few days before after a mid-air collision with one of his own side following an enemy engagement. His aircraft had fallen about 10,000 feet and had amazingly landed in a tree where Simpson had been trapped by the foot. He had been found hanging in the tree and rescued by the Maquis.[8]

Simpson was most surprised to find the SAS operating in the middle of occupied France. He and Bateman got on very well and soon became friends. Sadly, it was a friendship that was not to last. A few days later on 10 August, they woke to the sound of very heavy gunfire. *Capitaine* Albert, the commander of the camp, told them that the Germans were mounting a massive attack with armoured cars, flame-throwers, incendiary shells and heavy machine-gun fire. The situation was so hopeless that before long Albert advised them to get out of the forest as best they could.

Some time before his death, Fenwick had acquired a jeep and had given Bateman his old Citroen car. Bateman crammed his six men and the American into this rather un-warlike vehicle and followed by three Maquis trucks they made their way through the burning woods. They got out onto a 2 kilometre (1 1/4 miles) stretch of road, north of the Loire River, about a kilometre (1/2 mile) from Ouzoner-sur-Loire, intending to turn off into another spread of wood further on and hide up. Unfortunately, they were then attacked by German patrol cars. Bateman counted eighteen of them.[9] The first burst of German fire knocked out the engine and shattered the windscreen. Bateman heard a gasp from the American sitting beside him. He appeared to have been killed outright.

In the back, Trooper Wilson saw the German patrol car and shortly afterwards was shot just above the right eye and in the jaw.[10] Slowly, he slid sideways. Bateman tumbled out of the car and rolled across the road, in the process getting peppered with bits of stone chipped off the road surface by the bullets that were spewing up the ground all around him. The Germans had got out of their vehicle and were closing in, firing with machine-pistols. Amazingly, Bateman sustained only a few minor flesh wounds. One of his men had been shot a couple of times in the leg, but not seriously. Another man had also received only minor flesh wounds but had been temporarily blinded. The rest had got away. Still under German fire, Bateman and the two wounded managed to get off the road and away into the woods.[11]

In the back of the car, Wilson slowly came round. He was alone in the vehicle but then he realised that the American was lying on the road next to the open passenger door. He could do no more than watch as, painfully and slowly, the injured airman tried to crawl underneath the car. The slight movement caught the attention of the Germans who turned two bursts of fire onto the wounded man. But the Germans did not see Wilson and four of them began to approach the car. Wilson remained motionless. At fifteen yards' range, he raised his Colt .45 through the half-open shattered side door of the Citroen and fired in quick succession. Three of them dropped dead. The fourth let go of his weapons and fled. Wilson fell back exhausted.[12]

The Germans were still machine-gunning the vanishing Bateman and party and again directed their fire onto the car. The windscreen was blown in and Wilson was hit again and knocked out. When he came round, he was tied to a tree with his hands behind his back. A German staff car arrived and six Gestapo got out. They asked Wilson how many SAS men were with the Maquis. When he would not answer, they hit him in the mouth. In spite of being beaten about his wounded face, Wilson still refused to talk. He was taken to Orléans, along with a captured maquisard, where a similar interrogation process was repeated by the head of the local German Army unit. Knowing that his prisoner was SAS, the German threatened him with Hitler's edict and the firing squad. As if to make the point, and in the face of Wilson's obdurate silence, the Frenchman was then taken outside and Wilson heard a shot. He continued to say nothing and two Gestapo men took him back to Orléans and interrogated him again. After becoming unconscious again, he awoke some time later to find himself in hospital in Orléans.[13] He was looked after very well by the German doctors and even underwent an operation on his head where a metal plate was inserted into his skull.[14] Two days later, the Americans arrived. Against all the odds, another remarkable fighter had survived.[15]

Meanwhile, Leslie Bateman had only been able to make slow progress with his two injured men. Under his direction, he and the temporarily blinded man had to help the one with the wounded leg. They stopped and hid up in a large wood pile only about 20 yards from their car. Armed only with two hand grenades and a Colt automatic, they decided that if the Germans arrived, they would throw the grenades at them and fire the pistol to the last. In fact, the Germans never came. Bateman could not decide whether they were afraid to follow him into the woods or had imagined that they had disposed of their disappearing foe. All he knew was that they did not come. About three hours later, he returned to the scene. Wilson was gone. The American was lying dead on the ground.[16]

A little later, when things had calmed down, Batemen decided to make for the house of a forester friend of his called M. Boussogne. He had been a great helper and had actually stored petrol in his house for the Maquis. An 8 to 10 mile walk lay ahead of them, an ordeal for the man with two bullets still in his leg, and for those trying to help him. As they got near to the house, Bateman realised that all was not well. The whole place was on fire and Boussogne had been shot. Dawn was breaking, so they decided to lie up in a ditch for the day. Bateman used his field dressing to treat the wounded leg and they made themselves as comfortable as possible. They had no food and were by now very thirsty. Bateman went off with an empty water bottle but all he could find was a stagnant pond. Nevertheless, beneath the green slime on the surface, frogs were swimming about. Relying on his schoolboy biology which had taught him that such water was safe, Bateman filled the bottle and they all slaked their thirst.[17]

All day they watched German transport moving along a nearby road in front of General Patton's advancing Army. That evening, there was a cloudburst and the ditch began to fill with water. They clambered out and set off towards some woods. Before long, a Frenchman appeared pushing a bicycle and carrying a shoulder bag. 'Who are you?' he demanded. His attitude was at first fairly hostile. Bateman decided to give him the complete truth. The man's expression immediately changed. 'I'm a friend,' he said. 'Don't worry; I'll look after you.' The man turned out to be Gustave Bourge, the bailiff on a local estate. He took them to the house where he lived with his wife and two daughters, looking after the property of the owner, who was living there herself with her two children. Bourge's wife was an ex-nurse; she quickly attended to their wounds and the man who had been temporarily blinded regained his sight.[18]

Bateman and his men hid in the house while the Germans continued to clear the area. After a few days, he decided to make contact with Squadron HQ and Jock Riding. He knew roughly where they were so he borrowed a bicycle and some civilian clothes and set off. His instincts were right and he was received with great pleasure by Riding and Almonds. The new acting OC 'D' Squadron was also mightily relieved to discover that Bateman and his two men were alive. Having met the others, who had got away safely when the car was shot up, among them Corporal Baynham and Lance Corporal Essex, he had assumed that the three missing men were dead. In fact, all of the SAS men survived the escape from the battered Citroen that had seemed at the time a certain deathtrap. Only the unfortunate American was killed.[19]

Riding confirmed that Bateman and his men should stay at the safe house until the Americans forces arrived. About three days later, he heard the noise of tanks, went outside and discovered that they were indeed American. After explaining who he was to the officer in the leading tank, who did not believe him, Bateman was escorted to the US Army colonel, who had his story verified by radio. He was then given a captured car and a petrol requisition form, with which he made his way, with his men, to Dreux and caught a US Airforce 'plane to England.[20]

Despite these reversals, SAS operations continued. While Paddy Mayne was with them, he asked Almonds to go out, recce some enemy lorries and identify to which German unit they belonged. A continuous convoy of German troops was passing close to the edge of the forest and Mayne wanted to know more about them. Before Almonds set off, he stood with Mayne and Riding, chatting near a T-junction in the wood. *'Just as if we were watching a Regimental football match,'* Almonds thought. As he got down beside the road to cover the approaching vehicles, which in the event turned out to be French, he was aware that Mayne was watching him closely. It crossed his mind that Paddy was testing his nerve. Almonds assessed the convoy as he had been asked and then went back and reported. He had no idea who they were but they seemed to be retreating Infantry. 'Hmm. Good,' grunted Mayne, without further comment.[21]

The loss of Ian Fenwick and the enemy's attack on the Maquis, with whom the GAIN operators were at least co-operating, restricted active operations during August. By the middle of the month, the enemy was retreating in large numbers and by 18 August their area was clear of German troops.[22] Operation GAIN was officially terminated on 19 August. In all, nine officers (Fenwick, Riding, Watson, Bateman, Parsons, Garstin, Wiehe, Mayne and Sadler) and forty-nine other ranks had been parachuted in. Two officers and eight men had been killed and one man, Sergeant Dunkley, who had been with Fenwick when he was killed, was reported missing or a POW. His body was never found but may be that of the unknown soldier buried with Ion and Packman.[23]

The summary of confirmed damage inflicted on the enemy shows that sixteen railway lines had been put out of action and that one railway shed, two locomotive engines and forty-six trucks had been destroyed. There were two derailments and a set of points blown up. One of the unconfirmed bombing targets was 'C. 21', one million gallons of fuel that had been reported for the attention of Allied Airforces on 2 July.[24] These operational results were due to GAIN alone; the summary results for 1 SAS in France from June to September 1944 make grim reading. Enemy casualties were slight: it was not a specific objective of the Operation to kill personnel and Germans were attacked only if the occasion required it. In fact only six of the enemy were killed and five wounded.[25]

A few days after Paddy and Sadler had left, Almonds and Riding attended a Resistance meeting in Pithiviers about 15 miles away. On their way back in the jeep, they were suddenly aware of a commotion in a hedge bottom and American voices shouting 'Put those goddamn lights out!' Their vehicle was then approached by highly suspicious American soldiers. Almonds attempted to explain that they had been driving around the French countryside in jeeps at night, with lights on, for some months. But the Americans refused to believe him. He and Riding were taken to a basha alongside the road, where the American CO listened to their story with obvious scepticism. 'But how come you guys are in the combat zone anyway?' he drawled. Eventually, he seemed convinced but remained rather hung up on how they came legitimately to have a US jeep. Riding and Almonds described their role and explained how the jeeps had been parachuted in to them, realising even as they said it how far-fetched it sounded. It seemed even more incredible when they said that this was the first time they had ever been stopped when driving around at night. And so, for the second time during the war, Almonds was taken prisoner by the Americans. The US CO stroked his chin and shook his head. 'In the morning,' he said, rather wearily, 'you'll be taken to General Patton's headquarters.'[26]

Early next day, Almonds and Riding were taken back behind the Allied lines to Third Army HQ. They went into a small orchard where apples were already swelling on the branches, reminiscent of Stixwould and home. General George Smith Patton was sitting at a small table in front of the open flap of a tent. He looked old and tired. Almonds had of course heard of the controversial general who was an able tactician and an outstanding practitioner of mobile tank warfare in the European and Mediterranean theatres of war. He was known for his strict discipline and self-sacrifice which had led to his nickname 'Old Blood and Guts'. He it was who had captured Palermo the year before, when Almonds was still in Italy, in a campaign marked by his great initiative, relentless drive and complete disregard for classic military rules.[27] Since beginning operations in France on 1 August, he had lost no time in sweeping through and capturing Mayenne, Laval, Le Mans, Reims and Châlons.

The incognito SAS renegades could only wonder at how they would be dealt with by such a man. He had a noble patrician face, with a long thin nose and loose jowls. A 'fore-and-aft' side hat was pushed casually back on the grey-white hair. The eyes, half hidden under overhanging white eyebrows, looked down at a pile of documents between his brawny forearms. Almonds was transfixed to see that, just like a Wild West cowboy, Patton was wearing two pistols with pearl handles. After listening patiently to the statement being read by one of his aides, punctuated by the liberal use of the word 'Sir!', Patton put his head on one side, clenched his lips and without bothering to ask any questions, he pronounced 'If you're Brits, you'll be okay. If not, you'll be shot – even if I have to shoot you myself.'[28]

The two men were then handed over to a British Liaison Officer who questioned them at length. 'Look,' said Almonds, 'Forget all this. I'm really a Bristol policeman and I can prove it.' After various descriptions of divers elements of police work and more explanations, the Liaison Officer seemed satisfied and gave them a paper which remained valid as long as they reported to the occupying US Forces on a daily basis.

'Hang this for a lark,' Almonds said to Riding as soon as they were free, 'I'm going home'. Their job was done, the element of surprise was gone and the front line had caught up with them. Almonds had held his position since 15 June and Operation GAIN had been terminated. It was time to return to England.[29]

Ignoring the daily reporting requirement, he and Riding headed towards Chartres, with the intention of making their way back to the UK. Still in their jeep, they had only covered a few miles towards the city when they met a Sherman tank. Both drivers saw each other and stopped. The American tank commander stuck his head out of the turret and Almonds got out of the jeep. Just as in Italy, he said simply,

'Hello. I'm British and I'm going home'. He reported a clear road for 20 to 30 miles behind him and that they'd seen General Patton. The tank commander sent them on to find his unit, where they offered to swap the jeep for a flight back to the UK. This was an extremely good deal for the Americans and they accepted with alacrity.[30]

After a couple of weeks moving around in France, Mayne and Sadler had driven back to Le Mans and through the Falaise Gap. Back at the Forest of Orléans, they met up, quite by chance one evening, with Roy Farran. Farran had been with the Special Raiding Squadron in Italy and had taken part in the terrible engagement at Termoli. Ensconced in a local café, there then followed an evening shrouded in a cloud of alcohol.

'Paddy,' said Farran reproachfully, well on into the night, 'I think you 1 SAS chaps look down on us 2 SAS fellows.'

'No we don't,' said Paddy firmly. 'We never think about you at all.'[31]

The US Military Police began moving through the café. They were checking identity papers and generally interrogating the clientele. 'We'll speak French to them,' Paddy said. In due course, when the MPs, accompanied by a young US officer, reached their table, Paddy responded with waggling hands, shrugged shoulders and not very convincing French. 'No compris,' he repeated grinning and feigning complete surprise at being interrogated. 'Sir,' said one of the MPs to his officer. 'Don't you let these men fool you sir. With respect sir, I think these men speak better English than you do, sir.' The night ended with a combined 'feu-de-joie' from the Vickers-Ks over the sleeping Forest of Orléans.[32] The next day, Paddy was invited to go and see the US General Brigade Commander to explain the altercation with his military police. Having smoothed the situation over, Paddy ended with the equivalent to a 'have you stopped beating your wife question'.

'I do hope that we didn't frighten your men, General,' he said.[33]

When Almonds got back to England, he and Riding reported to the 1 SAS base which had moved to Nettlebed in Oxfordshire. After the usual debrief, one of his first, sad, tasks was to write to Ian Fenwick's next of kin, his sister Angela. As usual, he found exactly the right words to say:

SSM J. E. Almonds,
HQ SAS Tps (Fac)
HQ Airborne Tps (Main)
A.P.O. England

30-8-44

Dear Madam,

I was the sergeant major under your brother's command in France. He was a gallant officer and a gentleman, dearly loved by all members of his Squadron.

The French people in the area admired him greatly and his death was a blow to all. Before returning to England, I visited his grave in the little cemetery outside the village of Chambon-la-Forêt, which is situated 8 miles south of Pithiviers and 30 miles north-east of Orléans.

The graves of your brother and the two men who died with him are in the top right-hand corner of the cemetery, well kept and covered with flowers. A simple inscription on the major's grave reads 'a comrade'. I spoke to the villagers and gave them the major's initials as they were preparing a headstone. After paying my respects, I left the area to return to England.

I felt that you would like to know the position of your brother's grave and being in a position to forward you these facts I felt it my duty to do so.

Yours sincerely,
J. E. Almonds[34]

A Lieutenant's signature in the bottom corner of the letter showed that it had passed the censor. Little had changed in that respect since 1941.

For his part in Operation GAIN, the French awarded Almonds (by then a Lieutenant) the Croix de Guerre with Silver Star (*La Croix de Guerre avec Etoile de Vermeil*). The offer of this decoration came from France's General Juin and was accepted by the C- in-C, 21 Army Group, on behalf of him and others; amongst them was Bill Fraser, MC.[35]

The Citation from General Koenig referred to Almonds as 'Chef de Section' having parachuted 300 kilometres behind enemy lines and disrupted all communications channels useful to the enemy. In spite of being under attack from the enemy, he had demonstrated magnificent personal courage by leading his men, without any losses, and returning alone to their old camp location to destroy codes and other secret documents. It concluded 'N'a pas cessé durant sa mission d'être un magnifique exemple pour ses hommes.'

On 9 September, without any prior warning, Paddy Mayne told Almonds, 'Jim, get smartened up. I'm taking you to see Monty'. They drove to where General Montgomery's famous caravan was parked. The trees were tossing in the breeze below a cloudless blue September sky but already there was a crispness in the air that heralded the coming of autumn. Monty came out and down the steps. Army units were still in shirt-sleeve order but he was wearing battledress. He seemed even thinner than he appeared in the many photographs that Almonds had seen of him. Here was another outstanding Allied commander of the war. He had arrived to command the Eighth Army in North Africa in August 1942, just before the failed SAS Benghazi raid. By November 1942 when Monty had defeated Rommel at the Battle of El Alamein, the turning point of the war in the Western Desert, Almonds had been in an Italian POW camp. But the news had filtered through. He remembered that Monty was by all accounts a thorough strategist but a very cautious man who would refuse to make an attacking move until absolutely every last man and vehicle was completely ready. As a non-smoking teetotaller, his renowned asceticism meant that the men did not readily identify with him and yet he commanded an immense respect. He had instilled an attitude of positive thinking at all levels that made defeat seem impossible.

Paddy introduced Almonds and there were a few moments of pleasantries. Then Mayne said bluntly, 'As I mentioned to you the other day sir, I want this man commissioned.' Monty frowned and turned his hawkish gaze onto the prospective SAS officer. The General's face was bleak, his features hatchet sharp under the double badges of the beret worn scrupulously over his left eye. The long sharply pointed nose twitched slightly above the whippet-thin moustache.

After a pause, he said, 'Can you look after men?' A fleeting memory of the Army Recruiting office in Lincoln so many years before flashed across Almonds's mind. He straightened his back and squared his shoulders. He was tall and very lean, this time from the 'French picnic', but he was fit and determined. 'Well sir, actually,' he said, conscious that he was weighing his words carefully, 'I've been looking after men for some time.' It came out quite mildly and Monty did not seem to mind but accepted it as a statement of fact.

'Good,' he said. 'See that you do.' And with the briefest acknowledgement of their salutes, he turned on his heel and went back into the dim interior of the caravan.[36]

Without any more ado and with no ceremony, no passing out parade, no drum-head service, Almonds received his commission 'in the field' as a second Lieutenant. By October he was a full Lieutenant and promoted to Captain in November. From that day on, he moved around the world so frequently that I can remember his commissioning scroll from the Queen finally catching up with him ten years later when he was by then a major.

Meanwhile, Lockie had been planning her own 'under cover' operation. John was now almost four years old and she could see the gap between him and any future sibling becoming rather large. As the returning hero, Almonds's guard was completely down. All unsuspecting, he walked slap into the ambush Lockie had set for him. In no time at all she was pregnant. But the 'operational blueprint' was flawed and the plan rebounded on the perpetrator. Nine months later Almonds was in Norway, by then a Captain. The SAS had jumped ahead to grab war criminals because Churchill had promised the Norwegian government in exile that he would bring to justice the Quisling government.

Late one night a signal arrived in the Mess and Almonds found himself on the end of what he thought was some leg-pulling from his colleagues. 'Captain Almonds. Come home at once. Wife had twins,' the signal read. He ignored what he thought was a practical joke and Lockie was left to languish for a week with the completely unexpected double arrival – twin daughters![37]

But at last Almonds came back via Nettlebed, causing quite a stir among the neighbours as he roared up York Street in a specially modified jeep bristling with weapons. This vehicle was one of the jeeps that he had helped to convert to deal with special operations in Germany. Prior to going to Norway, he had gone with Paddy Mayne as part of Operation HOWARD from 6 to 29 April. While Lockie was in the last weeks of her pregnancy, the SAS were given the role of advancing ahead of the Allied tanks to take out the Panzerfaust teams who were armed with the German hand-held anti-tank weapons.[38]

This was not at all a real SAS role but Mayne had wanted to keep the SAS on active service. The work was not only active but extremely dangerous. As usual, Mayne continued to lead from the front. He was a superb soldier and the men knew it. On one occasion, a group of Germans was holed up in a schloss and it was proving difficult to take the position. Almonds watched as Mayne stood by impassively while the bursts of firing continued. He waited until one of the troopers turned to him exasperated.

'Can't seem to winkle Jerry out at all, sir.'

'Here, give me that,' said Mayne. He took the Bren and within a few minutes the firing from the schloss was silenced. It was true that the Bren was the most accurate slow-firing machine-gun of the Second World War but that particular result had more to do with Mayne than with the technology.[39] But there were light-hearted moments too, as the following extract from the annals of 'D' Squadron reveal, just after they had crossed the Rhine on 26 March and moved up to Brunnen:

> *Thursday, April 12* This day will go down as the greatest in the squadron's history. At 15.00 hrs, alone and without any supporting arms, it captured, at great risk to the personnel involved, a German

baggage. This was an attractive corporal in the LVAFF (sic).... She was removed as rapidly as possible to a prisoner of war cage by the Squadron Commander. There were no casualties.

The jeeps had to be specially adapted for the Operation HOWARD work. Almonds had designed an under-slung gun mounting, so that the weapons were easier to manipulate, and fitted an extension to a big bar beneath the front bumper. It came out to just in front of the vehicle and stuck up vertically to sever enemy trip wires intended to decapitate the men in the jeeps. He drove the first of these modified vehicles for about 2,000 miles around the coastal areas of Britain to put it through its paces, making further minor adjustments as he went along.

My brother John was waiting to be taken to the St Andrew's nursing home where my twin sister and I had been born. He was far more fascinated by the sight of all the guns than the prospect of having two sisters. Almonds walked into the hall of the little house by the lamp post with a .5 Browning machine-gun and ammunition belts. The boy stared at the rounds with their different coloured tips: red for tracer, blue for incendiary and black for armour piercing. Almonds could not take all this to the nursing home, or leave it in the house, so he drove off again and went to see his old friends at the police station. He tried to persuade them to lock up the weapons and ammunition in one of the cells. But there were no regulations to cover such an eventuality and so they refused. Even the war had not changed things at the Bridewell constabulary. So he resorted to the Co-op garage, who obligingly locked everything up overnight. Returning to York Street, he put my brother into the co-driver's seat, without a seat belt or even any doors, and roared off again to the nursing home.[40]

After the end of the war, Almonds had a short leave and went back on a goodwill mission to the people of Nancray-sur-Rimarde. He was sitting down at a reception held in his honour in the Mairie on 6 August 1945 (his thirty-first birthday and exactly a year after Fenwick's death) when the news of the bombing of Hiroshima was announced.

After returning to the UK, he was out driving one day with Leslie Bateman when they saw some Italian POWs toiling in the fields, helping to bring in the harvest.

'Stop the car, Les,' he said. He patted his pockets and looked at his friend. 'Have you got any cigarettes?' Bateman said he had, and Almonds had some on him too. He put them all together, got out of the car and picked his way across the field to the two POWs. They stopped work, amazed and slightly apprehensive at the sight of a British officer coming towards them.

'This', he said to them, 'is for you, because the Italian people were very kind to me and looked after me when I was an escaping prisoner of war in Italy.' The two men, at first stupefied, were quickly all smiles and responded with salutes and much bowing and scraping.

'Grazie, grazie, Il Capitano,' they said. It was a small gesture, but something about the simplicity of it brought tears to Bateman's eyes.[41]

It was not only for good manners and his lack of swearing that my father was known as 'Gentleman Jim'.

Notes and Sources

Note on early SAS Order of Battle
No particular logic was attached to the designation of early SAS units: on the contrary, nomenclature was often intended to confuse the enemy by disguising the order of battle. In mid-1941, the remnants of 'Layforce' were formed into the Middle East Commando. This subsequently became 1 Special Service Regiment, sometimes referred to as S.S. Brigade. Cf. *The SAS at War*, Anthony Kemp, Penguin, London, 1991, p. 45.

By September 1941, Brigadier Dudley Clarke, who was responsible for deliberate misinformation, had invented the fictitious First Special Air Service Brigade. He persuaded David Stirling to add verisimilitude to this imaginary unit by availing himself of its name. Stirling was known to hint that the letter 'L' stood for 'learner'. Cf. *David Stirling: The Authorised Biography of the Creator of the SAS*, Alan Hoe, Little, Brown & Company (UK) Ltd, London, 1992, p.70.

After the Benghazi raid in September 1942, General (later Field Marshal) Alexander accorded the unit regimental status, which gave it a clearer role and staffing establishment. Cf. *The Special Air Service*, Philip Warner, William Kimber & Co. Ltd, London, 1971, p. 66 and foreword by David Stirling making clear that in his view Warner's book achieved 'what was intended for the official regimental history'. 'L' Detachment was never officially re-designated but from September 1942 the SAS were increasingly known as 'the SAS'. Reorganisation did not stop there however.

On 1 April 1943, 1 SAS Regiment devolved into the Special Raiding Squadron under Paddy Mayne. It became 1 SAS again from the creation of the SAS Brigade on 1 January 1944, which also encompassed 2 SAS Regiment, the Belgian Independent Parachute Company, 3 French Parachute Battalion (2ième Régiment des Chasseurs Parachutistes). Cf. *The SAS at War*, Anthony Kemp, Penguin, London, 1991, Appendix A: The Organization of the SAS 1941-1945, p. 236.

Chapter 1: 'L' Detachment – SAS
1. John Edward Almonds Wartime diary, hereafter JEA diary. This contemporaneous diary of over 20,000 words consists of daily entries from 28 January 1941 to 28 March 1942. It has been cited for reference purposes by the authors of many SAS books, including the authorised biography of the creator of the SAS, Sir David Stirling (*David Stirling: The Authorised Biography of the Creator of the SAS*, Alan Hoe, Little, Brown & Company (UK) Ltd, London, 1992) but is used extensively here for the first time. I have been able to enhance its usefulness by cross-referencing from it to the researches I have carried out at the Public Record Office (PRO) and my interviews with other SAS originals.

2. Interview with Pat Riley, 11 November 1995, hereafter Interview PR. Sadly, he died in 1999.
3. Interview John Edward Almonds, hereafter Interview JEA; at time of writing he was alive and living in Lincolnshire; Interview PR.
4. Interview and correspondence with Jimmie Storie, 11 November 1997, 7 December 1997, 27 February 2000, hereafter Interview JS. At time of writing, he was alive and living in Scotland.
5. *The Times Atlas of the Second World War*, Times Books, 1989, p. 209.
6. Alan Moorehead, *The Desert War*, Hamish Hamilton Ltd, London, 1965, p. 118.
7. Years later when arrangements were being made for my father to lay a wreath at the Headquarters of the New Zealand SAS in Auckland in 1998, an answer came back affirmative via the New Zealand Chief of Defence Liaison Staff, with a 'PS. We want the piano back.'
8. Interview JS.
9. Ibid.
10. JEA diary.
11. Anthony Kemp, *The SAS at War*, Penguin, London, 1991, p. 12.
12. Alan Hoe, *David Stirling,* Little, Brown & Co (UK) Ltd, London, 1992, pp. 117–18.
13. JEA diary.
14. Interviews JEA, PR.
15. Interview JEA.
16. Ibid.
17. Mayne was IC No. 2 Troop, which consisted of Sections 3 and 4. Almonds was responsible for Section 3, consisting of Groups G to H. Nominal Roll, 'L' Detachment, 1.9.41 PRO/CAB/44/152 (Open).
18. JEA diary.
19. Interview and correspondence with Ernie Bond 11 July 1999, hereafter Interview EB. At time of writing he was alive and living in Kent.
20. Interview JEA.
21. Ibid.
22. JEA diary.
23. Ibid.
24. Interview EB.
25. Interview JEA.
26. Ibid.
27. Ibid The chemicals had a physical effect, possibly by absorption through the skin as well as inhalation.
28. Ibid.
29. Ibid It was probably an early version of napalm.
30. Interview Brigadier John H Almonds, late R Signals and SAS (my brother) hereafter Interview JHA.
31. Interview and correspondence with Mike Sadler, later Captain, September 1997, 10 November 1997, 11 July 1999, August 1999, hereafter Interview MS. At the time of writing he is alive and one of the most interesting and thoughtful survivors of that early period.

232   Gentleman Jim

32. Ibid.
33. JEA diary.
34. Ibid.
35. Ibid.
36. Ibid.

Chapter 2: Lincolnshire Poacher and Guards Commando
1. Thomas Cranmer sent his sister Alice to Stixwould as a Cistercian nun in 1525 and he was among the witnesses to its new royal foundation on 9 July 1537, Diarmaid MacCulloch, *Thomas Cranmer*, Yale University Press, London, 1996, pp 13 and 195.
2. George Almonds, letter, 13 November 1930, JEA letter, 7 December 1930, author's collection.
3. Interview JEA.
4. JEA letter, undated but shortly before Easter 1933, author's collection.
5. *The Daily Telegraph*, Thursday, 20 April 2000. Baillie-Stewart died in a Dublin bar in 1966.
6. The Army's usual description reference encompassing different forms of saluting.
7. In the British Army, all battalions of the Guards and the Line Regiments carry two colours: the King's colour and the Regimental colours. In the Brigade of Guards, the King's colour is crimson and the Regimental colour is the 'Union Jack'. Both have their Regimental Battle Honours emblazoned on them, recording all their past military victories. Like all Second Battalion colours in the Brigade of Guards, this one had its small 'Union Jack' in the top left-hand corner.
8. Interview JEA.
9. Interview JEA, Interview Iris May Almonds, née Lock, hereafter Interview IMA.
10. *Daily Sketch*, Monday, 4 September 1939.
11. Interview PR.
12. Ibid.
13. Ibid.
14. *The Times Atlas of the Second World War*, Times Books, 1989, p. 110. Eleven Commando units were formed within two months, each consisting of 500 volunteers.
15. Ibid.
16. Ibid; Interview and correspondence The Rt. Hon. The Earl Jellicoe, KBE, DSO, MC, FRS, PC, May 1999–June 2000.
17. Interview PR.
18. Interview EB.
19. Interview JEA.
20. Interview PR.
21. *Daily Mail*, 'For King and Empire', Tuesday 3 December 1940.
22. Interview IMA.

Chapter 3: Into the Breach
1. The original idea was to use them to attack Rhodes. Anthony Kemp, *The SAS at War 1941–1945*, Penguin, London, 1991 p. 2.

2. JEA diary.
3. In 1917, Keyes sent the 'Vindictive' to Ostend, where her volunteer crew sank the ship across the harbour entrance, curtailing German U-boat operations in Dover Command waters. Perhaps it was this feat that was to inspire Mayne to involve Almonds in a similar effort in the raid on Benghazi a year later.
4. Jane's *Warships of World War II*, Harper Collins, Glasgow, 1996, p. 192 ff LSIs could carry a battalion of troops, landing them from twelve LCAs (landing craft assault) stowed under heavy davits and from two LCM (landing craft medium) carried on deck. Over two hundred men were needed to crew the landing craft, almost as many as the number needed to man the *Glenroy*, bringing the total number aboard, together with some of the Special Boat Squadron personnel, to over sixteen hundred souls.
5. JEA diary.
6. Ibid.
7. A fish-shaped device, with fins or vanes, towed from the bow to deflect mines along a wire and sever their moorings, JEA diary, 2 February 1941.
8. Interview EB.
9. Alan Hoe, *David Stirling*, Little, Brown & Co (UK) Ltd, London, 1992, p. 43.
10. Evelyn Waugh, *The Letters of Evelyn Waugh*, Penguin, 1982, p. 149. It was common knowledge that David Stirling had a card game going most nights.
11. Ibid.
12. JEA diary.
13. Interview IMA.
14. JEA diary.
15. Interview EB.
16. JEA diary.
17. Ibid.
18. Ibid.
19. Ibid.
20. Ibid.
21. Ibid.
22. JEA diary, 12 March 1941.
23. JEA diary; Interview JEA.
24. Interview PR.
25. Interview JEA.
26. Interview PR.
27. JEA diary.
28. JEA diary, 16 April 1941.
29. Interview, PR.
30. JEA diary.
31. JEA diary, Interview PR.
32. Ibid.
33. JEA diary.
34. Ibid The 9th Australian division was at that time holding Tobruk.
35. Ibid.
36. Interview JEA.
37. JEA diary.

234   *Gentleman Jim*

38. Jane's *Warships of World War II*, p. 194 ff.
39. Ibid With a displacement of only 625 tons and 2,000 shaft horsepower they had originally been designed for use on the River Danube and had had to be towed out to China at the end of the Great War because of their alleged unseaworthiness. Following the addition of an extra bulwark to improve her going at sea, the leader of the class, the gunboat HMS *Aphis* had returned in 1940 under her own steam to make herself useful in the Mediterranean.
40. Interview PR.
41. JEA diary.
42. Interview EB.
43. Interview JEA.
44. Personal servant, usually a serviceman (or servicewoman outside theatres of war).
45. Interview PR.
46. JEA diary.
47. Ibid.
48. JEA diary; Interview.
49. Interview JEA Even when aiming at targets on land or sea, the 6-inch gun could only be traversed to fire out from the beam of the ship, where the deck reinforcements ran in the right direction, not over the bow or the stern, at risk of simply smashing up the deck under the force of the recoil.
50. JEA diary.
51. JEA diary.
52. Ibid.
53. Ibid.
54. Ibid.
55. Alan Hoe, *David Stirling*, Little, Brown & Co (UK) Ltd, London, 1992, p. 53.
56. Whom Almonds was later to accompany on the SAS raid to Sidi Barrani.
57. Untitled minute to Capt. Schott, covering a report by Guardsman D'Arcy, Irish Guards, dated May 1941, PRO, WO/218/173.
58. Alan Hoe, *David Stirling*, Little, Brown & Co (UK) Ltd, London, 1992, p. 61 ff.
59. Interviews JEA, PR.
60. The point is that Stirling and Lewes were at this time developing their ideas separately: one strategic and the other tactical.
61. JEA diary.
62. Ibid.
63. Alan Moorehead, *The Desert War*, Hamish Hamilton Ltd, London, 1965, p. 118.
64. JEA diary .
65. Interview PR.
66. JEA diary; Interview JEA.
67. Interview PR.
68. JEA diary.
69. Interview EB.
70. JEA diary.
71. Ibid.
72. Ibid.
73. Ibid.
74. Ibid.

75. Interview JEA.
76. *Jane's Guns Recognition Guide*, Harper Collins Publishers, Glasgow, 1996, p. 492.
77. JEA diary; Interviews JEA, PR.
78. Interviews JEA, PR.
79. Interview PR.

Chapter 4: The 'Tobruk Four'
1. JEA diary, 17 July 1941.
2. JEA diary.
3. Ibid.
4. Ibid, 20 July 1941.
5. JEA diary.
6. Probably the cable name for a section of the War Office.
7. PRO WO/201/731 Correspondence on Layforce reorganisation.
8. LECTURE: Operations of L Detachment SAS Bde – CYRENAICA Campaign up to December 1941, A: Brief History of 'L' Detachment NB: Part C of this document refers (erroneously) to the first parachute raids on Timimi and Gazala aerodromes as having taken place on 16/17 December, instead of November.
9. JEA diary, 25 July 1941.
10. JEA diary.
11. Ibid.
12. Ibid.
13. JEA diary, 3 August 1941.
14. Ibid.
15. JEA diary.
16. Interview JEA.
17. Ibid.
18. JEA diary.
19. Ibid.
20. Anthony Kemp, *The SAS at War*, Penguin, London, 1991, pp. 8–9.
21. Ibid
22. Alan Hoe, *David Stirling*, Little, Brown & Co (UK) Ltd, London, 1992, p. 73.
23. This eventually found its way home and was in my possession until I sent it to my brother, John H. Almonds, when he reached the rank of Colonel.
24. JEA diary.
25. Ibid.
26. Interviews JEA, EB.
27. Interviews JEA, PR.
28. Diary JEA.
29. Ibid.
30. My researches have consistently revealed the lower levels of pay and amenities endured by British soldiers in comparison to their Allied and Commonwealth counterparts.
31. JEA diary.

Chapter 5: Reserves of Courage
1. Interview EB.
2. Ibid.
3. Ibid.
4. Interviews EB, JS; *Mars & Minerva: The Journal of the Special Air Service*, December 1996, Vol 2, No 2, p. 28. This tragic incident made a huge impression on the others present and EB and JS agreed, after nearly sixty years, on this account.
5. Interview IMA.
6. He had waited with another man whose wife was also in labour. After a while, a doctor told this man that his wife had died. My grandfather was told that his wife and child were both fine. Then the doctor reappeared to say that it was my grandfather's wife who had died. A widower could not look after a baby and it was cared for by some relations. His way to work took him past their house and whenever he passed, he would hear the baby crying. Every day the baby got weaker and within three months it died. Then every day he had to pass the house and listen to the silence. Did he wish that he had done something?
7. Interview EB.
8. Interview JS.
9. Interview EB.
10. Interview JEA.
11. JEA diary.
12. Ibid.
13. Interview JEA. My brother now has them.
14. JEA diary.
15. Ibid.
16. Anthony Kemp, *The SAS at War*, Penguin, London, 1991, p. 6.
17. JEA diary.
18. Ibid.
19. Interview JEA.
20. Diary JEA.
21. Interviews JEA, EB, JS.

Chapter 6: First Strike and Regroup
1. Interview JS.
2. Codename for the attack by the Eighth Army, part of Auchinleck's command, to relieve Tobruk (18 November–6 January 1942).
3. Interview JS.
4. Ibid.
5. Ibid.
6. JEA diary.
7. Ibid, 17 November 1941.
8. JEA diary.
9. Ibid, 18 November 1941.
10. Ibid.
11. Interview JS.
12. JEA diary 20 November 1941.

Notes and Sources   237

13. JEA diary.
14. Ibid.
15. He had been taken prisoner but later escaped. He was killed during the crossing of the Rhine in 1945.
16. Bond was also captured and in spite of several 'near miss' escapes, remained 'in the bag' until the end of the war.
17. JEA diary.
18. Ibid, Interview PR.
19. Interview PR.
20. JEA diary.
21. Interview EB.
22. LECTURE: Operations of L Detachment SAS Bde – CYRENAICA Campaign up to December 1941, A: Brief History of 'L' Detachment, Part C, paragraph 3 (f)
23. JEA diary, 27 November 1941.
24. JEA diary.
25. Ibid.
26. Alan Hoe, *David Stirling,* Little, Brown & Co (UK) Ltd, London, 1992, p. 107.
27. Interview MS.
28. Ibid.
29. Ibid.
30. Ibid.
31. Reckoning of a position by log and compass when observations are impossible.
32. Interview MS.
33. Ibid.
34. JEA diary.
35. Ibid.
36. Ibid.
37. Ibid.
38. Ibid.
39. Ibid.
40. Ibid.
41. Ibid.
42. Ibid.
43. Ibid.
44. Ibid.
45. Ibid.
46. Interview JEA.
47. Ibid.
48. Ibid.

Chapter 7: Engaging the Enemy
1. Interview JEA.
2. JEA diary.
3. Ibid.
4. Ibid; Interview JEA.
5. Alan Hoe, *David Stirling*, Little, Brown & Co (UK) Ltd, London, 1992, p. 113.

6. Not to be confused with Sergeant 'Chalky' White who served with 1 SAS behind enemy lines in France in 1944 and won a Military Medal; Interview JEA; Anthony Kemp, *The SAS at War 1941–1945*, John Murray Ltd, London, 1991, p. 156.
7. JEA diary.
8. Ibid.
9. Ibid.
10. Ibid.
11. Ibid.
12. Ibid.
13. Ibid.
14. Interview JEA.
15. Ibid.
16. Ibid.
17. Interview JEA.
18. Ibid.
19. JEA diary.
20. JEA diary; Interview JEA; also in Anthony Kemp, *The SAS at War 1941–1945*, John Murray Ltd, London, 1991, p. 26.
21. Interview and correspondence Alan Nutt, January 1998, 16 May 1998, 12 July 1999, hereafter, Interview AN.
22. Interview JEA.
23. Ibid.
24. Ibid.
25. JEA diary.
26. Interview JEA.
27. Interview JS; it turned out to be Storie.
28. The wound in the leg must have happened as the rest scattered because the JEA diary entry makes quite clear that 'His second burst got our truck but did not hurt anyone or set us on fire.'
29. JEA diary.
30. JEA diary; Interview JEA.
31. Interview JEA.
32. JEA diary, 31 December 1941.
33. Ibid, 1 January 1942.
34. Interview PR.
35. Malcolm James, *Born of the Desert*, Collins, London, 1945, p. 26.
36. Interview JS.
37. Interview JEA.
38. PRO WO/201/731 Lengthy correspondence on 'Layforce' reorganisation and the proposed redeployment of the Commandos, 25 December 1941, Whitely to Smith.
39. Ibid, 26 December, Smith to Whitely.
40. JEA diary.
41. A small enemy held port on the coast about half way between Benghazi and Tripoli and north-west of Nofilia. When Benghazi was in Allied hands, Bouerat

was of strategic importance because Rommel's Afrika Korps needed to route their supplies through it.
42. JEA diary.
43. JEA diary 16 January 1942.
44. JEA diary; Interview JEA.
45. Ibid.
46. Interview Mrs Kate Bassett, New Zealand, January 1998.
47. Unfortunately, there has never been any further news of what happened to 'Chalk' White.
48. Ibid; interview JEA.
49. Ibid.
50. Ibid.
51. Interview JEA.
52. 'Report on operations at AGEDABIA, 19-25/12/41 and ARAE PHILAE-NORAM 25/12/41–11/1/42', by Lieut. W. Fraser, Gordon Highlanders, 'L' Detachment, SAS Bde., PRO WO 201/2847.
53. Interview JEA.
54. Interview JEA.
55. JEA diary.
56. Interview JEA.
57. JEA diary.
58. JEA diary.
59. George Almonds, letter, 13 November 1930, JEA letter, 7 December 1930, author's collection.
60. JEA diary.

Chapter 8: SAS to the Rescue
1. PRO WO/201/731 Special forces operational questions, Smith to Ritchie, 10 March 1942.
2. Ibid, 'Layforce' reorganisation papers, 29 December 1942.
3. PRO WO/201/732 Stirling minute to GHQ on future of 'L' Detachment, 3 May 1942.
4. Alan Moorehead, *The Desert War*, Hamish Hamilton Ltd, London, 1965, p. 149.
5. House servant.
6. Interview MS; Anthony Kemp, *The SAS at War 1941–1945*, John Murray Ltd, London, 1991, p. 29.
7. Interview MS.
8. Ibid.
9. Ibid.
10. Interview JEA.
11. Interviews MS, JEA.
12. Interview John H Almonds, hereafter Interview JHA.
13. Anthony Kemp, *The SAS at War 1941–1945*, John Murray Ltd, London, 1991, p. 38.
14. Alan Moorehead, *The Desert War*, Hamish Hamilton Ltd, London, 1965, pp. 153–4.

240   Gentleman Jim

15. Interview MS.
16. Alan Moorehead, *The Desert War*, Hamish Hamilton Ltd, London, 1965, p. 194.
17. Post-war notes by JEA; Interview JEA.
18. Ibid.
19. Interview MS.
20. Ibid.
21. Ibid; Interview Merlyn Craw, hereafter Interview MC.
22. Interview MC.
23. Interview Alan Nutt, hereafter Interview MC.
24. Interview MC.
25. Ibid.
26. Interview JEA.
27. Malcolm James, *Born of the Desert*, Collins, London, 1945, p. 43, 44.
28. PRO WO/373/46 The Citation is signed by David Stirling and approved by H. R. Alexander, General, Commander-in-Chief, Middle East Forces and franked MOST SECRET. It was not released to the PRO until 1994.
29. James G. Shortt & Angus McBride, *The Special Air Service*, Osprey Military Men-at-Arms Series 116, Osprey, London, 1981, p. 8.
30. Interview JEA.
31. Lord Jellicoe's account of attacks in July 1942 PRO/CAB/44/152 (Open).

Chapter 9: Partners in Crime
1. Interview JEA.
2. *The Times Atlas of the Second World War*, Times Books, 1989, p. 81.
3. Interview JEA.
4. Ibid.
5. PRO CAB/44/152 (Open).
6. Interview JEA.
7. Report of Western Desert Operation carried out by Capt. R.P. Schott K.A.R. [King's African Rifles] and party in July 1942, PRO WO/218/173; JEA Interview.
8. Ibid.
9. Report of Western Desert Operation carried out by Capt. R.P. Schott K.A.R. [King's African Rifles] and party in July 1942, PRO WO/218/173; JEA Interview.
10. Ibid.
11. Ibid.
12. Interview JEA.
13. Ibid.
14. Report of Western Desert Operation carried out by Capt. R.P. Schott K.A.R. [King's African Rifles] and party in July 1942, PRO WO/218/173.
15. Ibid.
16. PRO CAB/44/152 (Open); Malcolm James, *Born of the Desert*, Collins, London, 1945, p. 151.
17. Interviews JEA, MS.
18. PRO CAB/44/152 (Open).
19. PRO WO/201/732 Stirling's reports and signals of summer 1942 airfield raids.
20. Ibid, papers on ideas for the reorganisation.
21. PRO CAB/44/152 (Open).

22. Interviews JEA, MS.
23. Ibid.
24. Ibid.
25. Interview MC.
26. Ibid.
27. PRO CAB/44/152(Open).
28. Interview JEA; Malcolm James, *Born of the Desert*, Collins, London, 1945, p. 173.
29. PRO WO/201/728.
30. PRO WO/201/732 Papers on ideas for the reorganisation.
31. PRO WO/201/728.
32. PRO WO/201/732 Papers on ideas for the reorganisation.
33. Interview MC.
34. PRO WO/201/756, File note of conference with Stirling at Eighth Army HQ, 25 August 1942.
35. PRO WO/201/732 Operational Questions: Special Forces in the Middle East.
36. Alan Hoe, *David Stirling*, Little, Brown & Co (UK) Ltd, London, 1992, pp. 194, 196, 198.

Chapter 10: Attack on Benghazi
1. Interview JEA.
2. Interview MS.
3. *Sunday Times* News Review, June 1996. The BFC's leading light was Thomas Cooper who was tried for treason and sentenced to death in 1946 but escaped with a term of life imprisonment.
4. Interview JEA.
5. Interviews JEA, MS, MC.
6. Ibid.
7. Interview JEA.
8. Interviews JEA, AN, MC.
9. Report of Operations at Benghazi, September 1942, PRO WO/201/735.
10. Ibid.
11. Ibid.
12. Interview JEA.
13. Interview MS.
14. Ibid.
15. PRO/CAB/44/152 (Open).
16. Fitzroy Maclean, *Eastern Approaches*, Jonathan Cape, London, 1949, p. 239.
17. Malcolm James, *Born of the Desert*, Collins, London, 1945, p. 256.
18. Interview MS.
19. Report of Operations at Benghazi, September 1942, PRO WO/201/735.
20. PRO CAB/44/152 (Open) Section VII 'L' Detachment 1941–1942. A number of points made in a GHQ note on the lessons of the operations at Tobruk, Benghazi and Jalo apply to the failure at Benghazi, including several relating to security and pointing out [what everybody knew at the time] that too many people knew about the planned raid, including the enemy.
21. Interview JEA.
22. Interview MS.

23. Interview JEA.
24. Geneva Conventions – a series of international treaties concluded in Geneva, Switzerland, between 1864 and 1949 for the purpose of ameliorating the effects of war on soldiers and civilians. Amongst these, the 1929 Convention Relating to the Treatment of Prisoners of War provided, inter alia, for their protection and humane treatment by belligerents.
25. PRO WO/373/46.
26. Either the Sikh or the Zulu, Interview MC.

Chapter 11: Living with the Enemy
1. Interview JEA.
2. Ibid.
3. Ibid.
4. Interviews JEA, MC.
5. Ibid.
6. Interview MC.
7. Ibid.
8. Ibid.
9. Interview JEA.
10. Interviews IMA, MC.
11. Interview IMA.
12. PRO WO/373/46 1.
13. Interview AN.
14. Ibid.
15. Interviews JEA, MC.
16. Ibid.

Chapter 12: 'Empire' Effort
1. Interviews JEA, MC.
2. Ibid.
3. Ibid.
4. Italian for a woodman.
5. Interviews JEA, MC.
6. Ibid.
7. Ibid.
8. Ibid.
9. Interview JEA.
10. Interviews JEA, MC.
11. Interview MC.
12. Interview JEA.
13. Interview JEA; photograph on p. x.
14. *The Times Atlas of the Second World War*, Times Books, 1989, p. 209.
15. Ibid, pp. 130–1.
16. Interviews JEA, MC.
17. *The Times Atlas of the Second World War*, Times Books, 1989, p. 130.
18. Interview JEA.

Chapter 13: The Italian Picnic
1. *The Times Atlas of the Second World War*, Times Books, 1989, p. 130.
2. Ibid pp. 129–30.
3. PRO WO/208/3373 Soames to 'Dear Squad', 22 November 1943.
4. PRO WO/208/3373.
5. Ibid.
6. Interview JEA They met again in 1969 at Almonds's son-in-law's Commissioning Parade.
7. PRO WO/208/3373 minute from Major Herbert, No. Field Escape Section to Captain Soames i/c No. 2 Field Escape Section, 30 August 1943.
8. Interviews Beatrice Melton, née Almonds and MC.
9. Interview MC.
10. Ibid After the war, Craw learned from Aussie Wilkinson that these combined Italian and Grenadier Guards sentries actually fired on Allied escapees.
11. Interview MC.
12. Ibid.
13. Interview JEA.
14. Ibid.
15. Ibid.
16. PRO WO/208/3373.
17. Ibid.
18. Ibid.
19. A11 could have been a patrol because Squadron Leader Dennis was at No. 2 Field Section, 'A' Force.
20. Ibid.
21. Interview MC; PRO WO/208/3373.
22. Interview MC.
23. Interview JEA.
24. JEA diary; original in author's collection.
25. Interview JEA.
26. Ibid.
27. Ibid.
28. Interviews JEA, JHA. My brother remembers receiving at the age of four and a half a brown and green camouflage-painted wooden Thunderbolt aeroplane and noticing that that it had white American stars on the wings instead of the usual RAF roundels.
29. Ibid. It has proved impossible to find this intelligence in PRO POW debriefing files, or any record of my father's later POW debriefing in Croydon. The citation for his second Military Medal is a witnessed account but his unwitnessed account probably still exists.
30. PRO WO/208/3373.
31. Ibid.
32. Ibid.
33. Malcolm James, *Born of the Desert*, Collins, London, 1945, p. 319.
34. Interview IMA.
35. Interview JEA.

36. See illustrations.
37. Interview IMA.
38. Interview JEA.
39. Interviews JEA, IMA.
40. Ibid.
41. PRO WO/373/94, ff 535. My father did not see the recommendation for this Bar until I found it for him in the PRO in 1999.

Chapter 14: The French Picnic
1. Interview JEA. Twice in his life he had to cover fifty miles in twenty-four hours (once in Italy and once years later when chasing bandits while Military Adviser to Emperor Hailie Selassie in Ethiopia).
2. Interviews JEA, IMA, John H. Almonds.
3. PRO WO/218/114.
4. Ibid In fact, operations were not restricted to south-west France.
5. Ibid.
6. Interview JEA; photographs and cartoons on pp xx and xx.
7. Interview JEA.
8. PRO WO/218/192.
9. Interview JEA.
10. Interview IMA.
11. Interview JEA; Interview and correspondence with Leslie Bateman; October 1998, January 1999, August 1999, hereafter Interview LB.
12. PRO WO/218/114.
13. Ibid.
14. Ibid.
15. Interviews IMA, LB.
16. Interview JEA.
17. Interviews JEA, IMA.
18. Interview JEA, PRO WO/218/114.
19. Ibid.
20. Interviews JEA, IMA.
21. Interview JEA.
22. Interview LB.
23. Adolf Hitler: 'Captured SAS troops must be handed over at once to the nearest Gestapo unit...these men are very dangerous...they must be ruthlessly exterminated.' See D. I. Harrison, *These Men are Dangerous: The Special Air Service at War*, Cassell & Co Ltd, London, 1957, front page.
24. Interview LB.
25. Interview JEA.
26. PRO WO/118/214.
27. Interview JEA.
28. Report on Operation GAIN, by Lieut. J.M. Watson, 'D' Squadron, 1 SAS, PRO WO/218/192.
29. Ibid.
30. Report on Operation GAIN, by Capt. C.L. Riding, PRO WO/218/192.

Notes and Sources   245

31. Interview LB.
32. Report on Operation GAIN, by Capt. C.L. Riding, PRO WO/218/192.
33. When my father and I met Vic Long on 14 November 1998 at an SAS Remembrance Service and Reunion, the first thing he said to me was 'Your father was a gentleman.'
34. Interview JEA.
35. Interview JEA; Report by Lieut. Bateman, PRO WO/218/192.
36. Interview JEA.
37. Ibid Years later, he fitted it to the 32-ft ketch that he built by hand in Ghana and sailed back to England. Vic Long (see footnote 33) also said to me 'I'll never forget your father and that piece of rope!'.
38. PRO WO/218/114.

Chapter 15: No Gain without Pain
1. Interview JEA.
2. Interview JEA; Report by Lieut. Bateman, PRO WO/218/192.
3. PRO WO/218/114.
4. Ibid.
5. Ibid; Interview JEA.
6. PRO WO/218/114.
7. Interview JEA.
8. Interview MS.
9. Ibid.
10. Report of Corporal Jones and Corporal Vaculik, 'The Paddy Mayne Diary', SAS Association, Duke of York's Headquarters.
11. Summary of Captain Garstin's Operation. Report compiled by SQMS Wylie from information received from the first of the party to return to England – Trooper Norman, PRO WO/218/192.
12. See Chapter 14, fn 24.
13. Report of Corporal Jones and Corporal Vaculik, 'The Paddy Mayne Diary', SAS Association, Duke of York's Headquarters.
14. Interview JEA.
15. Ibid.
16. Report of Corporal Jones and Corporal Vaculik, 'The Paddy Mayne Diary', SAS Association, Duke of York's Headquarters.
17. Interview JEA.
18. Interview MS; Report by Captain Sadler: Investigation into the shooting by Gestapo of the SAS party commanded by Captain Garstin (investigation carried out by Captain Sadler and Major Poat), 'The Paddy Mayne Diary', SAS Association, Duke of York's Headquarters.
19. Account of escape at 3321165 Tpr CASTELOW M.I.9/S/P.G. (F) 2527, PRO WO/218/192; diagram on p. x.
20. Ibid.
21. Ibid.
22. See diagram on p. 201.

23. Summary of Captain Garstin's Operation. Report compiled by SQMS Wylie from information received from the first of the party to return to England – Trooper Norman, PRO WO/218/192.
24. Interview LB.
25. Summary of Captain Garstin's Operation. Report compiled by SQMS Wylie from information received from the first of the party to return to England – Trooper Norman, PRO WO/218/192.
26. Interview JEA.
27. Ibid.
28. Ibid; PRO WO/218/192.
29. Interview LB.
30. Interview LB and his contemporaneous official report PRO WO/218/192.
31. PRO WO/218/192 Report by Captain Riding.
32. Interview JEA.
33. PRO WO/218/192 Report by Captain Riding.
34. Ibid.
35. Interview JEA.
36. Ibid.
37. PRO WO/218/192 Report by Lieutenant Parsons.
38. Ibid; PRO WO/218/192 Report by Captain Riding.
39. Interview Mrs Angela Van Straubenzee, sister of Ian Fenwick, 21 November 1998.
40. PRO WO/218/192 Report by Captain Riding. NB: My father always maintained that had he been with Fenwick he would have been able to talk him out of it.
41. PRO WO/218/192 Report by Sergeant D. P. Duffy.
42. Ibid.
43. Interview LB.
44. PRO WO/218/192 Report by Sergeant D. P. Duffy.
45. Ibid.

Chapter 16: Mission Accomplished
1. Interview MS.
2. Ibid.
3. Interview JEA.
4. Interview MS.
5. PRO WO/218/114 War Diary.
6. Interviews JEA, LB.
7. Interview JEA; Witnessed statement made by No. 2655648 S.S.M. Almonds, J.E., 'The Paddy Mayne Diary', SAS Association, Duke of York's Headquarters; PRO WO/218/192 Report by Captain Riding.
8. Interview LB.
9. Ibid; Report by Lieut Bateman of 'D' Squadron, 1 SAS, AAC on Operations in France with 'D' Squadron (Operation GAIN), 27 August 1994, PRO WO/218/192.
10. Report by 7016991. Corporal WILSON, R. (from the time he left the Maquis Camp mentioned in report by Lt Bateman), 'The Paddy Mayne Diary, SAS Regimental Association, Duke of York's Headquarters, London, hereafter report by Wilson.

11. Interview LB.
12. Report by Wilson; Interview LB; D. I. Harrison, *These Men are Dangerous*, Cassell & Co Ltd, London, 1957, pp. 132–133.
13. Report by Wilson.
14. Interview LB.
15. There is a sad sequel to this story. He returned home to find his mother in bed with a strange man, whom he killed. He was sentenced to life imprisonment. Interview LB.
16. Ibid.
17. Ibid; Report by Lieut. Bateman, PRO WO/218/192.
18. Interview LB.
19. Ibid.
20. Ibid.
21. Interview JEA.
22. Ibid; PRO WO/218/114.
23. Interview LB.
24. PRO WO/218/114 War Diary.
25. Ibid.
26. Interview JEA.
27. Interview JEA. Patton's military achievements had in fact protected him from civilian criticism of some of his methods, including reportedly striking a hospitalised, shell-shocked soldier while still in Italy. Although he had later apologised, the incident had done nothing to redeem his reputation for ruthlessness. *Encyclopaedia Britannica*, 15th edn, 1992, Vol. 9, pp. 203–204.
28. Interview JEA.
29. Ibid.
30. Ibid.
31. Interview MS.
32. Ibid.
33. Ibid.
34. Interview Mrs Angela Van Straubenzee, 21 November 1998; original letter held.
35. PRO WO/373/185 letter to Sir Robert Knox, KCVO, DSO.
36. Interview JEA.
37. Interviews JEA, IMA.
38. Interview JEA.
39. Ibid; *Jane's Guns Recognition Guide*, Harper Collins Publishers, Glasgow, 1996, p. 430.
40. Ibid; Interview JHA.
41. Interview LB. Leslie Bateman wept when telling me about this incident.

Glossary

AEAF	Allied Expeditionary Air Force
ASDIC	Anti-submarine detection system, a sonic device that detects submarines
CGS	Chief of General Staff
C-in-C	Commander-in-Chief
CQMS	Company Quarter-Master Sergeant
DCRE	Deputy Commander Royal Engineers
DDGS	Deputy Director of General Staff
DDO	Deputy Director of Operations
DDSO	Deputy Director of Signals Operations
DZ	Drop Zone
EMFF	Etat-major des Forces Françaises de l'Intérieur (French General Staff in London)
FFI	Forces Françaises de l'Intérieur (name under which the Maquis, meaning 'brushwood heath' merged on 1 February 1944).
GSO 1	General Staff Officer (usually a lieutenant-colonel)
HMG	Heavy Machine Gun
HP	High Power
Hrs	Hours (time by the 24-hour clock)
IC	In Command
IO	Intelligence Officer
ISLD	Inter-Services Liaison Department (a euphemism for MI6)
LAF	Local Arab Forces
LCM	Landing Craft Medium
LG	Landing Ground
LMG	Light Machine Gun
LRDG	Long Range Desert Group
LSI	Landing Ship Infantry
MEHQ	Middle East Headquarters
MO	Medical Officer
MT	Motor Transport
OP	Observation Post
Op(s)	Operation(s)
OR(s)	Other Ranks(s)
Pct.	Parachutist (a private soldier in the SAS, later superseded by the rank of Trooper)
PI	Photographic Interpretation

Glossary

POL	Petrol, oil and lubricants
PTI	Physical Training Instructor
RE	Royal Engineers
RSM	Regimental Sergeant-Major
RV	Rendezvous
SF	Special Forces
SFHQ	Special Forces Headquarters
SHAEF	Supreme Headquarters Allied Expeditionary Force
SITREP	Situation Report
SOE	Special Operations Executive
SS	Special Service
Tps	Troops
WT	Wireless Telegraphy
2IC	Second-in-Command

Bibliography

UNPUBLISHED SOURCES

Contemporaneous diary of John Edward Almonds from 28 January 1941 to 28 March 1942 and one belated entry on 10 October 1943, after escaping from POW camp in Italy.

Contemporaneous collection of papers and photographs known as 'The Paddy Mayne Diary', courtesy of the Special Air Service Regimental Association.

Letters by George Almonds, 13 November 1930 and by John Edward Almonds, 7 December 1930, author's possession.

The National Archives, formerly the Public Record Office (PRO).

PRO/WO 118/214.
PRO/WO 201/248.
PRO/WO 201/728.
PRO/WO 201/731.
PRO/WO 201/732.
PRO/WO 201/735.
PRO/WO 201//756.
PRO/WO 208/3373.
PRO/WO 218/114.
PRO/WO 218/173.
PRO/WO 373/192.
PRO/WO 373/46.
PRO/WO 373/185.
PRO/CAB 44/152 (Open).

SECONDARY SOURCES

Bradford R. & Dillon M., *Rogue Warrior of the SAS: Lt-Col 'Paddy' Blair Mayne* [Foreword by Col David Stirling], John Murray, London, 1987.

Cooper J., *One of the Originals: The Story of a Founder Member of the SAS*, Pan Books Ltd, London, 1991.

Crawford S., *The SAS Encyclopaedia*, Simon & Schuster Ltd, London, 1996.

Daily Mail, 'For King and Empire', Tuesday, 3 December 1940.

Daily Sketch, Monday, 4 September 1939.

Daily Telegraph, Thursday, 20 April 2000.

Encyclopaedia Britannica, 15th edn, Vol. 9, 1992.

Harrison, D.I., *These Men are Dangerous* Cassell & Co Ltd, London, 1957.

Hoe, A., *David Stirling: The Authorised Biography of the Creator of the SAS*, Little, Brown & Co (UK) Ltd, London, 1992.

James, M., *Born of the Desert*, Collins, London, 1945.

Jane's Guns Recognition Guide, HarperCollins, Publishers, Glasgow, 1996.

Jane's Warships of World War II, HarperCollins, Publishers, Glasgow, 1996.

Jarrett, P., Series Editor, *Putnam's History of Aircraft, Aircraft of the Second World War, The Development of the Warplane* 1939-45. Putnam Aeronautical Books, London, 1997.

Journal of the Special Air Service Association, *Mars & Minerva*, December 1996, Vol. 2, No. 2.

Kemp A., *The SAS at War 1941-1945*, John Murray (Publishers) Ltd, London, 1991.

MacCulloch D., *Thomas Cranmer*, Yale University Press, London, 1996.

Maclean F., *Eastern Approaches*, Jonathan Cape, London, 1949.

Mather C., *When the Grass Stops Growing*, Pen & Sword Books Ltd, Barnsley, 1997.

Moorehead, A., *The Desert War*, Hamish Hamilton Ltd, London, 1965.

Pimlott, J. (General Editor), *Wehrmacht: The Illustrated History of the German Army in WWII*, Aurum Press, London, 1997.

Shortt, J. G. & McBride, A., *The Special Air Service*, Osprey Military Men-at-Arms Series 116, Osprey, London, 1981.

Sunday Times News Review, June 1996.

Times Books, *The Times Atlas of the Second World War*, London, 1989.

Waugh E., *The Letters of Evelyn Waugh*, Penguin, Harmondsworth, 1982.

Warner P., *The Special Air Service*, William Kimber & Co. Ltd, London, 1971.

Index

Abel Kerdair, 33
Abruzzi, 163
Abyssinia, 74
Acroma, 37
Aden, Gulf of, 30
Adriatic, 159, 163
Agedabia 76, 78, 82, 95-6, 109
Agheila 76-7, 95, 109-110, 130
'Agrippa', 217
Albert, *Capitaine*, 194, 218
Alexander, General, 124
Alexandria, 32-6, 51, 112
Algiers, 173
Alibert, Lance Corporal, 188
Allied, Allies, 6, 25, 30, 35, 38-9, 47, 69, 74, 82, 102, 105-106, 112, 114, 127, 136, 138, 141, 147, 150, 152, 154, 157-62, 166, 168, 170-72, 174, 182, 186-87, 193, 196, 203-204, 207, 217, 221-222, 225
Almonds, Beatrice, 160
Almonds, Edward, 16
Almonds, George, 16, 69
Almonds, Iris May ("Lockie"), 14-15, 20, 24, 26, 28, 30, 40, 45, 49, 52-5, 59- 62, 65-70, 72, 83, 91, 138-40, 146, 161, 169, 173-76, 181, 184, 186, 188-89, 226-27
Almonds, John Edward, "Gentleman Jim"
    advance into Germany, Op HOWARD, 227-8
    beginning of SAS, 21-2, 53-5, 97-8
    'Clerk of Works', 8, 100
    by ship to Middle East, 26-31
    by ship to Italy, 141-2
    Chequers, 175-6
    Childhood, 16-17
    Coldstream Guards, 17-19, 20-25
    construction:
        SAS parachute training equipment, 7, 14, 63-4, 66, 93, 98-100
        boat for Stirling, 64
    Croix-de-Guerre, 225
    death of Ian Fenwick, 212-13, 216-17, 221, 224-5
    death of Jock Lewes, 86, 88-9, 91-2
    Field Marshal Montgomery, 225-6
    escapes:
        February 1943, 149-54
        September 1943, 158-165, 168-71
    'game' with Messerschmitt, 85-6
    General Patton, 222-3
    Guards Commando, 22-55
    'Layforce', 26-36
    'L' Detachment, 3, 5, 8-10, 14-15, 59-68, 71-3, 77, 92, 98, 111, 113
    LRDG, 74-7, 85-90, 107, 109, 113, 115-16, 120, 122, 133, 140, 149, 217
    mapping enemy minefield, 170
    Military Medal, 110, 140, 149
        and Bar, 176
    nickname, 69
    Norway, 227
    Forest of Orléans, Op GAIN, 186, 199, 207-12, 217, 221
    POW, 136-58
    taken prisoner by the Americans:
        in Italy, 171
        in France, 222-23
    raids on:
        Agheila, 76-7
        Benghazi, 126-36
        Derna Road, 44-55

Mersa Brega, 78-80
New Zealanders, 6-7
Nofilia, 83-91
Sidi Barrani, 112-17
Sidi Haneish, 118-123
Tobruk enemy salient, 48
SAS training, 8-15, 59-62
siege of Tobruk, 37, 39-55
solitary confinement, 156-7
son John critically ill, 14-15, 60, 63-6
survives enemy minefields
  at Tobruk, 49-51
  in Italy, 170
'Tobruk Four', 44-55
Tower of London, 17-19
1st, SAS, Scotland, 176-86
wartime diary, 12, 15, 17, 31, 35, 37-8, 52-4
Almonds, Edward, 16
Almonds, George, 16
Almonds, John H, 14-15, 44, 53, 59-60, 63, 65-6, 68-9, 72, 171, 174-7, 181, 189, 226, 228
Almonds-Windmill, Lorna, 227
Alpini Regiment, 168
Altamura, 142, 146, 154-5, 158
Amaria, 112
Amasyria, 33
America, Americans, 3, 6, 29, 158-9, 161, 169-71, 187, 191-2, 196, 203-204, 206, 213, 215-24
Ancona, 157, 163, 169-70
Apennine Mountains, 159, 163-4, 170
Aphis HMS, 34-5
Aquila, 164
Arabic, Arab(s), 78, 94, 131, 133
Arae Philenorum (*see* Marble Arch)
Argentan, 186
Armistice, 158-60, 166
Army Air Corps, 111
Army Council, 111
Army Group(s):
  No. 15, 160, 166
  No. 21, 185-6
Arran, Earl of, 155
Arthur Smith, General, 33, 101

Artillery, Rhodesian 86
Ascoli Piceno, 163
ASDIC, 32
Ashtead, Surrey, 204
Aswan, 126
Asyut, 126
Atlantic, 25, 27
Auberge de la Cour Dieu, 190-91, 194
Auchinleck, General, Sir Claude 6, 51, 64-5, 73-4, 104, 113
Auneau, 205
Australia, Australian, 33, 39, 42-3, 47-8, 140, 150, 154
  9th Division, 113
  23rd Battalion, 46
  43rd Battalion, 40
Avon Gorge, 39
Axis, 6, 32, 77, 102, 106, 112, 132, 138, 141
Azores, 28

Badoglio, General, 159
  Government, 157
Baird, Corporal C., 113, 115
Baghdad, 6
Bagnold, Brigadier, Ralph, 75, 108
Bagoush, 37, 67, 71-3, 113
Baillie-Stewart, Lieutenant, Norman, 18
Bank of England, 19
Bantam jeep, 118, 135
Barce airfield, 129, 140, 147
Bardia, 33, 72
Bari, 142
Barrage, 100
Bassett, Dennis, 94
Bateman, Lieutenant, Leslie, 190-91, 204, 209, 217-21, 228-29
Battleaxe, Operation 6, 38
Baynham, Corporal, Bert, 190-91, 220
BBC, 189
Beauvais, 202
Beauvy, Léandre, 192
Belgium, Belgian, 130
Belgrave Harriers, 19
Bellegarde, 198

Benevento, 159, 170
Benghazi, 73, 76, 101, 104-105, 107, 125-6, 128-32, 134-5, 137-8, 146-7, 173, 181, 197, 225
Bennett, Corporal, Bob 4, 7, 9, 137, 140
Berbera, 30
Berneville-Clay, Lieutenant, The Hon., 126-27
Bersciglieri Regiment, 150
Bertrand, Bernard, 192
Bir Hekeim, 102
Bir Khal da, 120
Bible, 16, 69, 146, 148
Blakeney, Jim 3-4, 7, 21, 40, 42, 46, 49-50, 67, 70, 76
Blanchard, M., 188
Blitz, 24
Boulton, Matthew, 99
Bomba, 32
Bond, Ernie 4, 5, 7, 11, 23, 26-8, 36, 39, 59, 61, 69-71, 76, 82, 141
Born of the Desert, 110
Bouerat, 93, 98, 104-105
Bourge, M. Gustave, 220
Boussogne, M., 220
Boyne, Battle of the, 102
Boys Own Paper, 54, 130
Breconshire, HMS, 26
Breda(s), 35, 45, 73, 79
Bren, British Service LMG, 303, 28, 86, 120, 171, 200, 227
Brigade, International, 4
Brigade(s), British:
    4th Armoured, 38
    7th Armoured, 35, 38
    22nd Guards, 35, 38
    SAS, 181-2, 186, 188, 197
Brindisi, 159
Bristol, 14, 19, 175, 186, 223
    Bridewell, 228
    Bristol Evening Post, 20
    Castle Street, 20
    Filton, 24
    floods, 20
    Mina Road, 20
    Royal Infirmary, 60
    St Werburgh's, 19
    Tower Hill, 20
    York Street, 19-20, 174-5, 227-8
Bristol Bombay, 14, 59
Britain, British, 6-7 24, 28, 30, 32-3, 38, 41, 44-5, 65, 75, 95, 104, 106, 109, 134, 148, 154, 157, 159-62, 171, 206, 213, 216-7, 223, 228-9
    Battle of 15, 45, 52, 54
British Embassy, 102
British Free Corps (BFC), 127
British Somaliland, 30
British South African Police, 143
Brive, 182
Brize Norton, 216
Brno rifle, 91
Brodick, 26
Brough, Sergeant, Jimmy, 4, 113, 115, 117
Browning .5 machine gun, 228
Brunen, 227
Buckingham Palace 18-19, 110
BULBASKET, Operation, 182
Bunfield, Sergeant, 191, 210
'Bug Bug' (Buq Buq), 116
Burnham-on-Crouch, 27, 104
Byrne, Private, Jock, 5, 83, 96

Cairo 6, 8, 33, 51, 55, 72-3, 75, 93, 96, 100, 102, 106, 108, 124, 126
Caen, 187
Camberley, 8
Cameron Highlanders, 104, 139, 147
Campo Basso, 163, 165, 169
Capetown, 29
Carabinieri, 138, 154
Cassino, 159
Castellammare, 171
Castelow, Trooper, 203-4
Cator, Lieutenant Colonel, 124
Ceremony of the Keys, 18
Châlons, 222
Chambers, Jim, Lieutenant, 127
Chambon-la-Forêt, 212, 224
Champs de Mars, 201
Channel, English, 186-7

Index 255

Chartres, 186, 206, 213, 223
Château Chinon, 181
Château d'Ouchamps, 209, 217
Châteauroux, 181
Chelsea Barracks 18
Chelsea, Pensioners, 19
Chequers, 175-6, 181
Chesterfield, 24
Cheyne, Trooper, Jock, 70-71
Chief of the Imperial General Staff, 31, 124-5
Chilleurs-aux-Bois, 217
China, Chinese, 36, 45
  China gunboats, 34
Churchill, Captain, Randolph, 27, 29, 103
Churchill, Sir Winston, 22, 40, 125, 160, 227
Civitella Casa Nova, 164
Clark, General, Mark, 159
Clarke, Dudley, 160
Clerk of Works, 8
Clyde, 26, 31
Coapaulo, Liberato, 168-9
Colditz, 108, 173
Collins, Lieutenant, Ian 22, 24-6, 32, 35, 176
Colt .45 automatic, 187, 190, 219
Commander in Chief, Middle East, 6, 46, 64, 124
Commandos 4, 9, 22-3, 25-6, 31-3, 52, 92, 101
  Guards 3, 10, 19, 22-3, 26-7, 35-6, 43, 47, 53, 55, 65, 72, 104, 124, 155
  training 22-4, 41, 44, 181
Commonwealth 6-7, 30
Cooper, Brigadier, 171-2
Cooper, Sergeant, Johnny, 4, 103
Corbeille, 204
Corbreuse, 205
Corinth Canal, 142
  Gulf of, 142
Cowan, Rear Admiral, 35
CR 42(s), 137
Craw, Sergeant, Merlyn, 109-110, 122-3, 131, 140, 143, 145, 148-51, 153-4, 160-63, 166-8

Creden Hill, 104
Cricket, HMS, 362
Croix-de-Guerre, 225
Crouch River, 23
Croydon, 174
Crusader, Operation, 67
Cunningham, General Sir Alan, 73
Cumper, Captain, Bill, 128, 132-4
Cyrenaica, 64, 102-103, 109

DCGS, 51
DCRE, 98
Decoy, HMS 32-3
D-Day, 182
Dennis, Squadron Leader, 'Squad', 166, 171-2
Deputy Chief of General Staff, 65, 92, 124
Derna, 39, 42, 44, 46, 65, 107
Dhakla Oasis, 127
Dill, Sir John, 31
Diplomatic Service, 104
Distinguished Service Order (DSO), 104
Division(s):
  1st, Airborne, British, 159
  7th Armoured, British, 45
  5th Light Infantry, British, 45
  5th Light Infantry, German, 38
  9th Australian, 13
  15th Panzer, German, 45
  271, 272, 276, 277 Infantry, German, 182
  273 Panzer, German, 182
Djibouti, 30
Dobson, 'Woof woof', Company Sergeant-Major, 17
Dodecanese Islands, 28
Dorset, 185
Dorsetshire, HMS, 30
Doone, Valley, 20
Douglas, motor cycle engine, 17
Douglas airliner, 17, 72
Douglas Water, 23
Dourdan, 205
Dreux, 221

256   Gentleman Jim

Drongin, Corporal, 137
Duffy, Trooper, Joe, 59, 61
Duffy, Sergeant, 188, 211, 213-15
Duke of Kent, 19
Dunkley, Sergeant, 188, 211, 213, 221
Durban, 29
DuVivier, Sergeant, Geoff, 5, 83, 96

Eau de vie, 187
Edinburgh, 177
Egypt, Egyptian, 3, 6, 26, 31-2, 39, 93, 102-103, 105
Eight Bells pass, 128
Eighth Army, 6, 96, 101-102, 112, 117-18, 159-60, 225
Eisenhower, General, 159
El Abair, 131
El Adam, 37, 102
El Alamein, 106, 112-13, 226
El Daba, 111, 113, 118
El Grafia, 96
'ELKS', 166-7, 171-2
El Timimi, 65-6
England, English, 3, 28, 38, 41, 74, 93, 113, 123, 133, 149, 155-7, 163, 165, 167, 169, 173, 185, 187, 190, 196, 202-203, 206, 216-7, 221, 224-5
English Yeomanry, 108
Eritrea, 30, 124
Essex, Lance Corporal, 220
Etampes, 203
Ethiopia, 30
Europe, European, 22, 146, 164, 176, 222
Evans, 'Whacker', 5
Excalibur, 96

Fairford, 185-7
Falaise Gap, 223
Falvey, Captain, F.P., 147
Fanara, 99, 100
Farran, Roy, Captain, 223-4
Facism, Fascist, 157
Far East, 106
Fenwick, Ian, Major, 182-3, 186-7, 189, 191, 198, 207-213, 216-18, 221, 224, 228
Field Escape Section, No. 2, 150

Fieseler Fl 156 *Storch*, 88, 122, 212
Fifth Army, 159
Fig Tree sector, 53, 72, 84, 114
Finland, 21
First World War 10, 22-3, 26, 29, 34, 167
Fletcher, Guardsman, 133, 135-37, 139
Fly class gunboats, 40
Foggia, 159
Folscher, Johanne (Jan), 143, 146, 148-51, 153-4
Fontainebleau, 198, 213-4
'FORKS', 166-7, 172
Forth Bridge, 64
France, French, 25, 30, 135, 177, 183-7, 189-95, 199-200, 202, 205-206, 211, 213-14, 216-17, 219-224, 226
  4th French Parachute Battalion, 189, 211
  Foreign Legion, 73
  Maquis, 194-6, 198, 206, 209-210, 217-21
  Resistance, 182, 187-8, 192, 194, 196, 198-200, 203, 209, 211-12, 215, 217, 222
Franciscans, 156
Franco, 4
Fraser, Bill, Lieutenant, 76, 82-3, 85, 90, 94-6, 225
Freetown, 28
'Fritz', 196, 216
Fuhrer, 351
Fuka, 111, 113, 118

GAIN, Operation, 182, 186, 188-91, 193-4, 196, 198-9, 207, 210, 216, 221-3, 225
Garawla, 120
Garigliano River, 159
Garrison Engineer, 63
Garstin, Captain, Pat, 193, 199-203, 221
Gazala 39, 65-6, 102, 105-106
Geneifa 3, 31, 55, 98
General Field Hospital, 33
Geneva, 151
  Conventions, 138, 140, 155, 157, 201
Gerard, Gerry, 109-110

German, Germany, 'Jerry', 19, 22, 25, 28-9, 32, 34-5, 39, 43, 47-50, 53, 66, 71, 73, 76, 78-80, 83, 87-8, 90, 94-5, 112, 115, 120-24, 127, 130-31, 143, 146-7, 149, 158-60, 163-70, 172, 182, 186-8, 190-96, 198-205, 207-222, 227
Gestapo, 191, 201-202, 206, 219
Ghana, 138, 156
GHQ, 51, 92-3, 101, 124-5, 131
Gien, 186
Gilf el Kebir, 126-8
Girga, 126
Giry, *Capitaine*, 194
Glasgow, HMS, 30
Glenearn, HMS 26
Glengyle, HMS 26
Glenroy, HMS 26-31, 33
Glider Pilot Regiment, 111
Gloucestershire, 185
Gloucester Gladiator(s), 137
Gnat, HMS, 362
Goat Fell, 24-5
Gordon Highlanders 5, 76, 94, 96
Gourock, 26
Graham, Lieutenant Colonel, 92-3, 124
Grand Canyon, 39
Gran Sasso d'Italia, 163
Gravina, 155
Great Bitter Lakes 3, 31, 59, 64-5, 106
Great Depression, 19, 109
Great Sand Sea, 70, 73, 109, 129-30
Greece, Greek, 142
Griffiths-Jones, Captain 26, 29
Grimsby, 3
Guards 3, 17, 21, 23, 25, 42, 69, 104, 120, 148, 162, 195 (*see also* Commandos)
   Coldstream, 3, 17, 19-20, 29, 33, 39, 106, 160, 164
   Grenadier, 4, 161
   Irish, 133
   Scots, 'The Scottish', 4, 5, 9, 23, 108-109
   Welsh, 4, 21, 44
Gurdon, Robin, Lieutenant, 103, 112-13, 117
Gustav Line, 159

Haggard, Rider 16
Haifa, 124
Halfaya, 117
Halifax Bomber, 185, 192
Hasty, HMS, 55
Hereford, 60
Horsham Blue Star, 19
Hiroshima, 228
Hitler 19, 34, 191, 194, 200-202, 204, 207, 219
   Youth, 154
Holliman, Gus, 107-108
Holmes, Lieutenant General, 125
Honey tanks, 126
Hope, Driver, 113, 116
HOUNDSWORTH, Operation, 181, 216
HOWARD, Operation, 227-8
Hutoft, 17

India, Indian, 42-3, 45, 46, 51, 102, 106
Indian Ocean, 29
Insect class gunboats, 34
Intelligence, 171
   Officer (IO), 124, 200
International Brigade, 4
Inter Service Liaison Department (ISLD), 131, 135
Inverary 23
Ion, Trooper, 188, 191, 217, 221
Ionian Sea, 142
Ireland, Irish, 10, 72, 63, 194, 199
Ismailia, 55
Italian Somaliland 35, 74,
Italian, Italy, 24, 30, 35, 40-2, 44-6, 54, 71, 73, 76-8, 79-80, 94-5, 98-9, 105, 108, 114, 116, 126, 131, 136-43, 145-59, 161-9, 171, 173, 181-2, 184, 222-3, 226, 228-9 (*see also* Prisoner(s)-of-war, Italian)

Jaguar car, 18
Jalo Oasis, 72-3, 76, 80, 82, 88, 90-91, 93-4, 105, 109, 125-6, 129-30
Jebel Akhdar, 103, 107-108, 125, 127, 130-32, 137

Jedburgh radio, 188-9
Jellicoe, Lieutenant, Lord (George) 22, 26-7, 29, 32, 35, 42, 104, 113, 118, 120
Jellicoe, Admiral of the Fleet, The Earl, 22, 104
Joe Loss Orchestra, 46
Jones, Corporal 'Ginger', 201-203
Juin, General, 225
Junkers Ju 52, 121
Junkers Ju 87 B-2, 84, 115
Jutland, Battle of, 104
J Troop, 23

Kabrit 3-4, 7, 55, 59, 63, 70, 72, 82-3, 93, 96, 104, 106, 109, 111, 118, 124, 126, 189, 211
Kent, HRH, Duke of, 19
Kershaw, ("Honest") Dave 4, 7, 26, 31, 33, 39, 67
Kersing rifles, 33
Keyes, Admiral, Sir Roger, 26
Khan Al-Khalili, 55
Kharga Oasis, 126-7
King Farouk, 55
King George V, 19
King George VI, 44, 103, 149
King's Dragoon Guards, 96
Kiwis 6, 7
Klopper, General, 106
Knightsbridge 'box', 102
Koenig, General, 225
Kroutchelnitsky, Antoine, 192-3
Kufra Oasis, 126-8

La-Ferte-Allais, 203-204
Lambert, Sergeant, 195, 209
Lancia Trente Quatro, 73, 76, 78, 80, 116
Langston, Corporal, 188
La Pitié hospital, 204
Latimer House, 174
Laughlin, Captain, T. B., 36
Laval, 222
Lawrence, T. E., 109
Laycock, Colonel, Bob, 24, 33, 36

"Layforce" 26, 28, 36, 38, 46, 67
'L' Detachment 3, 5, 8-10, 14-15, 67-8, 71-3, 77, 92, 98, 101-102, 111, 113, 124-5, 189
Le Mans, 186, 222-3
Lewis gun, 28
Lewes, Captain, Jock, 4, 6-7, 10-13, 21, 36-8, 41-3, 44, 46-54, 63, 68, 76-81, 83-6, 88-92, 110, 113, 117, 130, 170
bomb, 14, 108
Libya, Libyan, 83, 102
Lilley, Corporal, Bob 3-4, 7, 21-2, 26, 32, 36, 39-40, 42, 46, 49-50, 53, 72, 76, 79, 82-4, 86-90, 92-4, 96, 104
'Little Audrey', 41-2, 77
Lincoln, Lincolnshire 16-17, 226
Lincolnshire Chronicle, 17
Stixwould, 16, 222
Local Arab Forces (LAF), 131
Loch Fyne, 23
Lock, Albert, 174
Lock, Emily, 174
Lock, May, ("Lockie") (*see* Almonds, Iris May)
Loire River, 182, 186, 218
London Gazette, 149, 176
London 22, 35, 46, 130, 176, 185
Tower of 21, 22, 40, 137, 160, 191, 206, 210
Long Range Desert Group (LRDG), 66, 70, 74-7, 82, 85-90, 93-4, 103, 105, 107-110, 112-13, 115-17, 120, 122, 125, 129, 140, 149, 188, 217
Long, Vic, 195
Lord Haw Haw, 49

Maaten Becleibat, 95
Maclean, Lieutenant, Sir Fitzroy Hew, 103, 105, 132, 135
Madagascar, Straits of, 29
Maintenon, 206
Malta, 65, 141
Marauder, 77, 80, 83, 89-90, 94-5
Marble Arch, 83, 94
Marde, 93
Marden, 'Scoffer', 44

Masterman Ready, 16
Mauritius, Mauritian, 204
Mayenne, 222
Maynard, 45
Mayne, Captain, 'Paddy', Blair, 9-10, 13, 63, 76, 81, 92, 103-105, 113, 116, 120, 126, 128-9, 131, 135, 173, 176, 181-2, 208, 210, 212, 216-7, 221-227
McCulloch, 'Snowy', 97
McGinn, Corporal, 'Magi', 133-4
MCR 1 'midget' radio, 188
McReery, Lieutenant General, 124-5
Mediterranean 28, 30, 51, 84, 141, 222
MEHQ, 5-6, 8, 11-12, 67, 74, 92-3, 97, 101-102, 104, 117-18, 125, 135
  Director of Military Operation, 8
Metz, 202
Mikeli, Lieutenant, Tinenti, 150-51, 156
Melot, Captain, Bob, 130-31
Menginou, Lance Corporal, 211, 213
Mersa Brega, 78, 95, 110, 130
Mersa Matruh 31, 34-6, 38-9, 112-13, 115-18
Messerschmitt 110, 85-8, 90, 92, 109, 116, 200
Messina, Straits of, 159
Meyer, Parachutist, 113, 115
M16, 131-2, 135, 160
Middle East 5-7, 8, 34, 36, 43, 54, 73, 92, 118, 124, 130, 173, 176
Mikeli, Lieutenant, Tinenti, 149-152
Military Medal, 110, 140, 149
  and Bar, 176
Milly, 214-15
Minister of War, 160
Ministry of Economic Warfare, 101
Mombasa, 29, 74
Montargis, 190, 198-9, 207-208, 217
Montgomery, Field Marshal, 159, 225-6
Monturano, 157-8, 160, 166-7
Moor Park, 185
Morris, Lieutenant, 'Bing', 90
Morrison, Trooper, 200, 204-206
Moselle River, 203-204
Mosley, Oswald, 19
Mortar bomb(s), 45

Moto Guzzi motorcycle, 40
Motukarara, 109
Movie Tone News, 146
Mussolini, 83, 143, 157, 159, 162-3

Nag Hammadi, 126
Nairobi, 74
Nancray-sur-Rimarde, 192, 211, 228
Nancy, 203
Naples, 159
  Bay of, 171
National Archive, (*see* Public Record Office)
Nazi(s), 85, 127, 194
Netheravon, 185
Nettlebed, 224, 227
New South Wales, 140
New York, 28
New Zealand, New Zealanders, 4, 6-7, 8, 85-6, 88-90, 93, 108-109, 113, 140
Nibelle, 190
Nielson, Captain, M., 169-71
Nile River, 55, 126
  Delta, 32, 116
  Theatre of war, 6
Ninth Army, 6, 125
Nofilia, 76, 83, 98, 109-110, 113
Norman, Trooper, 200, 204-206
Normandy, 203, 207
North Africa, 30, 126, 141, 173, 225
Norton motorcycle, 99
Norway, Norwegian, 25, 227
Nutt, Alan, 86, 90, 96, 109, 131, 145, 147-8

O'Neil, Colonel, 194
Orléans, 182, 186-88, 190, 193-4, 198, 209, 213, 216-17, 219, 223-4
Order of St John, 146
Ormidale Hotel, 25
Ouzoner-sur-Loire, 218
Overlord, Operation, 181, 186
Oxford, Oxfordshire, 185

Packman, Trooper, 188, 191, 217, 221
Padgett, John, Captain, 30

Palermo, 158, 222
Palestine, 6
Palestrino front 46, 51
Panzers, Panzerfaust, 38, 227
Parachute Regiment, 208
Paris, 186, 199, 201, 203-204, 206, 212, 217
Parsons, Lieutenant, 209, 221
Pathe News, 72
Patras, 142
Patton, General, 159, 221-3
Pensioners, Chelsea, 19
Pescara, 164
Philips, Trooper, A., 83, 96
Pirbright 17, 20-22, 160
Pithiviers, 187, 190, 193, 217, 222, 224
Playmate, The 23
Pleydell, Captain, Malcolm James, 110, 118, 123, 127, 145, 173
Pope, 156-7
Porcia, 167
Port Said, 31-2
Portsmouth, 185
Poulard, M., 187
Prendergast, Lieutenant Colonel, 117, 125
Prime Minister, 27, 53, 103, 124, 175
Prince of Wales, 18-19
Princess Marina, 19
Prisoner(s)-of-war, Allied, 93, 123, 137-8, 141-2, 149, 153, 160-61, 166-8, 196
 Camps, 142, 161-2, 166, 171
 'Complex', 171-3
 German, 76, 201
 Italian, 31, 35, 37, 76, 98-9, 228
Provins, 186
Prunay-sous-Ablis, 205
Public Record Office (PRO), 131, 147
Purple Heart medal, 215
Pyramids, 55

Qara Oasis, 117
Qattara Depression, 103, 109, 112, 116, 118, 120, 122

Qattara Springs, 122
Queen Mary, 19
Quinton, Spike, 79
Quisling, 227

Rambouillet, 186
Red Cross, 144, 146, 148-53, 155, 157, 162, 166
Red Sea, 30, 106
Reid, Denys, Brigadier 73, 93
Reims, 222
Resistance (*see* French Resistance)
'Rest and be thankful Bay', 46
Rhine River, 227
Rhodesia, Rhodesian, 74, 82, 108
Riding, Lieutenant, 'Jock', 188, 194, 209-211, 216-7, 220-24
Ridler, Parachutist, 113, 115
Riley, Pat 3-4, 7, 9, 11, 20-22, 24-6, 31-3, 35-6, 39-43, 46, 49, 52-3, 55, 70-72, 92-3, 98, 100, 103-104, 165
Rimini-Leghorn, 160
Ritchie, General, Neil, 51, 65, 72-3, 96, 101
Rocoimperialia, 154
Rome, Roman, 16, 108, 164
Rommel, Erwin, Field Marshal, 6, 15, 35, 64, 73, 75, 102, 105-106, 109, 113, 129, 143, 226
Rose, Corporal, Johnny 4, 7, 189
Rose Cottage, 176
Royal Air Force (RAF), 4, 21, 40, 59, 67, 71, 82, 117, 138, 142, 185
Royal Army Medical Corps (RAMC), 145, 161
Royal Army Pay Corps (RAPC), 108
Royal Engineers, (Sappers), 12, 14, 99-100, 128
Royal Marine Commandos, 138, 140
Royal Navy, 3, 28, 32, 35, 38, 138, 150
Royal Rhodesian Tank Corps, 107
Royal Scots Greys, 124
Royal Standard, 19
Royal Warwickshire Regiment, 96
Rue de Saussaies, 201
Russia, Russian 21, 39, 104, 213

SABU, 186, 188, 210
Sadler, Corporal, 188
'Sambo', Corporal, 77, 93
Sadler, Sergeant, Mike, 74-5, 103, 106-108, 120, 121-2, 132-3, 141, 199-200, 203, 216, 221-3
Sahara desert, 127
Salerno, 159
Sangro River, 159
San Giórgio, 158, 168
San Juliano, 168-9
Saronikos, Gulf of, 142
SAS (*see* Special Air Service)
Saults, 124
Schoeles, Parachutist, Sam, 163, 167-8
School of Hygiene, 55
Schott, Captain, R.P., 36, 112-17
Schwarzlose, 40
'Scoffer' Marden, 53
Scotland, Scottish, 4, 26-8, 70, 133-4, 139, 147, 155, 176
   Ayshire, 177
   Brodick, 31
   Carradale, 184
   Clyde, 26, 31
   Darvel 31, 37, 177, 181-2, 190
   Douglas Water, 28
   Edinburgh, 177
   Goat Fell, 24-5
   Gourock, 26
   Isle of Arran, 23, 28, 31
   Mull of Kintyre, 184
   Sleeping Warrior Ridge, 25
   Sorn, Ayrshire, 185
Scratchley, Captain, 'Sandy', 126, 128
Seaforth Highlanders, 18, 59
Second World War, 3, 18-19, 201, 227
Seekings, Corporal, Reg, 3, 4, 103, 128
Seine River, 186
Senussi, 96
'Sensor Box', 90, 97
Sfax, 173
SHAEF, 182, 185
Shepheard's Hotel, 106
Sherman tank, 223
Siberia, 127

Sicily, 150
Sidi Barrani, 31, 112-14, 116-17
Sidi Bishur, 32, 39
Sidi Haneish, 118-19, 123-4
Sidra, Gulf of, 76-7, 102
Sierra Leone, 28
Silvestri, 172
Sikhs, 144
Simmonds, Lieutenant Colonel, 147
Simpson, Edward, 217-18
Sinai, Mount, 30
Sirte, 76-7, 81, 83
Siwa Oasis, 70, 109, 112-13
Smith A. S., 92
Soames, Captain A.C., 160, 166, 171-2
Socotra, Island of, 30
Sofragi, 103
Sollum, 35, 38-9, 41, 69, 117
Somaliland, (see British Somaliland and Italian Somaliland)
Somme, 202
South Africa, South African, 106, 143, 146
   1st South African Division, 113
Spain, 4
Special Air Service (SAS)
   raids, 5-6, 15, 68, 70, 73, 76-8, 82-3, 87, 91, 93-4, 105, 107, 111-12, 117-18, 121, 123, 126, 130, 132, 135, 185
   founding of, 21-2, 46, 55, 97, 101-104, 124
   in England, 216
   in France, 187-225
   in Italy, 142-173
   in Scotland, 176-184
   joint operations with LRDG, 72, 125
   Order of Battle, 124-5, 173
   Raiding Squadron, 124, 173, 223
   Regiment, 3, 124-5
   Role, 13, 72, 74, 91-2, 95, 105-107, 111, 120, 125-6, 149, 183
   Selection, 60
   training, 14-15, 63, 96, 156, 182-3
   traitor, 127
Special Boat Section (Squadron) (SBS), 105, 124-5

Special Operations Executive (SOE), 101, 124
'S' landmines, German, 50
SS, 194, 203, 205, 217
Stalin, Stalinist, 104
Stanmore, 185
Sten gun(s), 202
Stirling, Captain, David, 4-8, 13-16, 22, 27, 29, 33, 36-7, 42, 46, 51-3, 62-7, 71-3, 75-6, 80-81, 83, 91-2, 97-8, 100-108, 110, 112-13, 116-18, 120-21, 124-8, 130-35, 149, 173, 181-2
Stirling, Bill, 102
Stirling, Peter, 102
Stirling Bomber, 185, 187, 200
St Chèron, 206
St James's Palace, 18
St John, Joint Council of Order of, 146
Stockton-on-Tees, 203
Stone, Trooper, Barney, 69
Storie, Trooper, Jimmie 5, 61, 67, 69, 83-4, 89, 92
Stuka(s), 35, 38-9, 49, 52-3, 83-4, 87-91, 122
Suez, 3, 69, 99-100
  Canal 6, 30-31, 61, 106
  Port of 30, Swedish Army, 21, 31
Swindon, 185
Switzerland, 150, 160, 201-202
Syria, 6

Table Mountain, 29
Tait, Sergeant, Bob, 5, 83, 96
Taranto, 142, 146, 159
  Gulf of, 152
Tel el Eisa, 113
Tel el Makh Khad, 113
Tempsford, 185
Tenth Army, 6
Termoli, 159, 173, 223
Thimory, 209
Third Army, 222
Thomas, Abbé, 192
Thompson, Parachutist, 113, 115-17
Thunderbolt aircraft, 168
Timpson, Captain, Alistair, 113-14

Tobruk 4, 6, 32-4, 36-9, 41-2, 46-7, 51-3, 55, 64-5, 69-70, 72-3, 76, 84, 102, 105-106, 114-17, 125, 129, 140, 143, 195
"Tobruk Four" 4, 21, 46, 52, 55
Toulouse, 182
Tours, 186
Tower of London, 17-18, 33
Trenfield, 'Tubby', 5
Trig el Abd, 130
Tripoli, 69, 77-8, 80
Tripolitania, 83
'Troopers', 46
Troyes, 186
Tuberculosis (TB), 145, 147
Typhoon Tank Busters, 213

U-boats, 32
UK, 45, 174, 182, 189, 223, 228
Union Jack, 216
US (*see* America)

Vaculik, Serge, 202
Vallée, M. Roger, 192
Varey, Sergeant, 204
Vatican, 160
Vendetta, HMS, 39
Verdun, 203-204
Verey pistol, 121
Vert-le-Petit, 203
Vickers-K machine-guns, 107, 134, 192, 199, 224
Vickers Valentia, 36
Victorious, HMS, 28
Vierzon, 182
Viktor Line, 159
Vitry-aux-Loges, 190
Volturno River, 159
Von Lutterotti, Baron, 123

Wadi Farag, 95
Wales, Welsh, 162-3
Wanderers of the Wasteland, 40
Warburton, Trooper, 59, 61
Ward, CQMS, Gerry, 6
War Diary, *SAS*, 186, 189, 193, 199

War Office, 139, 149, 176
Warr, Captain, 113, 115-17
Warwickshire Light Infantry, 5
Watson, Lieutenant, Jimmy, 188, 209-211, 221
Waterloo, Battle of, 102
Watt, James, 99
Waugh, Captain, Evelyn, 27
Wavell, General 6, 31
Welcome Sailor, The, 23
Wells, H. G., 146
Western Desert, 6, 34, 37-8, 66, 74, 182, 185, 208, 226
Western Libya, 64
White, 'Chalky', 83-6, 89, 94
White, Corporal H., 113, 115
Whitehall, 46, 176
Whitely, J.F.M Brigadier, 92

'Who Dares Wins', 96
Wiehe, Lieutenant, 'Johnny', 200, 204, 221
Wilder, Captain, Nick, 120, 122-3
Wilkinson, Tom, 'Aussie', 140, 142, 148-51, 153, 156, 161-2, 167
Williamson, Sergeant, 175
Willys Bantam jeeps, 107-108
Wilson, Trooper, 218-19
Wiseman, 'Johnny', 216
Woolton, Lord, 24
Woolwich, 8

Yemen, 30

Zbrojovka Brno, 42
Zeighen, 129